Citizenship in the American Republic

Citizenship in the American Republic

Brian L. Fife

UNIVERSITY OF MICHIGAN PRESS • ANN ARBOR

Copyright © 2021 by Brian L. Fife
All rights reserved

For questions or permissions, please contact um.press.perms@umich.edu

Published in the United States of America by the
University of Michigan Press
Printed and bound by CPI Group (UK) Ltd, Croydon, CR0 4YY
First published February 2021

A CIP catalog record for this book is available from the British Library.

Library of Congress Cataloging-in-Publication Data

Names: Fife, Brian L., author.
Title: Citizenship in the American republic / Brian L. Fife.
Description: Ann Arbor : University of Michigan Press, 2021. | Includes
    bibliographical references and index. |
Identifiers: LCCN 2020035276 (print) | LCCN 2020035277 (ebook) |
    ISBN 9780472074747 (hardcover) | ISBN 9780472054749 (paperback) |
    ISBN 9780472128501 (ebook)
Subjects: LCSH: Citizenship—United States. | Political participation—United
    States. | Democracy—United States. | Representative government and
    representation—United States. | United States—Politics and government.
Classification: LCC JK1759 .F44 2021 (print) | LCC JK1759 (ebook) |
    DDC 320.473—dc23
LC record available at https://lccn.loc.gov/2020035276
LC ebook record available at https://lccn.loc.gov/2020035277

Cover illustration courtesy of Shutterstock.com / Christopher Beahan.

To Carol and Noel,
stellar citizens, friends, and in-laws

Acknowledgments

I would like to thank my editor, Elizabeth Demers, for all her assistance throughout this process. I am greatly indebted to her and the anonymous reviewers for their insightful suggestions. In addition, I am fortunate to have worked with Haley Winkle, whose technical assistance was invaluable. Many thanks to Kevin Rennells as well, particularly for his counsel during the production process. I am also grateful for the students I have had at Lehigh University. Our class discussions and interaction have helped to shape the content presented in this book. In addition, the research assistance I have received at Lehigh has been instrumental in the completion of this book project. Finally, it is a blessing to have a supportive family, and I am fully cognizant of this reality and thankful beyond words.

Contents

Preface   xiii

List of Tables   xv

Introduction   1

One   Constitution and Federalism   9
Historical Evolution of the U.S. Constitution   10
Historical Evolution of American Federalism   17
U.S. Constitution and American Federalism Today   20
The Importance of Citizenship in a Republic   22
Knowledge Matters   26
Citizen Homework   27

Two   Civil Liberties and Civil Rights   28
Historical Evolution of Civil Liberties   30
Historical Evolution of Civil Rights   34
Civil Liberties and Civil Rights Today   39
The Importance of Citizenship in a Republic   41
Knowledge Matters   44
Citizen Homework   45

Three   Voting and Elections   47
Historical Evolution of Voting   49
Historical Evolution of Elections   53

Voting and Elections Today   59
The Importance of Citizenship in a Republic   64
Knowledge Matters   66
Citizen Homework   67

Four   Mass Media, Interest Groups, and Public Opinion   69
Historical Evolution of the Mass Media   71
Historical Evolution of Interest Groups   74
Historical Evolution of Public Opinion   76
The Mass Media, Interest Groups, and Public Opinion Today   79
The Importance of Citizenship in a Republic   82
Knowledge Matters   84
Citizen Homework   85

Five   Congress and Political Parties   87
Historical Evolution of Congress   89
Historical Evolution of Political Parties   94
Congress and Political Parties Today   102
The Importance of Citizenship in a Republic   105
Knowledge Matters   107
Citizen Homework   109

Six   Presidency and the Executive Branch   110
Historical Evolution of the Presidency   113
Historical Evolution of the Executive Branch   115
The Presidency and the Executive Branch Today   119
The Importance of Citizenship in a Republic   122
Knowledge Matters   125
Citizen Homework   126

Seven   Supreme Court and Federal Judiciary   128
Historical Evolution of the Supreme Court   130
Historical Evolution of the Federal Judiciary   134
The Supreme Court and Federal Judiciary Today   135
The Importance of Citizenship in a Republic   140
Knowledge Matters   145
Citizen Homework   146

Eight Social, Economic, and Foreign Policy 148
    Historical Evolution of Social Policy 150
    Historical Evolution of Economic Policy 152
    Historical Evolution of Foreign Policy 154
    Social, Economic, and Foreign Policy Today 156
    The Importance of Citizenship in a Republic 162
    Knowledge Matters 163
    Citizen Homework 165

Epilogue 166

Notes 169

Bibliography 181

Index 193

Digital materials related to this title can be found on the Fulcrum platform via the following citable URL: https://doi.org/10.3998/mpub.11606310

Preface

The fundamental message in this guide is very straightforward. The republic that the framers of the Constitution crafted in 1787 can be more responsive to the needs of Americans if citizens are willing to proactively engage in public affairs and politics. This is a very important duty for all American adults; we must be willing to be more effective citizens in order to pursue a more perfect union. If we care more about politics and public policy, know more about information about our form of government and current events, we will be better positioned to communicate what we desire to our elected leaders.

On January 26, 1883, a future president of the United States, Theodore Roosevelt, gave a speech in Buffalo, New York. This is what he said in a speech titled "The Duties of American Citizenship":

> But this is aside from my subject, for what I wish to talk of is the attitude of the American citizen in civic life. It ought to be axiomatic in this country that every man must devote a reasonable share of his time to doing his duty in the Political life of the community. No man has a right to shirk his political duties under whatever plea of pleasure or business; and while such shirking may be pardoned in those of small means it is entirely unpardonable in those among whom it is most common—in the people whose circumstances give them freedom in the struggle for life. In so far as the community grows to think rightly, it will likewise grow to regard the young man of means who shirks his duty to the State in time of peace as being only one degree worse than the man who thus shirks it in time of war. A great many of our men in

business, or of our young men who are bent on enjoying life (as they have a perfect right to do if only they do not sacrifice other things to enjoyment), rather plume themselves upon being good citizens if they even vote; yet voting is the very least of their duties, Nothing worth gaining is ever gained without effort. You can no more have freedom without striving and suffering for it than you can win success as a banker or a lawyer without labor and effort, without self-denial in youth and the display of a ready and alert intelligence in middle age. The people who say that they have not time to attend to politics are simply saying that they are unfit to live in a free community.[1]

This speech was delivered in the late nineteenth century; today we would add women to the discussion as well. All Americans need to participate in the national political discourse and debate. The very essence of citizenship entails awareness, knowledge, compassion, understanding, and citizen involvement. There are many ways to participate in politics and, undoubtedly, voting is typically the easiest mode of political participation. In reflecting on the realities of voter turnout in America, it is easy to conclude that countless millions of Americans do not participate at all in politics, to their general detriment. Consider this guide a call to arms. All adult citizens must find a way to become more engaged and involved. The 230-year-old democratic experiment in America requires a focused and participatory citizenry.

Tables

3.1 Voter Turnout in U.S. Federal Elections, 1932–2018   61
3.2 Voter Registration Laws in the American States   62
5.1 Party Divisions in the U.S. House of Representatives   96
5.2 Party Divisions in the U.S. Senate   99
6.1 U.S. Presidents   116
6.2 Presidential Approval Ratings, from Harry Truman to
    Barack Obama   119
7.1 Chief Justices and Associate Justices of the
    U.S. Supreme Court   137
7.2 U.S. Senate Confirmation Votes of U.S. Supreme
    Court Justices   143
8.1 Top 15 Nations in Military Spending   160
8.2 Top 16 Nations in Gross Domestic Product   161

Introduction

Citizenship is defined in the first part of the Fourteenth Amendment: "All persons born or naturalized in the United States, and subject to the jurisdiction thereof, are citizens of the United States and the State wherein they reside." The premise of the Fourteenth Amendment, following the Civil War, was that citizenship in the United States was a universal phenomenon and belonged to all people in this country, with the notable exception of Native Americans, who would not be granted citizenship until 1924.[1] There would no longer be first- and second-class citizenship in America; all Americans would be treated the same and have the same expectations. Citizenship is the theme of this book, and it is based on a steadfast belief that all Americans, regardless of gender, race, ethnicity, religious preference, sexual preference, ideology, or political party affiliation, should be equal in terms of the law. My conception of citizenship is also based on the premise that all citizens have a fundamental commitment to democracy and by being attentive to politics and public affairs can be better positioned to undertake their citizen responsibilities in a republic:

Supporters of Democracy → Knowledge → Citizen Action

Americans may differ on many issues, but they universally embrace democracy. They believe that the ultimate sovereigns in the United States, or rulers, are the people who consent to be governed by leaders whom they collectively select in popular elections. Some of the essential characteristics of a constitutional democracy include the following:

popular sovereignty, majority rule but at the same time the rights of the minority are protected, separation of powers, and checks and balances. Though we tend to focus and emphasize the differences between and among people, it turns out Americans agree on a number of very important issues.[2] Americans share a number of democratic values, including life, liberty, the pursuit of happiness, justice, equality, the belief that government officials need to pass laws that are beneficial to all segments of the population, and patriotism. Americans tend to have high reverence for those citizens who are devoted to the country above and beyond their own individual self-interest.

In 1931 a respected political scientist from the University of Chicago named Charles E. Merriam concluded a book titled *The Making of Citizens* with an optimistic, hopeful declaration:

> If present trends continue, the coming citizen will enter the political world far more adequately equipped than his predecessors for participation in the political behavior essential to the well-rounded life, and protected from many of the deformities, diseases, and obsessions that make political relations a zone of darkness and trouble to so many persons, and often so heavy a burden to the community itself. The long, long line of those who have marched to their doom, in slavery, prison, or the grave, in the tragic struggles for political readjustments, is not yet ended. But there is reason to believe that it is possible for humanity to train itself in such a way as to reduce the terrible and agonizing cost of men's adaptation to each other and to social change, and to release the finer, richer, more beautiful, and satisfying possibilities of co-operation in mankind.[3]

If we can only collectively accomplish what Professor Merriam suggested almost 90 years ago—find a way to train ourselves to be more effective participants in the political world in which we live—then better days are in our destiny.

Merriam was active in local Chicago politics for many years, serving as an alderman and a member of several investigatory commissions. He even ran for mayor in 1911, 1915, and 1919, albeit unsuccessfully.[4] During these years he became convinced that technology and science would ultimately enhance the role of the citizen in public affairs. Unquestionably, his vision was affected by the context of his time, namely the Progressive Era. He witnessed the expansion of democracy and the potential power of the people in action, as during his lifetime suffrage was expanded to include women, the American people were given the power to elect U.S. senators, and a great deal of corruption was curtailed in the guise of Progressive reform.[5]

Many observers of modern America, however, believe that the optimism Merriam expressed with regard to the untapped potential of citizens in the early 1930s has not been realized. Progress has been achieved on a number of issues (e.g., civil rights, gender equity, technology, health care, and education attainment), but we are still plagued by the reality that in the world's oldest democracy, tens of millions of citizens do not vote or otherwise participate in the political life of the nation.

This disinterest in politics and government has risen at the same time that news and information resources about the important issues of the day are in greater abundance than at any other time in history. In the 20th century, technological advancements changed politics dramatically, with the advent of radio, television, and the internet. Yet poll results show that Americans do not know very much about the Constitution, the institutions of government, or their political leaders. By way of illustration, officials at the Annenberg Public Policy Center at the University of Pennsylvania conduct an annual survey to coincide with Constitution Day (September 17). In 2018, center officials found that only 32 percent of American adults could name all three institutions of the national government, 27 percent incorrectly responded that the Constitution allows a president to ignore a Supreme Court ruling if the president believes it is wrong, and only 30 percent knew that the Senate has the sole power to confirm Supreme Court nominations.[6]

We can be better citizens in this republic. Admittedly, an operational definition of what it means to be a good or effective citizen is not an exact science. As political scientist David Ricci put it:

> Good citizenship is less tangible, more difficult to study, and sometimes overlooked in the national roster of political institutions. Americans admire good citizenship. But they are not always sure what citizens should do on behalf of the communities in which they live. This is so even though many people believe that, when civic practice does not measure up to its ideal, a vital element is missing from the national landscape. In truth, the concern for good citizenship, no matter how imprecisely defined, takes aim at something very important. That is, Americans understand not only that government officials should work properly but also that citizens must help assure the quality of public life. The point is self-evident: In a democracy citizens

rule, yet if they rule badly, all will suffer. Thus it is no exaggeration to say that not just constitutional checks and balances but also the practice of good citizenship has helped the nation to establish justice, insure domestic tranquility, provide for the common defense, promote the general welfare, and secure liberty.[7]

Collectively, citizens can make this a more vibrant democracy, as Merriam observed a long time ago. Conversely, as Ricci delineated, democracy becomes more dysfunctional when so many of us are not willing to take responsibility for our actions or our inactions.

What makes for an effective citizen? How can we identify or define effective citizenship? According to a position statement issued by the National Council for the Social Studies, an effective citizen can do the following:

- embrace core democratic values and strive to live by them
- accept responsibility for the well-being of the individual, family, and the community
- acquire knowledge of the people, history, and traditions at the local, national, and global levels
- gain understanding of the founding documents of the United States, civic institutions, and political processes
- become familiar with issues and events that have an impact on people's lives at the local, state, national, and global levels
- seek information from varied sources and perspectives to develop more informed opinions and creative solutions
- ask meaningful questions
- analyze and evaluate information and ideas
- use effective decision-making and problem-solving skills in public and private life
- collaborate effectively as a member of a group
- actively participate in civic and community life.[8]

This list is comprehensive and highly intuitive in a practical sense. As political theorist Michael Walzer indicated during the Watergate era, the essence of good citizenship involves loyalty, service, civility, tolerance, and participation.[9] All are important traits for being an effective citizen in a democracy. To that list I would add knowledge. In order to be effective citizens, people have to firmly grasp some fundamental and basic knowledge about institutions and principles of American democracy. Knowledge is power, and the citizen who has fundamental knowledge about public affairs and politics is well equipped to actively engage in the political process in a variety of ways, least of which is simply to vote in federal, state, and local elections.

If the United States had election rules that were structurally similar to those of other democratic countries, voting would be easier and more people would likely participate in elections. But a number of states have placed numerous restrictions on the electoral process. Our leaders could make it easier for residents (as well as transients, as many Americans relocate frequently) to participate in the electoral process, not more cumbersome. For example, many people can get thousands of dollars in credit to purchase a new automobile in five minutes, but if they are not registered a month before the actual election, in many states they are not allowed to vote. Democratic advocates contend that such restrictive laws have the cumulative effect of lowering voter turnout. Several states, on the other hand, have Election Day registration, where the citizen who is not registered can go to the polls on Election Day, register, and then cast a legal vote. Are election results somehow more fraudulent in states where officials make voting easier for their citizens than in states where lawmakers make it as restrictive as the law will permit? The answer to this rhetorical question is resoundingly negative, according to election experts such as the interdisciplinary team at the Caltech/MIT Voting Technology Project.[10] Elected officials who support restrictive laws will never publicly state that their intent is to discourage specific classes of people from voting. Their actions, however, prompt critics to question the motives of those who oppose making voting easier across the states. Some political scientists have concluded that officials who support voter suppression efforts are doing so strictly for partisan advantage. To many experts in the field, voter suppression efforts are clearly not motivated by a desire to reduce fraud in elections, for such activities have been relatively minuscule for many years.

Ample polling data suggest that citizens are not content with the political system today and yearn for change. Officials from the Gallup analytics company have been polling the public with the following question since 1979: "In general, are you satisfied or dissatisfied with the way things are going in the United States at this time?" The last time that at least half of respondents indicated they were satisfied with how things are going was in 2004. Typically, the percentage of people who report that they are satisfied is in the twentieth or thirtieth percentiles while those who report that they are dissatisfied is in the sixtieth or seventieth percentiles, or even higher.[11]

The status quo will not change unless our elected leaders recognize that interventions are absolutely essential in order to maintain good standing with the voters. American citizens who believe in changing structural rules governing elections to make voting more user-friendly are part of a rich history of democratizing the electoral process. Yet when it comes to political and social change, the history of this country is replete; change will not occur unless public opinion is attentive to the issue at hand and the people demand that some course of action has to be altered—in other words, when the people are focused, mobilized, and not willing to back down when political defeats occur, even over an extended period of time. Advocates for change simply do not quit. Suffragists first publicly demanded the right to vote at the Seneca Falls (New York) Convention in 1848, but the Nineteenth Amendment was not ratified by the states and added to the Constitution until 1920. Although slaves were first brought to this part of North America in 1619, the Thirteenth Amendment, which effectively banned slavery in the United States, was not passed until 1865, attesting to the fact that abolitionists endured a long struggle in their quest for justice and humanity. The civil rights advocates who sought equal protection under American law (guaranteed by the Fourteenth Amendment in 1868) or equal access to the ballot box (guaranteed for African American men in 1870 and all women a half century later) did not quit even in the face of decades of brutal race-based violence, intimidation, economic discrimination, and political repression—most infamously in the Jim Crow South but also in many other parts of the country.

We owe a duty to our predecessors, who believed that free people should have the authority to govern themselves to fulfill the dream and potential of the oldest democracy on earth. This republic that officially was launched in 1789 is currently plagued by a great variety of public policy challenges, including a relatively unhealthy population, an unacceptably high poverty rate, social and income inequality, a high national debt, climate change, and a host of other issues. Yet many people have become so alienated that they have opted out of our electoral system. Nevertheless, there is a great deal of untapped potential for political transformation in those millions of nonvoters. Collectively, the people have the power to effect change in this country. Many observers believe, however, that meaningful political and social reform will not come about unless "we the people" make politics and public affairs a priority and decide to fully engage ourselves in the national political debate.

The ideal scenario in the United States would be if citizens were both active and informed about the issues of the day. Unfortunately, this is not the present situation. In 2016 two political scientists, Jennifer Hochschild and Katherine Einstein, published a study on whether facts matter in American politics. They determined that there are four types of citizens in the United States: active-informed, inactive-informed, active-misinformed, and inactive-misinformed.[12] In reflecting on their study, Hochschild and Einstein said this:

> It is perhaps fortunate that there are relatively few cases in which a painful experience—a child's measles, a war in Iraq, or a sense of betrayal by a prominent member of one's racial group—is the only thing that moves people out of a state of misinformed activity. Nonetheless, a democratic polity would be much better off if other, less traumatic, strategies could move people away from the dangerous stance of political activity based on misinformation. As Will Rogers once remarked, "It isn't what we don't know that gives us trouble. It's what we know that ain't so."[13]

These scholars emphasize an important reality in politics. Perceptions are very important in the political arena. But sometimes our understanding and interpretation of political events are not based on concrete facts. If the information that we utilize to come to some conclusion about a political phenomenon is distorted, then facts do, indeed, matter. People should ideally make their political decisions based on facts and not contrived, exaggerated, or distorted information that is deliberately manipulative in nature.

Citizen engagement is sorely needed at this time in history. On January 21, 1961, President John F. Kennedy challenged all Americans to do the following:

> And so, my fellow Americans: ask not what your country can do for you—ask what you can do for your country.[14]

This famous line epitomized the 35th president's vision of America, one where all citizens were expected to give something back to the community through public service. We need to do the same thing now. Great civilizations cannot rest on past laurels and accomplishments. It is incumbent on this generation of Americans to give something back to their country and fellow citizens. Reformers urge those who feel alienated from the political process or who believe their leaders are indifferent to their problems and challenges to get engaged, for it is only through a proactive citizenry that meaningful and enduring political and public policy results can be attained.

In the 1820s and 1830s, the French aristocrat Alexis de Tocqueville traveled throughout this country. He subsequently wrote a two-volume account of his adventures and experiences titled *Democracy in America*.[15] He praised Americans for their level of political activity—but also observed a tendency for Americans to isolate themselves from one another. Tocqueville noted that when Americans withdraw from their communities and focus only on themselves and their families, they lose their ability to be empathetic toward one another. A society that is largely inward in its worldview can result in the creation of radical individualistic policies, where laws are made that benefit the few at the expense of the many. Collectively, we need to focus on how public policy affects society as a whole, especially vulnerable populations, and not simply on the politics of self-interest.

CHAPTER 1

Constitution and Federalism

Defenders of **democracy** (a form of government where the people are the ultimate sovereigns and typically elect representatives to govern on their behalf) can become effective citizens by increasing their knowledge of the American constitutional republic. The U.S. Constitution today, with all the amendments added since the framers drafted the document, has only slightly more than 7,500 words; thus, it is not cumbersome to read this foundational document in a relatively short time. It remains, of course, the bible of American politics because the Constitution is the supreme law of the land in the United States. The most important structural rules of the U.S. government are in it. The most compelling feature of the Constitution is that it established a **republican form of government** in the United States. The United States is a republic because the framers believed that the interests of the people are served best when they elect representatives to govern on their behalf. A republic is a representative democracy where the people are the ultimate sovereigns (rulers), but they do not establish public policy directly. Instead, Americans are charged with the task of electing members of the U.S. House of Representatives and U.S. Senate, who, in turn, make laws that govern the entire country.

The framers of the Constitution also established federalism in America. Another way of describing the American political system is that it is a federal republic. **Federalism** is the constitutional division of power between the national government and the states. The framers carefully assigned some powers specifically to the national government. In so doing, they also reserved some powers to the state governments. In addition, smaller local governments existed in 1787 when the framers drafted the Constitution. They are not specifically mentioned in the U.S. Constitution, however, because local governments are simply adjuncts to their respective state governments.

It is important for citizens to note that although the Constitution's language is clear in some parts, it is ambiguous in others. Americans have long debated how the Constitution should be properly interpreted. Citizens have to determine for themselves how the supreme law of the land should be interpreted and applied in the 21st century.

Historical Evolution of the U.S. Constitution

The colonial population rose from a few thousand in the early 17th century to about 2.5 million on the eve of the **Revolutionary War** in 1776. It was not until the end of the **Seven Years' War** in 1763 that some American colonists began to question their continued existence under British rule. The Seven Years' War was a global conflict fought between 1756 and 1763 involving the great European powers at the time. To some, the Seven Years' War is also known as the French and Indian War, and it entailed a struggle for colonial dominance between Great Britain and France. The British ultimately prevailed, but their victory over the French in the Seven Years' conflict had been financially costly, and the British determined that they could recoup some of those losses in the colonies through taxation. They imposed a series of direct taxes on the colonists, who increasingly believed that the British taxation scheme was unconstitutional because the colonists were not represented in Parliament. Though the American colonists were not eager for representation in the British Parliament, they nevertheless demanded "no taxation without representation." The reality of the time, according to Michael Kochin and Michael Taylor, is that Americans had developed a belief that only local assemblies should legitimately levy taxes in the colonies.[1]

A significant event occurred in 1773 with the **Boston Tea Party**, a famous gesture of colonial defiance in response to the passage of an unpopular tax on tea passed by Parliament. Protesters in Boston displayed their outrage by boarding British ships docked in Boston Harbor and dumping their cargoes of tea into the bay. The British response to this action was repressive, and relations between the colonists and the British Crown further deteriorated. After the Boston Tea Party, more Americans opposed a series of British taxes on the colonists and, over time, came to endorse the idea that they should not be taxed by the

British but by their own colonial legislatures. Tensions between Americans who supported independence and the British mounted until the first shots of what would later become the Revolutionary War occurred in Lexington and Concord, Massachusetts, in 1775. Later that year the Second Continental Congress appointed George Washington the commander of the Continental Army.[2]

During the American Revolution and in the years following the military victory over Great Britain, the states were governed by the **Articles of Confederation and Perpetual Union**, America's first written constitution. Following the **Declaration of Independence** in 1776, when Thomas Jefferson and members of the **Second Continental Congress** (1777) declared that the United States was independent of Great Britain, leaders from the states drafted the articles. The articles created a **confederal system of government**, which is a type of government where the states have more power than the national government. Economic chaos ensued after the end of the Revolutionary War in the mid-1780s, so a meeting of representatives from all 13 states was scheduled to discuss revising the articles. No national economy existed under the articles, and state officials generally placed an emphasis on states' rights over the greater national good. The Articles of Confederation caused a great deal of consternation in the new nation for a host of reasons. First, the articles did not permit the Confederate Congress to regulate interstate commerce, so officials from the various states pursued the interests of their own state, often to the detriment of other states in the compact. Second, there was only one branch of government at the national level under the articles, a Confederate Congress. It was a **unicameral** (one chamber) **legislature**, where ultimately each state had just one vote, meaning that a small state such as Delaware had as much political power as the largest states at that time (Virginia, Pennsylvania, and Massachusetts). There was no executive branch at the national level, so state governors had discretion in terms of whether or not federal laws would be enforced. In addition, there were no federal courts, so state judges interpreted the meaning of federal law. In short, state officials frequently implemented—or refused to implement—federal laws solely on the basis of whether the laws promoted the interests of their home states. Because of the fear that the new American democracy was succumbing to chaos, in 1786 **James Madison** (1751–1836) of Virginia invited states to send delegates to meet in Annapolis, Maryland, to discuss the possibility of revising the articles in order to make them more effective. Madison would later be considered the father of the Constitution for his contributions to the creation of the new American democracy and ultimately became the fourth president of the United States.

The **Annapolis Convention** was not a success, for delegates from only 5 of the 13 states participated (New Jersey, New York, Pennsylvania, Delaware, and Virginia). Many state officials were generally satisfied with the status quo and did not wish to change it. Nonetheless, another meeting was scheduled for Philadelphia in 1787. Between these two conventions, **Shays' Rebellion** occurred in Massachusetts. Many small farmers in the state were outraged that their farms were being foreclosed due to tax delinquency, even though many had served during the Revolutionary War and received very little compensation for their service. The farmers became so angry that they organized a rebellion. James Bowdoin, the governor of Massachusetts, knew he had to address the uprising directly, as requesting assistance from the Confederate Congress was not a viable option, since the national army was greatly reduced after the Revolutionary War to approximately 700 soldiers.[3] Bowdoin raised militia units from private financial contributions from Bostonians and seaport merchants, with the expectation that the donors would later be reimbursed from the state legislature, or at least profit from army procurement contracts.[4] The rebellion was defeated readily. Yet the importance of Shays' Rebellion was that many political leaders at the time, including George Washington, concluded that in a time of crisis, whether it took the form of a domestic insurrection or foreign invasion, the Confederate Congress—and by extension the national government—was too weak to effectively respond. To them, a stronger national government was needed to preserve the new democracy.

It was in this troubled, turbulent environment that the second Constitutional Convention was held in Philadelphia from May 25 to September 17, 1787. Today it is known as the **Philadelphia Convention,** though to many Americans it is popularly referred to simply as the Constitutional Convention. Fifty-five delegates from 12 states (Rhode Island did not send a delegation) participated in the debates that led to the creation of the Constitution that Americans still live by today. Most historical accounts of the debates in Philadelphia rely heavily on Madison, who took notes on the speeches and debates that occurred during the convention (although he did not allow for his notes to be published until after his death). He was the last of the participants in the Philadelphia Convention to die, and he revised his notes throughout his lifetime.[5] While there are other accounts of the Philadelphia Convention, Madison's is the most complete, because he provided information about what happened each day that the framers were in session. Some scholars believe that Madison may have altered his notes during the course of his lifetime in accordance with his own evolving understanding of past events and people.[6] His notes became more widely disseminated in the early 20th century, when the eminent Yale University historian Max Farrand published a multivolume account of the notes in 1911.[7]

In addition to being a key chronicler of the events of the Philadelphia Convention, Madison also played an important role in shaping the principles and provisions of the Constitution that resulted from the gathering. He sought to replace the articles with a new Constitution that would establish a stronger national government, which could protect citizens in a time of crisis and establish a national economy and true country. In that endeavor he succeeded. A federal republic was created in the new Constitution. In addition to the Constitution being established as the supreme law of the land, the framers also determined that federal law superseded state law.

Not all the framers supported the Constitution. Only 39 of the 55 participants actually signed the Constitution on the last day of the Philadelphia Convention. Several framers left Philadelphia early and for various reasons never returned. Some left the convention to attend to personal business; some decided to leave in protest because they felt that the proposed new national government would be too powerful; some wanted to include a list of citizens' rights in the original document; and some departed due to personal or familial health challenges.[8] Of the framers who remained in Philadelphia throughout the convention, three representatives opted not to sign the Constitution (George Mason and Edmund Randolph of Virginia and Elbridge Gerry of Massachusetts). Madison promised that if the new Constitution was ratified by the states, he would pursue the passage of constitutional amendments protecting civil liberties in the first session of Congress. As a member of the first House of Representatives, he proposed several protections for individual liberty and, ultimately, the states ratified 10 amendments in 1791 that became collectively known as the **Bill of Rights**.

The framers stipulated that ratification from nine of the states would be required for the Constitution to become the law of the land. After the Philadelphia Convention ended, three Americans started writing what became known as the *Federalist Papers* to drum up support for ratification. James Madison, Alexander Hamilton, and John Jay wrote anonymous letters to the editor in New York City newspapers and signed them "Publius" (the people). A total of 85 essays were produced by the three men (with Hamilton writing 51 of them), all of which encouraged citizens to endorse the new republican form of government. By the summer of 1788, nine states had ratified and the new Constitution went into effect in early 1789 (ultimately all 13 states ratified the document). The United States is the oldest democracy in the world.

The framers created three institutions at the national level (legislative, executive, and judicial branches). The sequence of the articles in the Constitution is significant. **Article I** established Congress and was the branch closest to the people, as in the original Constitution, the people could directly elect members of the U.S. House, and that authority was not given with regard to the other branches or the U.S. Senate. **Article II** created the presidency as an institution, and **Article III** established the Supreme Court. The creation of the first three articles permitted the framers to establish **separation of powers**, meaning members of Congress were empowered with making the law, the president was charged with enforcing the law, and the Supreme Court justices with interpreting the meaning of the law. With regard to presidential selection, the framers debated at great length how the president would be elected. Some delegates preferred that members of Congress be empowered to choose the president, while others favored direct election by the citizens of the young nation. The **Electoral College** was created as a result of the debates about presidential selection. The Electoral College is a body of individuals that is empowered by the Constitution to directly select the president. Under the rules of the Constitution, a candidate is required to receive a simple majority of the Electoral College in order to win the election and become the president. Today the most important number in a presidential election is 270 (a simple majority of the 538 total electors). A candidate can win the popular vote by several million votes, but still lose the election in the Electoral College. The framers also wanted to ensure that one branch would not exceed its constitutional authority, so they created an intricate system of **checks and balances** so that none of the three branches could dominate the other two. For example, the Constitution empowered the president to nominate all federal judges but gave the Senate the power to confirm or reject these nominations. Checks and balances are formal mechanisms created by the framers of the Constitution that allow one branch of government to have some power over the others.

Most of what was created in the Constitution was the product of political compromise. By way of illustration, the framers heavily debated the powers of Congress and how the ranks of its membership would be filled.

The **Virginia Plan**, which was supported by the "large state" delegates, proposed a **bicameral** (two-chamber) **legislature** with both chambers apportioned based on population. The **New Jersey Plan**, which was supported by delegates from the smaller states, proposed a basic replication of the Confederate Congress, which was a unicameral legislature, where states had equal political power. The resulting compromise between these two visions was the **Great (or Connecticut) Compromise**, which created a bicameral legislature, in which states enjoyed equal representation in the Senate (two senators per state) but representation in the House of Representatives was weighted based on population, with more populous states receiving higher numbers of representatives than less populated states. Another compromise occurred with regard to presidential selection. Some delegates at the Philadelphia Convention wanted direct election of the president by the people; others supported congressional selection. The compromise that was created at the time established the Electoral College, in which citizens vote for a slate of candidates that are pledged to them. This compromise would become one of the more notorious elements of the Constitution. Once the delegates decided to base representation in the House of Representatives on population, they faced the question of how and whether to count African American slaves in each state's population totals. Northern delegates felt that Southern states should not be able to count slaves in their population because slaves at the time were defined as property by the Southern delegates. Southern delegates wanted to include all slaves in their total population so that they would have more political clout in the House. The framers ultimately settled on a so-called **three-fifths compromise** in which for every five slaves living in a state, the state in question could add three people to its official population. Southern states were empowered politically as a result and received more representation; in return, citizens in the South paid more in taxes.[9]

The framers of the Constitution recognized that the document they created was not perfect. It had been crafted, after all, only after lengthy and contentious debate. The architects of the Constitution also recognized that the nation would face challenges in the future that they could not possibly anticipate. With these factors in mind, they included a mechanism whereby members of Congress could change the Constitution through amendments. An amendment proposal must have a two-thirds majority vote in both houses of Congress in order to be sent to the state legislatures for ratification (67 votes in favor in the 100-member Senate; 290 yes votes in the 435-member House). Amendment proposals that pass Congress are then sent to the states for ratification. For proposed constitutional amendments to pass this hurdle and become law, three-fourths of the states (38 of the 50 states) must formally approve it. The framers also included other mechanisms to amend the Constitution. Congress can propose an amendment with at least a two-thirds majority vote, and then the amendment can be ratified by at least three-fourths of state conventions called for the purpose of ratifying the amendment. This approach has been used only once (the repeal of Prohibition). Another method for amending the Constitution has never been used in history. An amendment can be proposed by a national convention that is called by at least two-thirds of the state legislatures. If approved, a proposal of this nature can be ratified by either three-fourths of the state legislatures or three-fourths of state conventions called for the purpose of ratifying the amendment. Clearly in the evolution of amendments in the United States, Congress has taken the lead role to date.

The U.S. Constitution has grown to include 27 amendments through 2020. Here is a brief summary of the amendments and when they were passed:

First: freedom of speech, press, religion, and assembly (1791)
Second: right to bear arms (1791)
Third: no quartering of soldiers (1791)
Fourth: protection from illegal searches and seizures (1791)
Fifth: right to grand jury, no double jeopardy, protection against self-incrimination, and due process (1791)
Sixth: right to speedy trial and counsel and right to confront opposing witnesses (1791)
Seventh: right to a jury trial (1791)
Eighth: no cruel and unusual punishment (1791)
Ninth: non-enumerated rights (1791)
Tenth: rights reserved to the states (1791)
Eleventh: suits against a state (1795)
Twelfth: election of the president and vice president (1804)
Thirteenth: abolition of slavery (1865)
Fourteenth: citizenship, equal protection, and due process (1868)
Fifteenth: voting rights for African American males (1870)
Sixteenth: Congress has the power to tax personal income (1913)
Seventeenth: direct popular election of U.S. senators (1913)
Eighteenth: Prohibition (1919)
Nineteenth: voting rights for women (1920)

Twentieth: moved the beginning and end of presidential and vice presidential terms from March 4 to January 20 and moved the beginning and end of terms for members of Congress from March 4 to January 3 (1933)

Twenty-first: repeal of Prohibition (1933)

Twenty-second: term limits for president (1951)

Twenty-third: presidential electors established for the District of Columbia (1961)

Twenty-fourth: poll tax abolished (1964)

Twenty-fifth: addresses issues related to presidential vacancy and disability (1967)

Twenty-sixth: voting rights for 18-, 19-, and 20-year-olds (1971)

Twenty-seventh: a sitting Congress cannot raise its own pay without an intervening election (1992)

Unlike most state constitutions, there have not been many amendments to the federal Constitution. Since the passage of the Bill of Rights in 1791, there have been only 15 sustained amendments (since the Prohibition experiment enshrined in the Eighteenth Amendment was subsequently repealed with passage of the Twenty-first Amendment).

Historical Evolution of American Federalism

In practical terms, think of federalism as the special relationship between the national government and the 50 state governments. In Article VI of the U.S. Constitution, a hierarchy of law was established in the new democracy. It was the vision of the framers not only to make the Constitution the supreme law of the land in the United States but also to specifically mandate that federal law supersedes state law, thereby establishing national supremacy.

Federalism has been debated throughout U.S. history. The first two political parties that developed in this country were organized largely on principles of federalism. Some believed that the key to economic prosperity existed in the centralization of more power and authority at the national level; others perceived that the economy would expand and that people would have better lives if power were decentralized at the national level and reverted back to the states and local governments. As was discussed with regard to the Articles of Confederation, early American leaders, leery of a powerful central government given their perceived experiences as bullied colonies of Great Britain, wanted to keep the central government limited in size and scope and embraced the doctrine of **states' rights**—that is, political power concentrated with states rather than national authorities. The relationship between the national government and the states has evolved throughout U.S. history, and some scholars contend that the United States has experienced three distinct phases of federalism in its history.

From 1789 to 1865 there was constant tension between two visions of federalism: **nation-centered federalism** versus **state-centered federalism**. Nation-centered federalism was predicated on a broad interpretation of the Constitution that held that Congress had wide latitude to regulate all aspects of the domestic economy. Chief Justice **John Marshall** (1755–1835) illustrated this belief in *McCulloch v. Maryland* (1819). He determined that the Bank of the United States, created by Congress, was constitutional because Congress had not only enumerated powers under Article I but also implied powers under the **necessary and proper clause** (also called the "elastic clause"). In Article I, Section 8, the framers stipulated that Congress has the power "to make all Laws which shall be necessary and proper for carrying into Execution the foregoing Powers, and all other Powers vested by this Constitution in the Government of the United States or any Department or Officer thereof." While the word "bank" does not explicitly appear in the Constitution, the members of Congress have the authority under the elastic clause to create the conditions for a strong national economy. Marshall and his colleagues thus unanimously rejected the charge that Congress had exceeded its mandate under Article I by creating a national banking system. To Marshall and the other justices, the Constitution clearly empowered Congress with wide latitude to regulate all aspects of the national economy.

This perspective, however, came under attack in the years leading up to the American **Civil War**, a battle between the North and the South in the United States from 1861 to 1865. Using a strict interpretation of the Constitution based on the Tenth Amendment, Chief Justice **Roger Taney** (1777–1864) endorsed state-centered federalism in *Dred Scott v. Sandford* (1857). In a 7–2 decision, Taney and the other justices in the majority concluded that persons of African descent were not citizens and therefore could not sue in the courts. The ruling also stipulated that the people in states and territories—not Congress—could decide whether they would have slavery. The Court's majority also invalidated the Missouri Compromise (1820), in which Congress had admitted two new states to the union, Maine and Missouri, under a specific arrangement. Under the terms of the Missouri Compromise, Maine would be a free state and Missouri would be a slave state.

The *Dred Scott* decision essentially stated that Congress did not have the constitutional authority to impose such deals on states. Seizing on the notion of popular sovereignty, Taney and his allies determined that states and territories would decide the slavery question and not federal officials. State-centered federalism emphasizes the doctrine of states' rights. It is based on a fairly strict interpretation of the Constitution and assumes that the national government has a limited mandate and that most citizens' lives are affected at the state and local levels of government.

After Abraham Lincoln was elected president in 1860 the Southern slaveholding states seceded from the Union. A Civil War ensued and had a devastating effect on society due to the high loss of life and suffering. Ultimately, the Union army prevailed and slavery was abolished. In addition, an important question in federalism was resolved on the battlefields. Once states were admitted into the union, they were expected to remain in the United States of America. As a result, the rebel state governments were absorbed back into the union upon the end of the war in 1865, even though Lincoln was assassinated shortly after he commenced his second term in office.

From 1865 to 1937, the doctrine of **dual federalism** was the norm in terms of how the federal government and the states interacted. The doctrine was based on an interpretation of the Tenth Amendment that members of Congress addressed policy issues that were specifically enumerated in Article I. All other policy issues were left for the states. This belief has historically been depicted as a **layer cake** by political scientist Morton Grodzins.[10] State officials addressed most policy issues and did not collaborate with federal officials. The states represented the top layer and the federal government represented the bottom layer. To many Americans of that era, the federal government was a relatively small operation that was focused mostly on security, immigration, and statehood. Most other policy issues were addressed at the state or local levels or in private sector organizations.

The primary point about the dual federalism era is that national officials did not collaborate much with state and local officials and that the lack of interaction between and among policy makers at the national and subnational levels of government was deemed preferable by officials at all levels of government. These distinct spheres of influence and responsibility largely stemmed from the fact that states then were much less dependent on federal dollars to operate. In practical terms, a very small amount of state revenue came directly from the national government. State officials and lawmakers thus had the freedom to operate independently from their counterparts at the national level.

U.S. Constitution and American Federalism Today

In 1937 a significant change occurred on the Supreme Court, the impact of which still reverberates today. In a series of cases in 1935–1936, a conservative-leaning Supreme Court overturned major parts of President Franklin D. Roosevelt's **New Deal**. The New Deal was a series of domestic economic programs and policies that Roosevelt advocated and persuaded members of Congress to enact during the early years of his presidency.[11] The conservative justices believed that in the case of the New Deal, Congress had exceeded its authority to regulate business under the federal Constitution. In other cases the justices pondered the extent to which state legislators could regulate businesses operating in their states. In the U.S. Supreme Court case of *West Coast Hotel Company v. Parrish* (1937), one of the justices, Owen Roberts, changed his mind on the matter of interpreting the federal Constitution and became the swing vote in a 5–4 decision. The Court's majority determined that the Washington state legislature did not violate the due process clause of the Fifth Amendment by establishing a minimum wage specifically for women in the hotel industry.[12] Thus, the justices ruled in favor of the legislature's authority to mandate a minimum wage. The following year (1938), at Roosevelt's urging, Congress passed a minimum wage (25 cents per hour) at the federal level for the first time in U.S. history. Justice Roberts's change of perspective with regard to the power of legislative bodies to regulate the economy is historically known as the "switch in time that saved nine."[13] Prior to this case, President Roosevelt attempted to pack the Court with additional appointees who would be more likely to support the constitutionality of New Deal laws and programs, but members of Congress rejected his proposal, which would have increased the size of the Court from 9 to 15 justices. His court-packing plan would have empowered the president to appoint additional justices if any of the sitting justices turned 70 years old but decided not to retire. Since all federal judges have lifetime tenure under the Constitution, a president cannot remove a justice simply because of political differences. Congress has the power to remove federal judges through impeachment, but a president does not participate. Under the Constitution, only Congress can change the size of the Court (and it did so on numerous occasions in the 19th century). While the president does have the power of the veto, changing the number of justices requires the consent of Congress. Roosevelt's attempt to pack the Court was rejected because it was perceived as an infringement on congressional authority, even by progressive members of Congress who were supportive of Roosevelt and the New Deal. Despite this rebuke, however, Roosevelt's long presidency (he served from 1933 until his death in 1945) gave him enormous influence over the membership of the Court. By 1942 all but two of the justices sitting on the Supreme Court were his appointees.[14]

A new era of **cooperative federalism** ensued as a result of this fascinating Supreme Court decision. This approach to federalism can be depicted as a **marble cake**, where all levels of government work together in the spirit of cooperation to address the needs of the people. In this new modern era, the federal government is supreme over the states due to the dependency relationship that states have with the federal government. State officials are dependent on federal revenue to fulfill their tasks, especially during times of crises. Unlike the era of dual federalism, state governments in the modern era receive almost one-third of their revenue directly from the federal government.[15] In the absence of these funds, state lawmakers would have to make very tough public policy choices to either increase state taxes or dramatically cut state services and programs. If revenue did not increase, then presumably cuts would be required to balance the budget. All states except for Vermont have a legal requirement that the budget must be balanced.[16] In many states, public education (K–12 and higher education) accounts for about half of the state budget. Cuts in programs would undoubtedly necessitate cuts in education, which is not something that officials in either major political party would like to do.

Federalism in action today occurs through the **grants-in-aid** system. A grant-in-aid occurs when members of Congress appropriate money to state and local governments. Generally, the two most popular approaches are **block grants** and **categorical grants**. Block grants are typically favored by conservatives, and the recipient has broad discretion in terms of how the funds are spent (e.g., community development). To conservatives, a block grant promotes independence from federal bureaucrats, as state and local officials, not lawmakers and officials in Washington, D.C., decide how revenue from such grants is spent. Liberals generally favor categorical grants, where the recipient has less discretion on how to spend the funds (e.g., drug prevention education in the public schools). To liberals, the federal government has a better track record of promoting social equality than many states. Not all grants, however, lend themselves to an ideological debate between liberals and conservatives.

The days of dual federalism are over. Since the time of FDR's presidency, federal, state, and local officials generally attempt to address the policy challenges of the day by collaborating and working together, understanding that the size and scope of the national government increased in the modern period. Thus, the doctrine of states' rights, while still in existence, does not mean the same thing today as it did earlier in U.S. history. Debates about how much power the national government should have with regard to the states will likely continue into perpetuity. As indicated explicitly in Article VI of the U.S. Constitution, however, federal law supersedes state law. Federal officials may choose to engage in **devolution**, which means to send power from the national government back to the states, but implementation of such an action will not likely result in massive cuts to the state and local governments.

The Importance of Citizenship in a Republic

All citizens should seek to empower themselves with knowledge of the basics of American democracy and the history of their own country. In doing so, they will be better equipped to hold their leaders accountable because their enhanced knowledge will assist them in the national debate concerning politics and public affairs. Consider what the researchers from the Annenberg Public Policy Center of the University of Pennsylvania report every year after their Constitution Day survey on civics knowledge. Our collective reverence of the Constitution is matched by our lack of awareness of what is in it.[17]

In 2008 two very prominent Americans served as the cochairs of the Campaign for the Civic Mission of Schools. Justice Sandra Day O'Connor is a Republican who became the first woman in U.S. history to be appointed to the U.S. Supreme Court, where she served from 1981 to 2006. Lee Hamilton was a Democratic member of the U.S. House of Representatives from 1965 to 1999. In a 2008 editorial in the *Christian Science Monitor*, they declared:

> If we hope to sustain American democracy, we need to treat civic learning as on a par with other academic subjects. To participate fully in our democracy, students need to understand our government, our history, and our laws. They need to appreciate the skills democracy imposes on us—consensus building, compromise, civility, and ratio-

nal discourse—and how they can be applied to the problems confronted by their communities and our nation as a whole. Restoring this civic mission of schools will require a concerted effort in school districts, at statehouses, and by the federal government.

The federal government should embrace civic education when it revisits education reform next year. Developing and then mandating civics standards—and increasing funding for civic learning—would go a long way toward jump-starting progress.

States likewise can elevate the importance of civic learning by creating commissions to review thoroughly the state's approach to civic education, instituting civics as a graduation requirement, and funding professional and curricular development.

Schools, which the noted education reformer John Dewey called the "midwife of democracy," should include civic learning in their mission statements and incorporate civics—including discussion of controversial topics and the responsibilities of citizen engagement—into their curricula for students of all ages.

The anniversary of the Constitution and the upcoming presidential election offer a chance to reflect on the health of American democracy. Still, democracy is a sustained conversation among citizens over how best to govern their communities. It is not enough for this conversation to take place on one day, or even over the course of one campaign.[18]

Scholars, educators, and lawmakers all emphasize that Americans owe it to their ancestors, their contemporaries, and future generations to be diligent and informed citizens willing to apply that knowledge in pursuit of a more perfect union.

Many Americans still have great reverence for the framers of the Constitution and what they accomplished in the late 18th century. It is now the 21st century, but certain realities have not changed in the United States. The framers of the Constitution created a republican form of government, and it has been in existence for over 230 years. By comparison with the authors of America's first constitution, the Constitution that has been in effect since 1789 was far more successful.

Bear in mind, however, that the architects of the Constitution were human, just like all of us today. Some of the same people who signed the Constitution also signed the Articles of Confederation, so they fully realized that even well-intended people could make mistakes. The Constitution is not perfect, for nothing created by humans achieves perfection. Even Madison did not agree with everything in it. For example, he believed it was unfair that each state, regardless of its population, was allowed two U.S. senators under the Constitution and instead supported proportional representation in both chambers of Congress. He determined that he had to compromise on some of his beliefs to achieve his greatest objective at the Philadelphia Convention: establishing a republican form of government.

As citizens in a republic, we need to understand how important it is for all of us to understand that in a democracy, citizens do not always get what they want. As **Benjamin Franklin** (1706–1790)—the oldest framer of the Constitution, as he was 81 in 1787—noted on the very last day of the Philadelphia Convention:

> Mr. President:
>
> I confess that there are several parts of this constitution which I do not at present approve, but I am not sure I shall never approve them: For having lived long, I have experienced many instances of being obliged by better information or fuller consideration, to change opinions even on important subjects, which I once thought right, but found to be otherwise. It is therefore that the older I grow, the more apt I am to doubt my own judgment, and to pay more respect to the judgment of others. Most men indeed as well as most sects in Religion, think themselves in possession of all truth, and that wherever others differ from them it is so far error. . . . I doubt too whether any other Convention we can obtain, may be able to make a better Constitution. For when you assemble a number of men to have the advantage of their joint wisdom, you inevitably assemble with those men, all their prejudices, their passions, their errors of opinion, their local interests, and their selfish views. From such an Assembly can a perfect production be expected? It therefore astonishes me, Sir, to find this system approaching so near to perfection as it does; and I think it will astonish our enemies, who are waiting with confidence to hear . . . that our States are on the point of separation, only to meet hereafter for the purpose of cutting one another's throats. Thus I consent, Sir, to this Constitution because I expect no better, and because I am not sure, that it is not the best.[19]

Nearly all of the delegates to the Philadelphia Convention could find something they opposed in the final Constitution. Yet those who signed it presumably did so because they felt this new experiment in democracy would be more successful than the first trial under the Articles.

But Franklin had a vision of democracy that is worth considering today. To him, democracy was messy and it was not easy. In his time, simplicity prevailed in the existence of monarchies. It was the job of the people to serve the monarch, not the other way around. This system of government, however, is not democratic. The framers did not seek to establish a new monarchy in their independent country. They clearly supported the concept of republicanism, at least in the 18th-century context. By definition, democracies are wrought with conflict on a continuous basis. This is actually a good thing, simply because people are free to express their opinions and government officials are accountable to the people for their actions.

There is no accountability in a country with an authoritarian regime. Democratic systems of government have to be fully accountable to the people, whether it is 1789 or 2021. When the American people consented to a new form of government through the constitutional ratification process in 1787–1788, they were giving the proposed Constitution a chance because they collectively believed that the Constitution would be an improvement over the articles. It is fine for citizens today to celebrate the accomplishments of the past, including the Declaration of Independence and the drafting and ratification of the Constitution. But we need to heed some of the historical lessons that Franklin shared in 1787.

Franklin agreed with Madison in believing that a republican form of government was the most advantageous choice for a country whose citizens wanted to establish a new governance structure in the New World. For a democracy to be stable and flourish over time, it must have a proactive citizenry that is informed about what is happening in public affairs and be willing to actively engage in American politics. As citizens in a democracy, it is our job not only to know what is in the Constitution but also to analyze the contents. Part of the wisdom of the framers is that they allowed their document to be changed with great consensus. As a result, American government is much more democratic now than it was in the late 1700s. The challenge for citizens today is to find ways to expand democracy for Americans today and in the future. Such an approach to citizenship is what Franklin and others envisioned a long time ago.

Politics is all about conflict, and there is plenty of disagreement in a democratic system of government. The great challenge for people in the contemporary era is to find a way not to eliminate the conflict that exists in society—which is impossible when people are free to express their opinions in a hopefully civil manner—but to manage the conflict in question. In that manner, we can collectively continue to do what our ancestors started a long time ago. Our job as citizens is to make this republic better for those who may succeed us.

Knowledge Matters

It is very difficult to engage in citizenship with little or no fundamental knowledge about the structural rules embedded in the Constitution. The Constitution is the supreme law of the land, so it behooves all American citizens to review it carefully from time to time. A central message in this chapter is that information going back to the founding of the republic is important because all citizens can learn from history. If we do not understand the context of the founding of this republic, we are destined to repeat the mistakes of the past.

Reflect on what the eminent Supreme Court Justice Oliver Wendell Holmes offered in his analysis of studying law:

> At present, in very many cases, if we want to know why a rule of law has taken its particular shape, and more or less if we want to know why it exists at all, we go to tradition. . . . The rational study of law is still to a large extent the study of history. History must be a part of the study, because without it we cannot know the precise scope of rules which it is our business to know. It is a part of the rational study, because it is the first step toward an enlightened scepticism, that is, toward a deliberate reconsideration of the worth of those rules.[20]

Holmes was reflecting on the importance of studying history and past precedents so that one could gain a better understanding of the legal field. His fundamental premise—that it is essential to study history and to learn from it—is extremely important to citizens today. It is our business to know what is in the Constitution and to understand how the structural rules in the Constitution have evolved since the document was written in 1787. Understanding the brief history (compared to many nations) of the United States will not only enhance Americans' understanding of contemporary politics but will also, hopefully, increase the probability that the citizenry is equipped to address the policy challenges of today and those into the future.

Citizen Homework

Here are some sources available on the internet that can enhance citizen knowledge of both the Constitution and federalism in general:

U.S. Constitution: https://www.archives.gov/founding-docs/ constitution. There is no better way to understand the Constitution and its 27 amendments than simply reading it. It is a relatively short read, which delineates the fundamental democratic principles of the U.S. government. A basic overview of the Constitution can be obtained at https://www.whitehouse.gov/ about-the-white-house/the-constitution/.

Declaration of Independence: https://www.archives.gov/founding-docs/declaration. Read about the natural rights that apply to all citizens, the grievances against the British government, and the major announcement promulgated by Thomas Jefferson and his colleagues on July 4, 1776.

The Federalist Papers: http://avalon.law.yale.edu/subject_menus/fed.asp. Peruse these essays to gain a more enhanced understanding of all aspects of the new republic that the framers of the Constitution presented to the American people in 1787.

Layer cake federalism, cooperative federalism, and grants-in-aid: https://www.youtube.com/watch?v=J0gosGXSgsI. Learn more about the evolution of federalism in the United States by viewing this brief video.

Philadelphia Convention and the art of political compromise: https://www.youtube.com/watch?v=kCCmuftyj8A. Learn more about the Articles of Confederation and the political compromises that took place at the Philadelphia Convention in 1787.

CHAPTER 2

Civil Liberties and Civil Rights

Americans tend to believe they have the "right" to do many things in this republic. The inherent challenge is that sometimes these beliefs are tangible; at other times they are not.[1] Since they are often assumed, civil liberties typically come first and civil rights struggles commonly follow. **Civil liberties** are areas of personal freedom that government officials cannot infringe upon. A prime example of a civil liberty is the **First Amendment**, which protects freedom of speech, press, religion, and assembly. **Civil rights** are legal and moral claims that citizens are entitled to make on their government. Civil rights claims are based primarily on the **equal protection clause** of the Fourteenth Amendment. The Fourteenth Amendment generally guarantees citizenship, equal protection, and due process rights to the former slaves who were emancipated when the Union prevailed in the Civil War in 1865. The equal protection clause stipulates that both the federal and state governments must treat all citizens in an impartial manner so that the law does not discriminate against a specific category of individuals.

It is important for citizens to know and understand their rights in the American republic. Yet it is also essential for people to comprehend that not all rights are entirely clear and are thus subject to interpretation, most notably by federal judges. For example, the text of the Second Amendment reads:

> A well regulated Militia, being necessary to the security of a free State, the right of the people to keep and bear Arms, shall not be infringed.

The language used in the Second Amendment has created a great deal of debate, particularly in the modern era. To some citizens, the phrase "the right of the people to keep and bear Arms" means that individuals have an unfettered right to own a gun. To them, state legislatures or the federal Congress cannot prohibit gun ownership nor can legislative bodies restrict gun ownership. Other citizens have a much different interpretation of the Second Amendment. To them, the phrase "a well regulated Militia" suggests a collective right so that citizens of the colonial era could protect themselves from tyranny. From that perspective, individual citizens do not have the right to own a gun; therefore, federal and state legislators have the legal authority to regulate gun ownership.[2]

No rights are absolute, even though American citizens live in a democratic republic. None of us have the right to infringe on the rights of others. A historic example of this was a test created in free speech cases a century ago. Justice Oliver Wendell Holmes Jr. devised the **clear and present danger test** in a case after World War I. Justice Holmes used the example of shouting "Fire" in a crowded movie theater in *Schenck v. United States* (1919):

> The most stringent protection of free speech would not protect a man in falsely shouting fire in a theatre and causing a panic. . . . The question in every case is whether the words used are used in such circumstances and are of such a nature as to create a clear and present danger that they will bring about the substantive evils that Congress has a right to prevent. It is a question of proximity and degree.[3]

If people leave in panic and injuries happen, the instigator of the chaos will be responsible and held accountable for his or her actions. No civil liberties are absolute; all civil liberties are balanced in the context of protecting the greater common good. It is incumbent upon Americans to understand this reality in order to help guide them in civil liberties debates now and into the future.

A tenuous balance that has always existed in the United States is preserving civil liberties while simultaneously keeping the people safe. Here is what Benjamin Franklin said about this balance in a 1755 letter to the governor of Pennsylvania:

> Those who would give up essential Liberty, to purchase a little temporary Safety, deserve neither Liberty nor Safety.[4]

In the aftermath of the terrorist attacks on September 11, 2001, Americans supported the USA Patriot Act because they sought security and protection by federal officials. Since the original act, and its successor in 2015, the USA Freedom Act, critics have contended that the law violates fundamental constitutional rights, allows government officials to spy on them without due process and search their homes without consent, and increases the risk of citizens being accused of crimes without just cause.[5] Many years later, the premise that diminished liberties are the price to pay for more security still pervades the political arena. The lessons of history suggest that at some point Americans will opt for higher protections of civil liberties and that the willingness to negotiate some civil liberties protections for more perceived safety will diminish.

Historical Evolution of Civil Liberties

Over time, civil liberties have expanded in the United States. Starting with the Bill of Rights in 1791, 10 amendments were added to the Constitution to specifically protect civil liberties. After the First Amendment, such freedoms as the right to bear arms (Second Amendment), protection from illegal searches and seizures (Fourth Amendment), protection against self-incrimination (Fifth Amendment), the right to a speedy and public trial with an impartial jury (Sixth Amendment), and protection from cruel and unusual punishment (Eighth Amendment) were guaranteed in the federal Constitution.

In addition, both the Fifth and Fourteenth Amendments guarantee **due process clause** protections. The Fifth Amendment has typically applied to the federal government and the Fourteenth Amendment applied to the states. Under both amendments, no person can be denied life, liberty, or property without due process of law. Civil liberties vastly expanded in the United States in the 1960s through the judicial process of selective incorporation. Up to this time, the Supreme Court justices interpreted the Bill of Rights provisions as applicable to only the federal government. This interpretation of the Constitution would later evolve in the 1960s in a series of cases that are discussed later in this chapter.

The **Civil War Amendments** (Thirteen, Fourteen, and Fifteen) expanded civil liberties following the Union victory in the Civil War. Slavery was abolished under the **Thirteenth Amendment** (1865). The intent of the Fourteenth Amendment (1868) was to make the former slaves citizens and to provide equal protection. To illustrate how civil liberties come first, and may be followed by a civil rights struggle, the **Fif-**

teenth Amendment (1870) can be used. As presented in chapter 3, African American men were granted suffrage and started voting for the first time. After Reconstruction ended and the Jim Crow era commenced, countless barriers were established in order to prevent many African American men from voting, especially in the South. It took a civil rights movement in the 1950s and 1960s to implement a civil liberty that was explicitly added to the Constitution about a century before.

When the outcome of the disputed 1876 presidential election was determined, it hindered the causes of civil liberties and equality for generations. In a contentious election between Democrat **Samuel Tilden** (1814–1886) and Republican **Rutherford B. Hayes** (1822–1893), the election came down to the electoral votes of Florida, Louisiana, and South Carolina. At that time, the South was a Democratic region. However, Hayes agreed to end **Reconstruction** by withdrawing federal troops from the South. Reconstruction was a federal policy of reorganizing and reestablishing the former Confederate states after the Union victory in the Civil War. It lasted from 1865 to 1877. Southern states were rebuilt during this time and brought back into the Union. Union troops occupied the South in order to ensure that the former slaves were not mistreated. In exchange for his willingness to end Reconstruction, Hayes was able to prevail in the electoral contest and gain a simple majority in the Electoral College in the closest electoral vote in U.S. presidential history: 185 votes for Hayes and 184 votes for Tilden in spite of the fact that Tilden won the popular vote by 3 percent. This informal agreement was known as the **Compromise of 1877** and earned Hayes the nickname "Rutherfraud" by his political opponents.

A period of overt racism arose during the **Jim Crow** era. African Americans were clearly not treated as political equals to white Americans in the South as well as the other regions of the country. Jim Crow laws were passed by state and local government lawmakers that mandated segregated public facilities by race. African Americans were depicted in popular culture in an blatantly discriminatory manner. First- and second-class citizenship existed in the United States, and the Supreme Court justices later upheld segregation laws in *Plessy v. Ferguson* (1896) as long as the tangible physical facilities were "separate but equal." During the segregation era, facilities were separate but they were clearly not equal. African Americans experienced overt discrimination for many generations after the end of Reconstruction.

Plessy was decided by a 7–1 vote. The lone dissenter, Justice **John Marshall Harlan** (1833–1911), said:

The white race deems itself to be the dominant race in this country. And so it is in prestige, in achievements, in education, in wealth and in power. So, I doubt not, it will continue to be for all time if it remains true to its great heritage and holds fast to the principles of constitutional liberty. But in view of the Constitution, in the eye of the law, there is in this country no superior, dominant, ruling class of citizens. There is no caste here. Our Constitution is color-blind, and neither knows nor tolerates classes among citizens. In respect of civil rights, all citizens are equal before the law.[6]

Harlan's interpretation of the equal protection clause was later vindicated in *Brown v. Board of Board of Education of Topeka, KS* (1954). In this case the justices banned segregation laws and agreed that the Fourteenth Amendment does not allow distinctions based on race, because all citizens are equal in terms of the law. The justices outlawed **de jure segregation**, or segregation created by law or public policy. However, they did not invalidate **de facto segregation**, or segregation by the fact of where people reside.

Historically, the Bill of Rights expanded greatly through a process known as selective incorporation. The Fourteenth Amendment provided the basis to make the Bill of Rights applicable to the states, but it would take almost 100 years for that to happen. The Fourteenth Amendment was passed, in part, to ensure that state officials would not deny the newly freed slaves the full protection of the law. The due process clause of the Fourteenth Amendment led to an important expansion of civil liberties in America, because the justices of the Supreme Court had determined earlier that the due process clause of the Fifth Amendment applied to Congress; the new due process clause therefore applied to the state governments.

In *Barron v. Baltimore* (1833) the justices ruled that the Bill of Rights provisions applied only to Congress and not the state governments. Even after the passage of the Fourteenth Amendment, the justices were largely unwilling to apply the Bill of Rights to the states. It was not until *Gitlow v. New York* (1925) that the justices reversed the precedent that had been established in 1833 regarding the Bill of Rights.

Benjamin Gitlow was a socialist who was arrested in 1919 for distributing a "Left Wing Manifesto," which touted the establishment of socialism through strikes. Gitlow was convicted under New York's Criminal Anarchy Law. This law criminalized advocating for the overthrow of the government by force. The Court's majority reasoned that state officials in New York could punish speech that threatens its existence due to concerns over public security. The importance of *Gitlow* is that the precedent established in *Barron v. Baltimore* was partly reversed, for the **selective incorporation** principle allows the Fourteenth Amendment to be applicable to the states. Selective incorporation is a judicial process by which the due process clause of the Fourteenth Amendment becomes a funnel through which the Bill of Rights provisions become applicable to state governments. Until the 1960s, when selective incorporation became more widely used in practice by the Supreme Court justices, the Bill of Rights applied only to the federal government. When state officials were also bound by the first 10 amendments, selective incorporation had the effect of vastly expanding civil liberties in the United States.

In the 1960s the Supreme Court, under the leadership of Chief Justice **Earl Warren** (1891–1974), issued several rulings that had a significant impact on civil liberties in America. The most important cases included *Gideon v. Wainwright* (1963), *Escobedo v. Illinois* (1964), and *Miranda v. Arizona* (1966). In all of these cases, the justices used the due process clause of the Fourteenth Amendment to apply the Bill of Rights provisions to the states.

In *Gideon* the justices determined that Florida state officials denied Clarence Gideon the right to counsel under the Sixth Amendment when he was tried for breaking into a pool hall. Gideon requested an attorney due to his indigence but was denied one under Florida law, which, at the time, provided public defenders only in cases involving capital crimes. In *Escobedo* the justices concluded that the defendant, Danny Escobedo, was denied the right to counsel under the Sixth Amendment, similar to *Gideon*. In this case, however, Escobedo was arrested and questioned in a police station about a murder. He repeatedly requested his attorney, but the police would not allow him to see his lawyer. He subsequently confessed to the crime. The justices ruled that the police violated the Constitution because they would not allow Escobedo to confer with his legal representative. The most controversial case, however, was *Miranda*. In this case there was no question that Ernesto Miranda was guilty of some violent crimes. He was released upon order by the justices, however, because the police denied Miranda his Fifth Amendment protection against self-incrimination, as they did not explain his constitutional rights to him before he confessed to the crimes in question. This case led to the education of police across the country about the Bill of Rights.

There are a number of other civil liberties issues in the United States. Among some of the more prominent include the following: freedom of religion (First Amendment), freedom of speech (First Amendment), freedom of assembly (First Amendment), freedom of the press (First Amendment), the right to bear arms (Second Amendment), unreasonable searches and seizures (Fourth Amendment), protection again self-incrimination (Fifth Amendment), the right to counsel and a jury trial (Sixth Amendment), protection against cruel and unusual punishment (Eighth Amendment), and privacy rights, which may be implied by a multitude of constitutional protections. Political conflict is omnipresent concerning civil liberties because Americans have differing perceptions about the practical applications of civil liberties in contemporary society. Many Americans believe there is too much gun violence in this country, particularly when a mass shooting occurs in a school or some other public or private locale. Some citizens espouse more stringent gun control measures, especially to protect children in their school environments. Others believe that any restrictions on guns by federal, state, or local officials are an impingement on their right to bear arms. Crafting a compromise measure has proven elusive to policy makers at the federal level in recent years.

Historical Evolution of Civil Rights

The pursuit of equality for all Americans has a long history in the United States. When the Fourteenth Amendment was added to the Constitution, all citizens were supposed to be equal in terms of federal law. Equality, however, has not always been afforded to all citizens. After slavery was abolished in 1865, members of Congress passed civil rights legislation in 1866 and again in 1875, but there was no enforcement mechanism. Following the end of Reconstruction in 1877, segregation laws were passed in many Southern states during the Jim Crow era. Laws enacted during this time were vastly discriminatory and hurtful. Segregation was mandated in neighborhoods, schools, restaurants, hospitals, restrooms, drinking fountains, cemeteries, hotels, and many other public places, and it was upheld as constitutional in the *Plessy* decision. For the first few decades after Reconstruction, the plight of African Americans was ignored by the rest of society, as most African Americans at this time lived in the South. In the early 20th century, thousands of African Americans migrated to the North, so the race dilemma in the United States was no longer an issue relevant just to the South but to the whole country. The issue of segregation was particularly salient during World Wars I and II, when African Americans served in the military but only in segregated units.

Progress in civil rights in America was achieved in the *Brown* decision in 1954. Unfortunately, though segregated public schools were declared to be unconstitutional by the justices in this case, very little progress was witnessed in the school desegregation movement until the late 1960s and early 1970s.[7] In a series of cases, the justices of the Supreme Court helped to accelerate the process of desegregating public schools.[8] Some civil rights advocates contend that much of the progress toward achieving racial balance in the public schools was stymied in *Milliken v. Bradley* (1974).[9] In this case the Supreme Court justices determined that federal district court judges did not have the authority to order a metropolitan school desegregation remedy in situations where segregation existed in the urban school districts but not in the outlying suburban districts.

Much of the focus on civil rights in U.S. history has been related to slavery and then racial segregation. **Martin Luther King Jr.** (1929–1968) led the civil rights movement from 1954 until he was assassinated in 1968. Through nonviolence and civil disobedience, a great deal of progress was achieved in the United States with the passage of the **Civil Rights Act of 1964** and the **Voting Rights Act of 1965**. The Civil Rights Act of 1964 is the most comprehensive civil rights law in U.S. history. The act ended segregation in public places and banned employment discrimination on the basis of race, gender, religion, or national origin. The Voting Rights Act of 1965 is a landmark federal law that prohibited racial discrimination in voting in the United States. In 1963 King articulated his vision for an equality in America in his "I Have a Dream" speech:

I say to you today, my friends, though, even though we face the difficulties of today and tomorrow, I still have a dream. It is a dream deeply rooted in the American dream. I have a dream that one day this nation will rise up, live out the true meaning of its creed: "We hold these truths to be self-evident, that all men are created equal."

I have a dream that one day on the red hills of Georgia sons of former slaves and the sons of former slave-owners will be able to sit down together at the table of brotherhood. I have a dream that one day even the state of Mississippi, a state sweltering with the heat of injustice, sweltering with the heat of oppression, will be transformed into an oasis of freedom and justice.

I have a dream that my four little children will one day live in a nation where they will not be judged by the color of their skin but by the content of their character. I have a dream. . . . I have a dream that one day in Alabama, with its vicious racists, with its governor having his lips dripping with the words of interposition and nullification, one day right there in Alabama little black boys and black girls will be able to join hands with little white boys and white girls as sisters and brothers. . . .

When we allow freedom to ring—when we let it ring from every city and every hamlet, from every state and every city, we will be able to speed up that day when all of God's children, black men and white men, Jews and Gentiles, Protestants and Catholics, will be able to join hands and sing in the words of the old Negro spiritual, "Free at last, Free at last, Great God a-mighty, We are free at last."[10]

King was an advocate for full implementation of the equal protection clause of the Fourteenth Amendment. This was the primary legal basis for the civil rights movement of the 1950s and 1960s.

Several other groups have experienced lengthy civil rights struggles that continue into the 21st century. Women have endured discrimination throughout U.S. history. They were not granted suffrage in the federal Constitution until 1920, though women in some states, such as Wyoming, were granted suffrage as early as 1869.[11] Additionally, women in many states did not control their own property upon marriage. In *Bradwell v. Illinois* (1873) the justices upheld an Illinois law that forbade women from practicing law based on this reasoning by Justice Joseph Bradley:

It certainly cannot be affirmed, as an historical fact, that this has ever been established as one of the fundamental privileges and immunities of the sex. On the contrary, the civil law, as well as nature herself, has always recognized a wide difference in the respective spheres and destinies of man and woman. Man is, or should be, woman's protector and defender. The natural and proper timidity and delicacy which belongs to the female sex evidently unfits it for many of the occupations of civil life. The Constitution of the family organization, which is founded in the divine ordinance as well as in the nature of things, indicates the domestic sphere as that which properly belongs to the domain and functions of womanhood. The harmony, not to say identity, of interest and views which belong, or should belong, to the family institution is repugnant to the idea of a woman adopting a distinct and independent career from that of her husband. So firmly fixed was this sentiment in the founders of the common law that it became a maxim of that system of jurisprudence that a woman had no legal existence separate from her husband, who was regarded as her head and representative in the social state, and, notwithstanding some recent modifications of this civil status, many of the special rules of law flowing from and dependent upon this cardinal principle still exist in full force in most states. One of these is that a married woman is incapable, without her husband's consent, of making contracts which shall be binding on her or him. This very incapacity was one circumstance which the Supreme Court of Illinois deemed important in rendering a married woman incompetent fully to perform the duties and trusts that belong to the office of an attorney and counselor.[12]

The premise that women should not have their own careers is contrary to the equal protection clause of the Fourteenth Amendment. Rather, Title VII of the Civil Rights Act of 1964 prohibits employment discrimination based on sex. While measurable progress has been achieved for women in American society (e.g., more women serving in Congress, numerous professions, and in management positions), there is still a significant difference in earnings in the United States in terms of gender. Women typically make between 80–83 percent of what their male counterparts earn in this country.[13]

For much of American history, gay and lesbian Americans had to live secret lives for fear of abuse and discrimination. The gay rights movement, however, was launched in 1969 as a result of a police raid at the Stonewall Inn in New York City.[14] At that time it was common for police to raid gay bars to harass patrons. A crowd gathered outside the bar in the street and, rather than dispersing, several hundred to thousands of people protested law enforcement and hurled objects at the police. The Stonewall rebellion lasted for several days and galvanized the gay community when many supporters came to conclude that they could promote the cause of civil rights through collective action.

The Supreme Court justices ruled in *Bowers v. Hardwick* (1986) that the Constitution did not include a fundamental right for homosexuals to engage in consensual sodomy and that state legislatures could outlaw such practices. This was a devastating defeat for the gay rights movement. In *Lawrence v. Texas* (2003), however, the justices reversed the ruling in *Bowers*. Under the due process clause of the Fourteenth Amendment, the justices ruled that citizens do have the right to engage in private consensual affairs and that state legislators have no legitimate interest in criminalizing such conduct.

Other groups, such as Native, Latino, and Asian Americans have struggled for equality as well. Native Americans were in the United States long before European immigrants arrived. As more and more settlers arrived, Native Americans were pushed from their ancestral lands and forced to live on reservations. Perhaps the most startling illustration of this devastating human rights issue occurred when President Andrew Jackson signed the Indian Removal Act of 1830. This began a process of forced relocation of thousands of Native Americans that became known as the Trail of Tears because more than 4,000 of the 46,000 Native Americans that were relocated died because of harsh conditions, starvation, and disease. After Oklahoma became a state in 1907, Native American lands were gone forever.[15] Native Americans were subsequently afforded citizenship by members of Congress under the Indian Citizenship Act.[16]

Latinos have long endured prejudice and discrimination in the United States. Between 1846 and 1848, the United States absorbed a great deal of territory from Mexico, which today makes up most of the Southwest. The pursuit for economic equality was highlighted by César Chávez in the 1960s and 1970s. The struggle for equality for Latino Americans is particularly challenging, as they vote at low levels due to the language barrier and about one-third of Latino adults cannot vote because they are not citizens. While many Mexican Americans have had roots in the United States for generations, most Latinos have only been in the United States for a relatively short period of time. They are currently gaining in political clout, though, as Latinos are now the largest minority group in the United States.

Asian Americans immigrated to the United States beginning in the mid-19th century. Many Chinese Americans experienced violence as a result of the California Gold Rush. A great number of Chinese immigrants worked on the transcontinental railroad after the Civil War and lost their lives, as they were given the most dangerous jobs. After the completion of the railroad project, numerous Chinese Americans returned to the West Coast, where they were the victims of racial prejudice and violence. In 1882 members of Congress passed the Chinese Exclusion Act. This was the first significant law in America that restricted immigration into the United States. Chinese immigration was suspended for 10 years (this restriction was later renewed) and Chinese Americans were ineligible for naturalization.[17] Later, during World War II, President Franklin Roosevelt issued an executive order that placed more than 110,000 Japanese Americans in internment camps during World War II. Members of Congress in the 1980s later apologized for this activity and provided reparations for the survivors.[18] As with other groups, there is a great deal of diversity in culture and political views with Asian Americans, as a broad range of Asians have immigrated to the United States, including Koreans, Cambodians, Vietnamese, Hmong, Filipinos, in addition to their peers from China and Japan.

Civil Liberties and Civil Rights Today

The debate about whether Americans have a **right to privacy** continues to this day. The phrase "right to privacy" does not exist in the federal Constitution in an explicit manner. The right to privacy is the implied right to be left alone in the federal Constitution based on an interpretation of the First, Fourth, Fifth, Ninth, and Fourteenth Amendments. Despite the lack of a specifically enumerated right to privacy, **Samuel Warren** (1852–1910) and **Louis Brandeis** (1856–1941) wrote an article titled "The Right to Privacy" in an 1890 article in the *Harvard Law Review*.[19] Basically, the two Boston lawyers defined the right to privacy as the right to be left alone from undue government interference. Brandeis was later appointed to be the first Jewish American to serve on the Supreme Court, a position he occupied from 1916 to 1939. In the 20th century the justices determined that a right to privacy does exist in the Constitution because it is implied by the existence of other civil liberties identified in the amendments mentioned above. Later, in a landmark decision, the justices extended the right to privacy to abortion, at least in the first trimester of the human gestation period, in *Roe v. Wade* (1973).

Another contentious issue with regard to civil liberties and civil rights is same-sex marriage. For most of U.S. history, same-sex marriages were denied to gay Americans by the states. In *Obergefell v. Hodges* (2015), however, the Supreme Court justices determined by a 5–4 vote that the due process and equal protection clauses of the Fourteenth Amendment provide a fundamental right for same-sex couples to legally get married. This ruling continues to be critiqued by many political conservatives today, as they view the matter as a states' rights issue and not one that should be mandated by federal officials.

A prominent civil rights debate for the past several decades is **affirmative action**. Affirmative action is a public policy designed to redress past and continuing discrimination against women and nonwhites in the employment and higher education sectors in particular. In the mid-1960s, affirmative action was a bipartisan issue in that adherents in both major parties generally supported it. About a quarter century later, a schism developed, and for the past few decades, Democrats generally support affirmative action and Republicans generally oppose it. The

Supreme Court justices upheld the constitutionality of affirmative action in *Regents of the University of California v. Bakke* (1978). At the same time, the justices determined that quotas, or automatic slots for specific classes of individuals, were unconstitutional. Allan Bakke, a white student, was denied admission to the medical school at the University of California, Davis. When he discovered that 16 of 100 slots in the entering medical school class were reserved for minority students, he challenged the constitutionality of this policy, contending that it resulted in reverse discrimination against him as a white male. He prevailed in the case.

Twenty-five years after *Bakke*, the justices decided two cases involving the University of Michigan. With regard to undergraduate admissions, the justices overturned a policy of awarding 20 points to African, Latino, and Native Americans as unconstitutional (100/150 total points were needed for admission to the institution) in *Gratz v. Bollinger* (2003). In another case, *Grutter v. Bollinger* (2003), the justices upheld the *Bakke* ruling with regard to the constitutionality of affirmative action. The admissions policy used by law school officials was upheld because the justices concluded that officials at the University of Michigan had a compelling interest to promote diversity at their institution. Thus, as it was in 1978, affirmative action continues to be constitutional from the perspective of the justices. It is important to note, however, that the justices do not view affirmative action policies as permanent in nature. In her majority opinion in *Grutter v. Bollinger,* Justice Sandra Day O'Connor determined the following:

> It has been 25 years since Justice Powell (the prevailing vote in the *Bakke* decision) first approved the use of race to further an interest in student body diversity in the context of public higher education. Since that time, the number of minority applicants with high grades and test scores has indeed increased. We expect that 25 years from now, the use of racial preferences will no longer be necessary to further the interest approved today.[20]

I believe that O'Connor was suggesting that in the pursuit of a more perfect union, it is conceivable that at some point affirmative action policies will no longer be needed in the event that all citizens are treated the same, regardless of a wide variety of demographical factors.

Civil liberties and civil rights struggles continue. Presumably in a democracy they will always persist, and as free citizens Americans will be able to continue to express themselves in a differential manner. Given the subject areas of civil liberties and civil rights, gaining more knowledge of these key areas of democracy is an essential starting point for maintaining this right. Information is essential, but awareness is as well. It is important for citizens to understand that they have important liberties as a consequence of living in a democratic republic. But people also have responsibilities that coincide with being citizens in a democracy.

The Importance of Citizenship in a Republic

As Benjamin Franklin astutely noted in the 18th century, civil liberties are central to adherents of democracy. Citizens should understand the importance of their constitutional guarantees. A first step in this process, naturally, is to become more familiar with the federal Constitution itself. Reviewing it is a fundamentally important exercise that should be revisited on frequent occasions. Beyond that is a realization that although liberties are guarantees for citizens, all of us also have responsibilities that are associated with citizenship. Jane Grant published a book in 2008 titled *The New American Social Compact: Rights and Responsibilities in the Twenty-First Century*. In the book, she concludes:

> The nation faces many dangers at this moment in time. It is adrift, lacking the needed resolve to fulfill its commitments to its own citizens and future generations. It has abdicated its responsibilities or has been unwilling to recognize what it owes to the other people, other nations, and other species in the world. Americans and their leaders need to newly rededicate themselves to protecting the cherished rights of all citizens, while pledging to acknowledge what we are ethically bound to honor in each other. By respecting the precious autonomy of individuals and recognizing our essential interdependence, we can fully address the problems of our own nation, those of the larger world community, and of those of the earth upon which we all depend in the 21st century.[21]

Indeed, citizens should rightly protect their most fundamental civil liberties, for they are essential components of democratic governance. Yet all of us must embrace the notion that we must contribute to the greater community as well. A fundamental reality is that the United States is not a nation of about 330 million isolated individuals, whose collective actions do not affect their fellow citizens. Rather, our individual decisions about an array of policy issues likely have broad implications not only for people in this country but also for the world as a whole. We are interconnected and interdependent whether we choose to accept this reality or not.

Thus, citizens can repudiate the politics of individualism and seek to view public policy issues from more of a societal perspective. In other words, what effect does policy X have on general society as opposed to what policy X does for the individual and her or his family. In fact, it was Alexis de Tocqueville who provided a succinct overview of individualism in America during his travails in this country in the 19th century:

> I have brought out how, in centuries of equality, each man seeks his beliefs in himself; I want to show how, in the same centuries, he turns all his sentiments toward himself alone. *Individualism* is a recent expression arising from a new idea. Our fathers knew only selfishness. Selfishness is a passionate and exaggerated love of self that brings man to relate everything to himself alone and to prefer himself to everything. Individualism is a reflective and peaceable sentiment that disposes each citizen to isolate himself from the mass of those like him and to withdraw to one side with his family and his friends, so that after having thus created a little society for his own use, he willingly abandons society at large to itself. Selfishness is born of a blind instinct; individualism proceeds from an erroneous judgment rather than a depraved sentiment. . . . As conditions are equalized, one finds a great number of individuals who, not being wealthy enough or powerful enough to exert a great influence over the fates of those like them, have nevertheless acquired or preserved enough enlightenment and goods to be able to be self-sufficient. These owe nothing to anyone, they expect so to speak nothing from anyone; they are in the habit of always considering themselves in isolation, and they willingly fancy that their whole destiny is in their hands. Thus not only does democracy make each man forget his ancestors, but it hides his descendants from him and separates him from his contemporaries; it constantly leads him back toward himself alone and threatens finally to confine him wholly in the solitude of his own heart.[22]

Individualism is often portrayed in popular culture in a very positive manner. It is always compelling to learn of individuals overcoming seemingly insurmountable challenges to accomplish noteworthy achievements. Yet individualism taken to an extreme can lead citizens to become too inward in their focus and worldview. This practice can be antithetical to promoting the greater common good and can prompt people to avoid being empathetic. Empathy is the ability of one citizen to understand the experience and perspective of another citizen. In order to have empathy, people must care enough about their fellow citizens to consider their plight in society. Some social scientists believe that contemporary Americans have succumbed to the politics of individualism at a substantial cost to society.[23] In order to have a facilitative public debate over civil liberties and civil rights, it is incumbent upon citizens to at least attempt to balance the needs of the greater community with individual civil liberties. The balance in question will not be easy to address and it will result in political conflict. Yet if a balance is to be achieved and preserved into the future, it will be indicative that citizens today contributed to the democratic foundation of this republic. After all, most people would endorse empathy over selfishness without hesitation.[24]

Many Americans associate democracy, in part and rightfully so, with the existence of constitutional rights. There are certain areas of personal freedom where no legitimate government interest exists. Given the history of this republic, it was clear to many Americans in the late 18th century that their fundamental freedoms were being violated and that they needed to do something about it in order to establish democracy in the New World. Today some Americans make exaggerated claims based on their perceptions of their "rights." One political scientist noted:

> The language of rights in the United States is a central element of law and legal meaning. Rights language is also prevalent within public consciousness, discourse, and practice. We live in a society in which people see themselves as rights-bearing beings and in which legal, political, and social relationships are commonly defined in terms of rights. Appeals to rights are regularly heard both within and beyond the courtroom. In short, rights language is a dominant component of the legal, political, and social realms, and it is embedded within thought and practice.[25]

Our collective tendency as Americans to focus on our rights likely precludes us from making reasonable political compromises on serious public policy issues. A prime example as noted in the beginning of this chapter is gun control. There is too much gun violence in American society. Mass shootings, while shocking in nature, have become somewhat commonplace in this country. The image of schoolchildren running for their lives is etched in the American experience. Yet even the most incremental, arguably reasonable, legislative measures designed to keep citizens, including children, safe are routinely blocked from passing. Unquestionably, the gun lobby is powerful in American politics. This political reality cannot be disputed. Yet the manner in which the debate is constructed is also problematic. Instead of focusing on public safety, especially keeping vulnerable elementary schoolchildren safe, some Americans tend to focus first on their perceived rights. The history of gun legislation is replete in that when the debate is framed mostly in terms of rights, proposals designed to restrict, not forbid, gun ownership are routinely defeated in spite of public opinion on the matter.[26]

The existence of various freedoms in a democracy comes in the context that other citizens have rights as well. Accordingly, none of us has the right to abridge the rights of others. It is for this reason that civil liberties are not absolute under the Constitution; they must be carefully and properly balanced, which is why conflicts regarding liberties tend to be very strident, and many are resolved by federal judges when they tell us in their rulings what the law does and does not mean.

Knowledge Matters

Many of our predecessors struggled mightily for years in pursuit of a more perfect democracy. Any human endeavor is, of course, imperfect by definition. All humans make mistakes. A more perfect democracy is one that affords its citizens equality of opportunity, a concept that the vast majority of Americans embrace as fundamental in the United States. The history of the republic is well documented. The Constitution has become more democratic since the late 18th century. Civil liberties have been extended to groups that had been discriminated against in the past. In general, amendments to the U.S. Constitution have expanded civil liberties and not restricted them. This is fundamentally important information for citizens to ponder, for it compels all of us to consider specific proposals in perhaps a different way.

The case of flag burning provides a concrete illustration. We know through public opinion polls that many citizens, especially military veterans, find flag burning to be patently offensive. This issue was brought to the Supreme Court justices in 1989 in the case of *Texas v. Johnson*.[27] During the 1984 presidential election, Greg Johnson burned an American flag in front of Dallas City Hall to protest Reagan administration policies. Texas had a law that outlawed the desecration of the flag, so Johnson was convicted and sentenced to one year in jail and was assessed a $2,000 fine. The Texas Court of Criminal Appeals reversed his conviction, and then the case went to the U.S. Supreme Court. By a 5–4 decision the justices determined that burning the flag was protected expression under the First Amendment.[28]

Liberal justice William Brennan wrote the majority opinion. In it, he said, "If there is a bedrock principle underlying the First Amendment, it is that the government may not prohibit the expression of an idea simply because society finds the idea itself offensive or disagreeable."[29] Furthermore, Brennan determined the following:

> We are tempted to say, in fact, that the flag's deservedly cherished place in our community will be strengthened, not weakened, by our holding today. Our decision is a reaffirmation of the principles of freedom and inclusiveness that the flag best reflects, and of the conviction that our toleration of criticism such as Johnson's is a sign and source of our strength. Indeed, one of the proudest images of our flag, the one immortalized in our own national anthem, is of the bombardment it survived at Fort McHenry. It is the Nation's resilience, not its rigidity, that Texas sees reflected in the flag—and it is that resilience that we reassert today. The way to preserve the flag's special role is not to punish those who feel differently about these matters. It is to persuade them that they are wrong.[30]

Conservative justice Antonin Scalia, who was part of the Court's majority, said a few months before he passed away in 2016, "If it were up to me, I would put in jail every sandal-wearing, scruffy-bearded weirdo who burns the American flag. But I am not king."[31] There are times when many citizens will not embrace the views of others. In fact, they may find them downright abhorrent. Nevertheless, constitutional protections are in place that safeguard certain civil liberties. The constant challenge in a democracy is to balance civil liberties protections for individuals with the right of citizens to live peaceably in a civil society. Awareness of this omnipresent reality is beneficial to citizens in a republic; what citizens choose to do with this information is entirely up to them.

Citizen Homework

Here are some sources on the internet that can enhance fundamental knowledge about civil liberties and civil rights in general:

The Bill of Rights: https://www.youtube.com/watch?v=xgtrp66i2S8.
Information about the first 10 amendments, which came after
the original Constitution was put into effect, is available by viewing this brief video.
American Civil Liberties Union: https://www.aclu.org/. Information about a prominent civil liberties organization that was
formed about a century ago in the United States is available at
this website.
University of Pennsylvania Annenberg Public Policy Center Survey
(September 2017): https://cdn.annenbergpublicpolicycenter.
org/wp-content/uploads/2017/09/Appendix_Civics_sur-
vey_2017.pdf. Find out how much adult citizens know about the
Constitution. About 40 percent of Americans cannot name a
single right protected by the First Amendment. About one-third
of citizens cannot name just one of the three branches of government at the national level.
The right to privacy: http://law2.umkc.edu/faculty/projects/ftri
als/conlaw/rightofprivacy.html. Read more about the history of
the right to privacy in the United States.
The right to bear arms: https://www.youtube.com/
watch?v=BDvlqFBJh1o. CNN legal analyst Jeffrey Toobin dis-
cusses varying interpretations of the ambiguous Second Amendment in this brief video.

CHAPTER 3

Voting and Elections

Undoubtedly, the most apparent aspect of citizenship to many Americans involves voting in federal, state, and local elections. **Election Day** was established by Congress by law dating back to the mid-19th century. Federal elections are held every even-numbered year (e.g., 2020, 2022, 2024, etc.) on the Tuesday after the first Monday in November. There are two types of elections in the United States: **primary elections** and **general elections**. A primary election is held before the general election; in a primary election, citizens select nominees for the political parties in the general election. A general election is held at least every two years; in a general election, voters cast their ballots for U.S. House members, U.S. senators (if applicable), president and vice president (if applicable), as well as state and local officials (if applicable).

The role of citizens in voting and elections in the United States is paramount. In a democratic republic, proactive citizens have the serious responsibility of holding their elected leaders accountable. It is the duty of the people of this republic, in a collective sense, to reward officials for doing an effective job but also to punish those who do not represent their constituents in a reasonable manner. Accordingly, while we tend to view voting as a right, it is imperative that voting and participating in elections should be commonly defined as a responsibility as well.

It is my contention that a shift in culture toward more political awareness and involvement would be a positive sign for the health of the world's oldest democracy. It is difficult to counter the premise that Americans are comparatively disengaged from the political process, at least as measured by voter turnout (more about this issue will be covered later in this chapter). Americans vote at low numbers compared to citizens in other democracies. In addition, citizens do not appear to be enthralled with the political system in terms of their responses to fundamental questions posed by pollsters. For example, Gallup conducts an annual poll that solicits citizens' confidence in institutions of the United States. Pollsters ask citizens whether they have a great deal of confidence, quite a lot of confidence, some confidence, very little confidence, or no confidence at all in various institutions. For 2018, here are the results:

38 percent had a great deal/quite a lot of confidence in organized religion;
37 percent had a great deal/quite a lot of confidence in the Supreme Court;
11 percent had a great deal/quite a lot of confidence in Congress;
26 percent had a great deal/quite a lot of confidence in organized labor;
25 percent had a great deal/quite a lot of confidence in big business;
29 percent had a great deal/quite a lot of confidence in the public schools;
23 percent had a great deal/quite a lot of confidence in newspapers;
37 percent had a great deal/quite a lot of confidence in the presidency;
36 percent had a great deal/quite a lot of confidence in the medical system;
30 percent had a great deal/quite a lot of confidence in banks;
20 percent had a great deal/quite a lot of confidence in television news; and
22 percent had a great deal/quite a lot of confidence in the criminal justice system.

Positive ratings using this index were given to only three entities in 2018: the military (74 percent); the police (54 percent); and small business (67 percent).[1] These polling results do not suggest a high rate of satisfaction with crucial institutions in contemporary American society.

A central measure of citizen satisfaction with government in general is the basic survey that Gallup pollsters have been administered since the Watergate era: "Do you approve or disapprove of the way Congress is handling its job?" From January 2009 to March 2019, 126 surveys were taken. The average approval rating for Congress during this decade is 18 percent.[2] Only one-fifth of Americans typically approve of the way Congress is handling its job. This figure is hardly an affirmative vote when it comes to an evaluation of job performance. Simply put, if we do not collectively have faith in our national leaders, or many of our own societal institutions for that matter, it is incumbent upon all of us as citizens to make the republic work more effectively, even if that means making fundamental changes. In other words, if the status quo is not acceptable, perhaps there are plausible ways to make our institutions more responsive to the needs of citizens.

Historical Evolution of Voting

When the framers wrote the Constitution in 1787, they did not say much about voting and elections in the document. Nevertheless, they did make election administration an issue of federalism in Article I:

> The times, places and manner of holding elections for Senators and Representatives, shall be prescribed in each state by the legislature thereof; but the Congress may at any time by law make or alter such regulations, except as to the places of choosing Senators.

State legislators were afforded the opportunity to create rules governing the electoral process, yet members of Congress could intervene and establish more standard practices if they so desired. In short, state legislators were empowered with the task of running elections, although members of Congress could create laws that would govern all the states. In 1845, for example, a national Election Day was established for the first time in U.S. history. Prior to this time, states could conduct their presidential elections during a 34-day period (before the first Wednesday in December) pursuant to a law passed by the members of Congress in 1792.[3]

In 1787 elites had a much different view of citizen participation in the democratic process in terms of **suffrage** (the right to vote in political elections). This belief system was contextual in that only white males with a sufficient amount of property (e.g., some states required 50 acres of land) were eligible to vote in the states. Since the late 18th century, democracy has expanded in America. By the 1830s most state legislatures had eliminated the property requirements for voting. In 1848 feminists at the Seneca Falls Convention proposed suffrage for women. After the Union prevailed in the Civil War, African American men obtained the right to vote with the passage of the **Fifteenth Amendment** in 1870. Unfortunately, many barriers to voting were created in a number of states following the end of Reconstruction in 1877. Barriers that prevented thousands of African American men from exercising their right to vote included violence and intimidation, the "grandfather clause," literacy tests, poll taxes, and the white primary.

In 1898 legislatures in seven Southern states passed laws stipulating that those who had the right to vote prior to 1867, or their lineal descendants, would be exempt from educational, property, or tax requirements for voting. Thus, these **grandfather clause** laws had the effect of denying African American males the right to vote while assuring suffrage for impoverished and illiterate whites.[4] The justices of the Supreme Court later struck down the grandfather clause laws as unconstitutional in 1915.[5]

Literacy tests were administered by various state governments in the United States from the 1850s to the 1960s. A literacy test assesses a citizen's ability to read and write. In 1855 Connecticut became the first state to require a literacy test, and it was designed to keep Irish immigrants from voting. After the Civil War, many Southern states implemented literacy tests after Reconstruction so that African Americans would not be able to exercise their right to vote.[6] Literacy tests were not banned in this country until the Voting Rights Act of 1965 was passed.[7] Bear in mind that this is 95 years after all African American males were guaranteed the right to vote in 1870.

Poll taxes, or essentially a fee for voting, was another way to prevent African Americans from voting in Southern states. Eligible voters beginning in the 1890s were required to pay for the privilege of voting. While the corresponding grandfather clause excused a number of poor whites from paying the tax if they had an ancestor who voted before the Civil War, no such exemptions existed for African Americans.[8] Under the **Twenty-fourth Amendment** (1964), poll taxes were banned in federal elections. Two years later the justices of the Supreme Court determined that poll taxes were also invalid in state elections as well.[9]

The **white primary** was particularly devastating for African Americans during its utilization in the South. Texas became the first state in 1923 to pass a law stipulating that only white citizens could vote in a primary election. State legislators passed this law to disenfranchise African Americans and also Mexican Americans in the southern part of the state. Lawmakers in Texas argued that the Democratic Party in Texas was a private organization and thus had the right to limit who could become members in its own organization.[10] From the end of Reconstruction to the 1960s, the

"Solid South" was a stronghold for the conservative Democratic Party. Winning the primary was tantamount to winning the general election, as the Democratic Party maintained overwhelming support by white citizens. The Supreme Court justices later determined that the white primary was unconstitutional in *Smith v. Allwright* (1944).[11]

After the departure of Union troops in the South after Reconstruction, the Jim Crow era began in the American South. Segregation laws were created throughout the South and were based on extreme racist attitudes. White Southerners sought to preserve a caste system that subjugated African Americans throughout the region. After the Civil War was over, the **Ku Klux Klan (KKK)** was first organized. The KKK is an overt white supremacist organization that advocates for white supremacy and white nationalism while condemning immigration, Catholicism, and Judaism.

Although the first iteration of the Klan did not last long after the Civil War, it would reappear and spread throughout the country in the early 20th century. When the Klan started in 1866, it became a way for white Southerners to oppose Republican Party policies that had the objective of establishing political and economic equality for African Americans.

The Klan was in a period of decline in terms of membership until around 1915, when it reemerged as a group not only committed to oppressing African Americans but also espousing hatred against Roman Catholics, Jews, foreigners, and organized labor. Klan membership peaked in the 1920s at more than 4 million people across the country. Today it is estimated that Klan membership has declined to about 8,000 active members, mostly in the South.[12]

In other ways, however, voting has been expanded to include more groups in American society throughout the history of the country. Due to the eras of Jeffersonian democracy (1801–1809) and Jacksonian democracy (1829–1837), many state legislatures abolished property qualifications and allowed all white males who were 21 years of age the right to vote. In 1913 the **Seventeenth Amendment** was added to the Constitution, allowing the people the right to directly elect U.S. senators. Under the original Constitution, the people could only directly elect U.S. House members, which is why the House is known as the "people's House." U.S. senators were selected by state legislatures and the president was directly selected by the Electoral College. Seven years later, in 1920, women were finally granted the right to vote in federal elections as a result of the **Nineteenth Amendment**. It literally took seven decades of struggle to achieve this fundamental right for women. Before passage of the amendment, women in several states had no way to hold federal lawmakers accountable. Demographics played an important role in the action by the Wyoming legislature to confer voting rights to women in its territory shortly after the end of the Civil War. It would take another half century for women to secure suffrage across the nation.[13]

In 1961 electors for the District of Columbia were established under the **Twenty-third Amendment**. The amendment is interesting in that it stipulates that the district would appoint "a number of electors of President and Vice President equal to the whole number of Senators and Representatives in Congress to which the District would be entitled if it were a state." Thus, the District of Columbia has three electors, as it would have one congressional representative, based on its population, and two senators, if it were designated by Congress as a state. District residents have been arguing for many decades that it should not be taxed without representation, given the historical importance of the "no taxation without representation" mantra dating back to the American Revolution.

In 1971 the **Twenty-sixth Amendment** was added to the federal Constitution, thereby allowing 18-, 19-, and 20-year-olds the right to vote. During the height of the Vietnam War, many young people questioned the fact that even though they could serve their country in battle, they were not afforded the right to vote. In this context the right to vote was extended to include more young people.

The procedure for adding amendments to the federal Constitution is delineated in Article V:

> The Congress, whenever two thirds of both houses shall deem it necessary, shall propose amendments to this Constitution, or, on the application of the legislatures of two thirds of the several states, shall call a convention for proposing amendments, which, in either case, shall be valid to all intents and purposes, as part of this Constitution, when ratified by the legislatures of three fourths of the several states, or by the conventions in three fourths thereof, as the one or the other mode of ratification may be proposed by the Congress; provided that no amendment which may be made prior to the year one thousand eight hundred and eight shall in any manner affect the first and fourth clauses in the ninth section of the first article; and that no state, without its consent, shall be deprived of its equal suffrage in the Senate.

As delineated in chapter 2, constitutional amendments require a super majority at both the national and state levels of government. This is why there are only 27 amendments to the federal Constitution, the first 10 of which came early in 1791. James Madison did not want to debate amendment proposals in the Philadelphia Convention in 1787. Rather, he wanted a civil liberties debate to take place with the new government after the Constitution was already put into effect. In this context the Bill of Rights was added to the Constitution. Thus, since 1791 there have been only 17 amendments to the Constitution and, when factoring out the social experiment of Prohibition, only 15 successful amendments since the late 18th century. Assuming that all 435 House members and 100 Senate members are present, a two-thirds majority vote in the House is 290 votes and 67 votes in the Senate. This sizable majority is required simply to forward an amendment proposal to the state legislatures. Since a three-fourths majority ratification vote is constitutionally required, 38 of the 50 state legislatures must vote to ratify the proposal and add it to the federal Constitution. Such political consensus is very difficult to achieve most of the time.

Historical Evolution of Elections

Unlike most democracies in the world, political party leaders in the United States no longer select their nominees. The American voters select the candidate for the parties in primary elections. State legislatures typically create either **open** or **closed primaries**, though some hybrid structures are employed as well. An open primary allows any registered voter to participate, regardless of party affiliation. In a closed primary, only registered members of a particular political party are eligible to vote. Some states, such as Iowa, use **caucuses**. In a caucus, citizens do more than simply enter a polling site and vote for the candidates of their choice. They often listen to speeches by advocates for the candidates who are running for office. Turnout in a caucus is typically lower than it is for a primary. Political campaigns are important, for if a candidate does not prevail in an election, her or his policy agenda will not be addressed, because the winner of the election takes the contested position, even if the margin of victory is only one vote. The loser of the election gets nothing in the U.S. winner-take-all system.

In the early decades of the republic after political parties evolved, presidential candidates were selected by **King Caucus**, meaning that in the early 19th century, presidential candidates were selected by national party leaders in Congress. This approach to nominating presidential candidates was replaced by **nominating conventions** in the 1830s. A nominating convention was a meeting held by each political party every presidential election year where delegates from all of the states selected a presidential and vice presidential nominee for their respective parties and approved party platforms. While nominating conventions still exist to this day, presidential candidates in the modern era are selected through the accumulation of pledged delegates through competitive primaries across the states.

Under the Constitution there are only three requirements for serving as president, a member of the U.S. Senate, or a member of the U.S. House: age, residency, and citizenship. Presidents have to be at least 35 years old, a resident of the United States for at least 14 years, and a natural-born U.S. citizen. Senators must be at least 30 years old, a resident of the state they wish to represent, and a U.S. citizen for at least 9 years. House members must be at least 25 years old, a resident of the state, and a U.S. citizen for at least 7 years.

Electoral campaigns are very important in the modern era, not just in presidential elections but also in Senate and House races as well. The development of key messages, or themes, in a campaign is very important, and raising sufficient money so that candidates can communicate their messages is vital in federal campaigns today. Recall that the successful candidate must compete in two election cycles (primary and general). In both election cycles, candidates must focus on such issues as name recognition, policy positions on a wide range of issues, getting supporters or potential supporters to actually vote, fundraising, and participating in televised debates. The importance of money in federal campaigns cannot be overemphasized. In modern federal election campaigns, about 80 percent of all campaign expenditures are used for television advertising. However, the candidate who raises more money than the opponent does not always prevail.

In presidential elections under Article II of the Constitution, a candidate is elected president directly by the **Electoral College**:

> Each State shall appoint, in such Manner as the Legislature thereof may direct, a Number of Electors, equal to the whole Number of Senators and Representatives to which the State may be entitled in the Congress: but no Senator or Representative, or Person holding an Office of Trust or Profit under the United States, shall be appointed an Elector.

Thus, for example, Indiana currently has 11 electoral votes because the state has 9 representatives in the U.S. House and 2 U.S. senators. As indicated by the framers, a person currently serving in any office of the United States government cannot be an elector. About five weeks after the popular vote in November, the electors who are selected at their state party conventions in presidential election years, and are pledged to the winner of the popular vote in that state, convene in the state capital and cast their ballots for president and vice president. These ballots are sealed and sent to Congress, where they are opened at the beginning of the new session in early January.[14]

To win the presidency, the following must happen under the Twelfth Amendment:

> The person having the greatest number of votes for President, shall be the President, if such number be a majority of the whole number of electors appointed; and if no person have such majority, then from the persons having the highest numbers not exceeding three on the list of those voted for as President, the House of Representatives shall choose immediately, by ballot, the President. But in choosing the President, the votes shall be taken by states, the representation from each state having one vote.

Today there are a total of 538 votes in the Electoral College, which correspond to the 435 members of the U.S. House, 100 members of the U.S. Senate, and, since the Twenty-third Amendment was added to the Constitution, 3 electors allocated for the District of Columbia (even though it is not a state). A simple majority of the Electoral College is 270 votes. A person can become president under the current structural rules, even if she or he loses the popular vote, by prevailing in the Electoral College.

In U.S. history five presidential candidates have won the popular vote but lost the election. This happened first in 1824, when Andrew Jackson (Democrat) won the popular vote but did not get a simple majority of the Electoral College. Accordingly, the House of Representatives determined the outcome of the election in a contentious election, and John Quincy Adams (National Republican) prevailed. The next time it happened was in 1876. Democrat Samuel Tilden won the popular vote, but in a controversial election Republican Rutherford B. Hayes won the presidency. This election was the closest in the history of the republic in terms of the Electoral College vote: the margin of victory for Hayes was exactly one vote (185–184). Twelve years later the popular vote winner lost again. Grover Cleveland (Democrat) won the popular vote in his bid for a second term; Benjamin Harrison (Republican) defeated him in the Electoral College. Four years later, both candidates represented their respective parties again as their nominees, and this time Cleveland won both the popular vote and the electoral vote. Cleveland remains the only president in U.S. history to have staggered terms (1885–1889 and 1893–1897), thus making Cleveland both the 22nd and 24th president.

It would be another 112 years before the people's choice lost in the Electoral College again. In 2000 Democrat Al Gore defeated Republican George W. Bush in the popular vote by about 540,000 votes nationally; however, Bush became president because he won 271 Electoral College votes. In 2016 Hillary Clinton (Democrat) defeated Donald Trump (Republican) by almost 3 million votes across the country. Nevertheless, Trump won the electoral vote handily, 304–227. In a very unusual occurrence, seven electors voted for people they were not pledged to support (Clinton lost five electoral votes and Trump lost two). In the official presidential electoral tally in 2016, Colin Powell received three votes and four officials received one vote each (John Kasich, Ron Paul, Bernie Sanders, and Faith Spotted Eagle). Typically, there is usually no more than one faithless elector in a presidential election and often there are none.

The **gender gap** is the measurable difference in the voting behavior between women and men in presidential elections. Ever since 1980, women have been more inclined to support the Democratic presidential candidate and men have been more likely to support the Republican presidential candidate. The gender gap is the difference in the percentage of men and women voting for a presidential candidate. The measure is calculated by subtracting the percentage of women supporting the winning candidate (in the Electoral College) from the percentage of men supporting that candidate. In 1980 the gender gap was 8 percent, and in subsequent years it has been 6 percent (1984), 7 percent (1988), 4 percent (1992), 11 percent (1996), 10 percent (2000), 7 percent (2004), 7 percent (2008), 10 percent (2012), and 11 percent (2016). Note that the highest gender gap in presidential election history is 11 percent (1996 and 2016). In one election, the Democratic candidate, Bill Clinton, prevailed in 1996, and the Republican candidate, Donald Trump, won in 2016, despite losing the popular vote.

Why is there a measurable gap in presidential elections between women and men? Fundamentally, it has everything to do with opposing visions of public policy and the role of the federal government in society and in the economy. Women tend to favor higher levels of social spending at the federal level than men. Thus, women are more likely to support presidential candidates who will pledge more resources to support such initiatives as health care, education, and assistance to the impoverished and the elderly than their male counterparts. Conversely, men tend to favor less spending on social programs and more spending on such priorities as national defense and security. Thus, women are more inclined to support Democratic contenders for the White House while men are more likely to support Republican presidential candidates.

Accordingly, the gender gap is both good news and bad news for both major political parties. The good news for Democrats is that women are an important part of their electoral coalition. The bad news for Democrats is that they struggle to secure support from men, especially white males. The good news for Republicans is that they do very well with white men in particular; correspondingly, the bad news is that they are challenged when it comes to receiving support from women as an aggregate group.

Another important fact is that congressional elections are typically not that competitive. In a normal federal election cycle, about 95 percent of all **incumbents** (an elected official who currently holds the job and is seeking another term for the office) in the U.S. House will be reelected, and about 80 percent of all Senate incumbents will be given another term by the voters. These figures accentuate the importance of **name recognition** in American politics. Name recognition involves the ability of citizens to identify a political candidate's name due to a certain amount of previous exposure. Exposure to a candidate's name can increase her or his likability to the voters. Many Americans do not pay much attention to politics. They are more likely to be familiar with an incumbent than a challenger, and the incumbent gets rewarded accordingly with another term most, but not all, of the time. Both major political party leaders are quite attentive to **open seats**, which are elected positions where there is no current incumbent seeking another term. Open seats are viewed by both party leaders and potential candidates with great interest, because if there is no incumbent there is an opportunity for either party to enhance its numbers in either the House or the Senate. In other words, open seats are often viewed as more winnable than seats that are held by political incumbents.

Though name recognition is extremely important in federal elections, other factors are crucial as well. A prevailing issue of importance is undoubtedly fundraising. Frequently, incumbents vastly outraise and outspend their challengers in both primary elections and in the general election. Incumbents have a number of advantages compared to many challengers. Heightened name recognition often leads to more financial contributions to the campaign. Leaders in political action committees are more likely to donate to incumbents, because the campaign donations are often viewed as investments. Since incumbents almost always win, the donation(s) in question may prompt the member of the House or the Senate to meet with big donors and listen to their policy viewpoints. While most political scientists contend that elected members of Congress are not controlled by their big donors, they do believe that big donors have access to their leaders that most citizens do not have. Generally, conservative individuals and groups tend to donate to conservative candidates, and liberal individuals and groups tend to donate to liberal candidates. Another advantage that incumbents have is the **franking privilege**, which is the right of elected members of the U.S. House and Senate to legally send mail to their constituents at the federal government's (taxpayers) expense.

Under federal law there are two types of money in political campaigns: **soft money** and **hard money**. Soft money involves political donations that cannot be made directly to the candidates who are seeking office. The donations are made to mobilize voters, promote a specific public policy proposal, or even advance a specific political viewpoint. Soft money donations are not made directly to political campaigns and they are not regulated. Direct hard money contributions to political candidates are regulated by law. Hard money entails political donations that are regulated by law that are given directly to a specific candidate for U.S. House, U.S. Senate, or the presidency.

Congress created a federal agency in 1974 to oversee and collect financial records for all federal campaigns: the **Federal Election Commission (FEC)**. The FEC is an independent regulatory agency that enforces election laws in federal campaigns. It consists of six presidential appointees; no more than three of the six members can be from the same political party.

The contribution limit for individual House, Senate, and presidential candidates in 2019–2020 was $2,800 per candidate per election (remember, the United States has primary and general elections). Thus, a person committed to a specific candidate could give the candidate $2,800 in the primary and, if that candidate won the primary, another $2,800 in the general election.[15] There is a significant loophole in existing law, however.

There is no limit currently on **independent expenditures**. An independent expenditure is an amount of money that is used for a communication that expressly advocates the election or defeat of a specific federal candidate and is not coordinated with a candidate, a candidate's committee, party committee, or her or his agents.[16] In theory millionaires and billionaires can spend lavishly to promote their candidates or oppose candidates they do not like. The key word is "independent," as these expenditures cannot be made in concert with the campaigns themselves.

The Supreme Court ruling in *Buckley v. Valeo* (1976) still has important implications in federal campaigns. Members of Congress do not violate the First Amendment when they restrict how much citizens can give directly to a federal candidate. Originally in the 1970s, the amount was $1,000 per candidate per election. In 2002, however, Congress revised the Watergate-era laws on campaign finance when the **Bipartisan Campaign Reform Act** was passed and doubled the figure to $2,000. The act also allowed indexing for inflation, which is why citizens could give $2,800 in the 2020 presidential election cycle. However, members of Congress do not have the authority to regulate independent expenditures or the amount of money that candidates spend on their own campaigns. Thus, billionaires can currently spend as much as they want to in pursuing an elected position in the federal government.

In the important Supreme Court decision of *Citizens United v. Federal Election Commission* (2010), the justices determined by a 5–4 vote that free speech under the First Amendment prohibited the federal government from restricting independent expenditures for communications by corporations, labor unions, or other groups. A portion of the Bipartisan Campaign Reform Act was challenged under constitutional grounds. Part of the law forbade corporations or labor unions from funding "electioneering communications," or radio, television or satellite broadcasts that referred to a federal candidate within 30 days of a primary election or within 60 days of a general election. To the justices in the majority, these restrictions were tantamount to a free speech violation. Consequently, the impact of *Citizens United* has been profound in the last decade. Before the decision, contributions from political action committees (PACs) were limited to $5,000 per candidate per election. Since 2010, however, spending by so-called super PACS is essentially unlimited, meaning that a relatively small group of wealthy individuals and corporations are able to exert a great deal of influence with regard to federal, state, and local elections.[17]

Voting and Elections Today

Voter turnout (the percentage of the adult population who actually vote in an election) in the United States in the modern era is depicted in table 3.1 and is noticeably low compared to most democracies in the world.

The **voting age population** has been 18 and older since 1972. Voter turnout in the rest of the free world is typically in the 60th to 80th percentile in events that are analogous to a presidential election in the United States. In the United States turnout is typically 50 to 55 percent in a **presidential election** (federal elections held every four years—2020, 2024, 2028, etc.) where the presidency is contested, along with all 435 U.S. House seats and one-third of the U.S. Senate, and turnout of about 33 to 38 percent in a non-presidential election year (i.e., **midterm election**). A midterm election is held near the midpoint of a president's four-year term of office (e.g., 2018, 2022, 2026, etc.). Thus, by definition the presidency is not contested during this type of election, but elections for all 435 U.S. House seats and one-third of U.S. Senate seats are conducted. A very unusual increase in voter turnout occurred in the 2018 midterm elections, however. In the three previous midterm elections, turnout was 33.2 percent in 2014, 37 percent in 2010, and 36.1 percent in 2006. In 2018, 46.5 percent of the voting age population participated in the election. The last time voter turnout exceeded 45 percent in a midterm election was in 1966, before 18- to 20-year-olds were allowed to vote. It is too early to know if this trend will continue, as some analysts speculate that the surge in voter turnout may be at least partly attributable to President Donald Trump (in terms of supporters and opponents alike).

Unlike many other democracies, citizens in 49 states and the District of Columbia must register in order to be eligible to vote. In most democracies the burden of registration is on government officials for citizens, but in America, if individual citizens do not register to vote, they waive their right to vote. The only exception is the state of North Dakota. The government in that state has been responsible for registering citizens to vote since 1951. Citizens there must have proper identification to vote on Election Day; if people meet the requisite age and residency requirements, they are already registered without physically having to do it themselves. There is a significant consequence with placing the burden of proof on citizens for voter registration. In some other democracies, voter turnout in theory could be 100 percent, as all citizens who meet the voting requirements are automatically registered and thus eligible to vote. In the United States, however, more than 20 percent of citizens 18 and older are not registered and are therefore not eligible.[18] As a result, in any federal election today in the United States, the highest voter turnout possible of the voting age population (those 18 and older) is about

Table 3.1. Voter Turnout in U.S. Federal Elections, 1932–2018 (Percentage of Voting Age Population That Voted)

Election Year	Voter Turnout
1932	52.6
1934	42.1
1936	56.9
1938	*Not available*
1940	58.8
1942	32.5
1944	56.1
1946	37.1
1948	51.1
1950	41.2
1952	61.6
1954	41.7
1956	59.3
1958	43.0
1960	62.8
1962	45.4
1964	61.4
1966	45.4
1968	60.7
1970	43.6
1972	55.1
1974	35.7
1976	53.6
1978	34.5
1980	52.8
1982	37.7
1984	53.3
1986	33.6
1988	50.3
1990	33.6
1992	55.2
1994	36.5
1996	49.0
1998	33.1
2000	50.3
2002	34.8
2004	55.7
2006	36.1
2008	57.1
2010	37.0
2012	53.6
2014	33.2
2016	54.7
2018	46.5

Sources: (1932–2010): U.S. Census Bureau, *Statistical Abstract of the United States: 2012,* Section 7: Elections, https://www.census.gov/prod/2011pubs/12statab/election.pdf; and (2012–2018): U.S. Elections Project, "Voter Turnout," http://www.electproject.org/home/voter-turnout/voter-turnout-data

80 percent, and that would occur only if all registered citizens actually voted in the election in question.

Voter registration laws vary considerably in the United States. Some state lawmakers have made voting procedures more facilitative for citizens. In other states this is not the case at all. As of early 2020, 19 states and the District of Columbia have **Election Day, or same-day, registration,** where citizens are entitled to register up to and including Election Day prior to voting. As reported by officials at the National Conference on State Legislatures, states with Election Day or same-day registration have between 3 and 7 percent higher voter turnout than states that do not, with an average of a 5 percent increase.[19] Included in table 3.2 is a current compendium of state voter registration laws.

Twenty-one states have either no registration or Election Day registration. Another five states have registration in advance of the election requirements between 11 and 20 days. The remaining 25 states have laws that require citizens to register between 21 and 30 days before the election. In **Dunn v. Blumstein** (1972), the justices of the Supreme Court determined that given the computer technology at that time, it was reasonable for states to have laws that required their residents to register up to 30 days before the election. States could not have laws that exceeded

Table 3.2. Voter Registration Laws in the American States (2020)

Voter Registration Law	States with This Law	N
No registration law	North Dakota	1
Same-day (Election Day) registration	California, Colorado, Connecticut, District of Columbia, Hawaii, Idaho, Illinois, Iowa, Maine, Maryland, Michigan, Minnesota, Montana, Nevada, New Hampshire, Utah, Vermont, Washington, Wisconsin, and Wyoming	20
11 days before election	Nebraska	1
15 days before election	Alabama, Pennsylvania, and South Dakota	3
20 days before election	Massachusetts	1
21 days before election	Kansas, New Jersey, Oregon, and West Virginia	4
22 days before election	Virginia	1
24 days before election	Delaware	1
25 days before election	New York, North Carolina, and Oklahoma	3
27 days before election	Missouri	1
28 days before election	New Mexico	1
29 days before election	Arizona, Florida, Georgia, Indiana, and Kentucky	5
30 days before election	Alaska, Arkansas, Louisiana, Mississippi, Ohio, Rhode Island, South Carolina, Tennessee, and Texas	9

Source: National Conference of State Legislatures, "Voter Registration Deadlines," November 1, 2019, https://www.ncsl.org/research/elections-and-campaigns/voter-registration-deadlines.aspx

that 30-day registration in advance of the election requirement. Bear in mind that computer technology has evolved greatly since the early 1970s, yet the constitutional standard has not changed. Maine was the first state to establish Election Day registration, in 1973.

Though voter turnout is a complicated issue when comparing countries, it is fairly clear that voter turnout in the United States is lower than other nations because laws in this country are still comparatively stringent (e.g., voter registration requirements, voter identification requirements, and laws governing felons). In addition, the United States is essentially a two-party, **winner-take-all** system (an electoral system where the person with the most votes gets the job, even if the candidate with the most votes does not achieve a simple majority) as opposed to a country that has multiple viable political parties with proportional representation in the national legislative body. Though structural reforms to make voting easier in this country should occur, one thing is clear: countless millions of Americans do not understand that voting is an important duty in a representative democracy. Thus, it is incumbent on either state or federal officials to make voting easier for citizens. In the world's oldest democracy, it is a shame that people in this country vote at such low levels. Not only does it suggest that our laws are in need of reform, but low voter turnout can also be indicative of a population where many people believe that policy makers are indifferent to them and their needs. Unfortunately, when people feel alienated, they tend to isolate themselves and disengage from the electoral process.

Some states have laws that encourage citizens to engage in direct democracy. **New England town meetings** have been held since the 1630s, beginning in Massachusetts, where the residents determine public policy issues directly.[20] In other states, citizens can also make some decisions directly without a representative body. Citizens in 36 states have the opportunity to have **recall elections** for certain elected officials at the local or state level. This means that people can remove elected officials before their terms expire if they conclude that the officials are not doing a reasonable job.[21] While recall elections are not a traditional form of direct democracy, they do give the people the authority to remove ineffective political representatives and replace them altogether.

Currently, 26 states and the District of Columbia permit **initiative** or **referendum** rights to their citizens.[22] Initiatives allow voters to bypass their state legislatures and decide specific issues directly. A referendum is a policy measure that must appear on the ballot for voters by law. This often occurs in states where a constitutional amendment, bond issue, or tax change must be approved by the voters under the rules delineated in the state's constitution.[23]

The Importance of Citizenship in a Republic

Adults in the United States can do a number of things to be more effective citizens in this republic. It is absolutely crucial for all of us to be more attentive to politics and public affairs and enhance our own knowledge base. In so doing, we make ourselves less vulnerable to exploitation by those who would use our ignorance against us in order to pursue their own agenda. What else can people do to engage in their own democracy? It turns out that there are many ways to participate in the American democracy. Voting is an obvious choice. Our voter turnout rates are not a particularly flattering depiction of the health of democracy in America. We can collectively do better and we must. Reforming election laws in the United States is also necessary. Whether the state officials automatically register their own citizens, as in the case of North Dakota, or state lawmakers provide for Election Day registration, laws in many states are too rigid and stringent where citizens are required to register weeks before the actual election. Computer technology has truly been revolutionized since the Supreme Court's ruling in 1972; if California, the largest state in the union in terms of population, can have same-day registration without fraudulent elections, then presumably other state legislators could do the same within their own borders. By way of illustration, if due to computer technology thousands of dollars in credit can be given to citizens in order to purchase expensive items, then certainly the same technology can be employed by the respective secretaries of state across the country in order to register citizens so that they can more easily participate in democratic governance. Democracy is always more effective with more input and citizen participation, not less.

There are other ways to engage in politics and public affairs. Citizens can form alliances with like-minded and cause-oriented people by joining interest groups. Sharing ideas by writing a letter to the editor of a local, state, or national newspaper is another way to encourage civic debate in this country. Some citizens choose to run for office themselves; others opt to join a campaign and volunteer their time accordingly. Yet others decide to volunteer in their community in numerous ways. There is not a singular formula for participating in American politics; citizens should decide for themselves how they wish to do so and implement their plans en masse.

Public service is about the opportunity to make people's lives better. This is what we hope we get when leaders are sent to the federal government to work in Washington, D.C., state capitals, or local corridors of power. Yet all of us can engage in public service in our local communities by volunteering our time to promote a particular cause, by donating to worthwhile causes, or simply by helping a neighbor or person in need.

All Americans, regardless of their plight, should aspire to be better citizens of this republic. As I highlighted in my book *Winning the War on Poverty*, one indicator of a healthy democracy is the extent to which people accept their duties and responsibilities as citizens.[24] According to officials at U.S. Citizenship and Immigration Services, citizenship comes with many civil liberties (freedom of expression; freedom to worship as one pleases; the right to a trial by jury; the right to vote in elections; the right to run for public office; and the freedom to pursue life, liberty, and happiness). Citizenship also involves a number of civic responsibilities, such as supporting and defending the U.S. Constitution; staying informed about the public policy issues of the day; participating in politics through voting and other means; respect for the rule of law; respect for the rights, beliefs, and opinions of others; paying taxes in an honest manner; serving on a jury if called upon at the local level; and defending the country if the need ever arises.[25] Balancing individual rights with civic obligations is essential to making America a more vibrant democracy. The challenges that exist in the 21st century on a number of fronts (e.g., climate change, poverty, national debt, and health care) should not be passively deferred to the members of Congress and the president. By being more engaged and proactive, citizens can help address some of the many policy and moral challenges that exist in contemporary society. The diversity that exists in American society should collectively collaborate in the pursuit of a more perfect union.

America's best days are not in the past. Americans cannot simply rest on their past laurels and hope to maintain the nation's status as the sole superpower on the planet. As citizens, we have a civic responsibility to view public policy in terms of how government officials can create policies that would promote the greater common good. Too many citizens view public policy debates only in individualistic or familial terms. This libertarian approach to public policy will only promote more isolationism and will not sufficiently address a wide variety of policy challenges. It is incumbent upon Americans at this time to advocate together for policies that will make American society better for the many, as opposed to the few. Such a communitarian ethos could unleash the boundless potential for citizen involvement in the American democracy.

Knowledge Matters

The history of voting and elections in this country is abounding. Many groups have had to engage in extensive struggles to obtain the franchise. In the much-followed presidential election dispute of 2000 in Florida, the Florida Supreme Court justices highlighted the importance of voting in a republic: "The right to vote is the pre-eminent right in the Declaration of Rights of the Florida Constitution."[26] Access to the ballot is the primary way that citizens can hold their elected leaders accountable for their decisions and non-decisions alike.

Knowledge is powerful in this context, for its judicious use can result in avoiding the same mistake on multiple occasions. At present there are numerous attempts across the nation to suppress the vote. According to officials at the Brennan Center for Justice at New York University, since 2010, lawmakers in the following 25 states have instituted new restrictions that make voting more cumbersome for voters: Alabama, Arizona, Arkansas, Florida, Georgia, Illinois, Indiana, Iowa, Kansas, Mississippi, Missouri, Montana, Nebraska, New Hampshire, North Carolina, North Dakota, Ohio, Rhode Island, South Carolina, South Dakota, Tennessee, Texas, Virginia, West Virginia, and Wisconsin.[27]

Voter suppression efforts are not acceptable. Such political strategies are crafted not in order to reduce alleged fraudulent voting but to disenfranchise a specific class of voters. In the annals of history, such efforts are typically used to limit the number of votes from people of color, the less affluent, immigrants, the less educated, and a host of other disadvantaged groups in society. Voter suppression efforts are reflective of past practices of denying democracy to individuals based on discriminatory attitudes. We should be beyond these sinister, but highly transparent, political practices today. Unfortunately, we are not, as evidenced by the reality that half the states are restricting voting at a time when election experts report that fraudulent voting is not problematic; our leaders should be much more concerned about foreign influence in American elections, as there is tangible evidence demonstrating that Russia, in particular, interfered with the 2016 election.[28] In short, officials who seek to suppress the vote in a democracy need to be accountable for their actions. All political party leaders, regardless of party and ideology, should compete to get political support from citizens; they should never seek to deny certain Americans from voting based on a perception that they will not support their fellow partisans. Voter suppression and other unsavory actions need to be artifacts of the past, never to resurface.

Citizen Homework

There are many ways to participate in politics. In several aspects, voting is undoubtedly the easiest. Given the turnout rate in American federal elections, however, it is apparent that millions of adults in the United States are clearly not that engaged in voting. Whether people choose to understand this or not, public policy affects all citizens, and they should seek to empower themselves accordingly. The American democracy will not function in a more effective manner unless more citizens engage in the political process. There are a number of sources that can enhance citizens' understanding of this republic and hopefully promote more citizen interest and knowledge of the political process. Here are some sources available on the internet that can enhance citizen knowledge of both voting and elections:

Basic information about U.S. elections: https://www.youtube.com/ watch?v=48EZKXweGDo. Watch a nine-minute video titled "Election Basics: Crash Course Government and Politics #36."

Voting Rights Act Timeline: https://www.aclu.org/files/assets/ voting_rights_act_timeline20111222.pdf (March 4, 2005). Read about the historical evolution of voting rights since the late 18th century.

Seneca Falls Convention: http://www.history.com/topics/seneca-falls-convention. Read about the first women's rights convention in the United States. The women's suffrage movement began as a result of this event.

Political campaign commercials: https://www.nbcnews.com/ politics/politics-news/six-political-ads-changed-game-n607281. View six important political advertisements in television history ("Daisy," "Morning in America," "Willie Horton," "Rock," "It's 3:00 am," and "Smoking Man").

Presidential elections in U.S. history: https://www.270towin.com/. At this website, one can visualize the results of all presidential elections starting in 1789 with George Washington's first victory.

Identify local, state, and federal representatives: https://www.usa. gov/elected-officials. Not all citizens know who works for them at the local, state, and federal levels. This website provides the basic information that citizens need in order to hold their leaders accountable.

Voter registration rules in each state: https://www.vote.org/voter-registration-rules/. Citizens in every state except for North Dakota must register to vote in order to exercise the franchise. This website provides information that will assist citizens in this process.

CHAPTER 4

Mass Media, Interest Groups, and Public Opinion

The mass media, the existence of interest groups, and public opinion are all vital components of a democratic republic. The **mass media** includes all sources that provide information to large numbers of citizens (e.g., newspapers, television networks, radio stations, internet websites, and podcasts). **Interest groups** are organizations of people who share common political interests and goals and seek to influence public policy making by engaging in election activities and lobbying. **Public opinion** is the collective views of the people on politics and public policy issues. In a democracy the people rely on a free and open press for their political information. Without journalists Americans would have little knowledge of governmental and societal activities. Citizens rely on a free and open press for their information. In a letter to Edward Carrington written on January 16, 1787, Thomas Jefferson said this about a free press:

> Were it left to me to decide whether we should have a government without newspapers, or newspapers without a government, I should not hesitate a moment to prefer the latter. But I should mean that every man should receive those papers and be capable of reading them.[1]

In a republic, checks and balances provide a structural framework for the government. Yet the structure of the government itself does not ensure democracy without a fundamental role for the people. Jefferson was espousing two things in the late 18th century. He was highlighting the importance of citizens having the right to know what is happening in their government and society. In addition, he was promoting the duty of citizens to consume the news. At a time when the literacy rate was low, he was advocating the idea that citizens be educated sufficiently in order to consume the news on a consistent basis. Journalists report to the public, and in so doing they educate citizens about the state of current affairs. Accordingly, journalists are an independent check on the government and industry alike. Without them, how could the people attempt to hold their leaders accountable?

Criticism of the press is nothing new in American history. Leaders sometimes take exception with news coverage and offer their criticism. Having a free and open press often requires a rebuke of journalistic coverage. Yet it is important for citizens to understand that the role played by the mass media in a democracy is crucial. Professional journalists promote the cause of democracy every day when they do their jobs. While many would contend that some journalists are better at their job than others in their field, and undoubtedly so, the absence of a free and open press would be indicative of a dictatorship. In authoritarian countries the government controls the flow of information to the citizens, meaning that the people who live in such nation-states have to endure overt propaganda all the time. Clearly, this would run counter to the cause of democracy.

President Donald Trump is not the first president to criticize journalists. However, he and his supporters have regularly sought to undermine the credibility of the mass media as an institution of democracy. He has regularly referred to specific news outlets as "fake news" and as "the enemy of the American people."[2] Such rhetoric commonly emanates from authoritarian regimes, not from elected leaders in the democracies of the world.

Similarly, interest groups are essential in a democracy. They serve as a link between the people and their elected leaders. Interest groups provide another mechanism for citizens to be involved in politics. In the Gallup Poll's annual survey of the professions in 2017, however, lobbyists ranked last (of 22 professions) in terms of honesty and ethics. Only 8 percent of respondents reported that they have a very high or high level of honesty and ethics.[3] **Lobbying** is a practice of interest group officials in which they contact public officials and try to influence them on public policy issues. By definition, lobbyists are advocates for whatever causes they endorse. There are thousands of interest groups in the United

States; each is reflective of the diversity that exists in American society. Hence, the existence of interest groups allows people with a wide variety of perspectives on the issues of the day a chance for their voices to be heard in public policy making, through interest group lobbying efforts. Most lobbyists conform to the law when they engage in their activities. The results of the Gallup survey, however, are clear: most Americans do not believe that lobbyists are honest and trustworthy.

Although the United States is not a direct democracy, public opinion plays an instrumental role in the political system. Elected leaders who depart from what the people want may find themselves in a tenuous position when they go to the voters and ask for another term in office. There is always a method to recall an elected leader in that citizens can reject the leader's request for another term in office. In the original Constitution, the framers avoided incorporating term limits in the final document. Ultimately, they decided as a group to allow the voters (a small subset of the population in the late 18th century) to decide whether an official had earned another term in office. There are still no term limits for members of Congress, and federal judges are appointed for life. Ever since 1951, however, when the Twenty-second Amendment was ratified, presidents are limited to two terms or no more than 10 years in office (they can serve up to two years of another president's term if they ascend to the presidency because they were vice president when a vacancy in the presidency occurred).

Historical Evolution of the Mass Media

The mass media have evolved dramatically over time due to technological advancements. When the republic began in the late 18th century, newspapers and pamphlets were primary ways to disseminate information about American politics. Newspapers, in particular, were a way for political parties to reach out to their loyal partisans, as newspapers at that time had a very overt political ideology (e.g., some were pro Federalist Party and others were pro Democratic-Republican Party). Newspapers were expensive to produce, so only the more affluent could afford to purchase them. In the 1830s, however, this changed with the advent of the **penny press**. The dissemination of the news became widespread and transcended social classes. In 1833 Benjamin Day founded the *The Sun* in New York City with the motto of "It Shines for All." His newspaper cost one cent as opposed to the others at the time, which cost five or six cents a copy. For the first time in U.S. history, all citizens had the economic opportunity to consume the news, not just upper-class people. In 1800 about 200 newspapers were published in the United States; by 1860 that number had jumped to about 3,000. The annual circulation of newspapers increased dramatically all across the nation. Some media scholars attribute the increase in readership not only to technology and the lowering of the cost of the newspaper but also to higher rates of literacy and increased leisure time. The one-cent newspapers at this time were not subsidized by political party officials; they operated independently and targeted new audiences. Partisan newspapers typically printed speeches and provided scant news coverage. Publishers for newspapers like *The Sun* relied more on circulation rates and an issue interconnected with it: advertising revenue.[4]

A significant invention regarding the dissemination of knowledge and information occurred in 1844. An electric telegraph message was successfully sent for the first time in U.S. history. Samuel Morse was in the chamber of the U.S. Supreme Court in Washington, D.C., and sent a message to his assistant in Baltimore, who transmitted the same message back to Morse by telegraph. Members of Congress watched this demonstration and were amazed that a long-distance message could be conveyed so quickly. Morse's message simply said "What Hath God Wrought."[5] At the beginning of the 19th century, the United States was largely an agrarian society in the vision of Thomas Jefferson. Most Americans were small subsistence farmers. Yet around the mid-19th century, significant technological advances were made in addition to the penny press and the telegraph. Print media affected virtually all aspects of American life. The dissemination of newspapers, magazines, and books was partly made possible by the common school movement. A literate population made the consumption of the print media possible, as did an enhanced transportation system. Americans became less isolated from one another, and their lives became more intertwined in terms of economics, politics, and culture.[6]

Toward the end of the 19th century, some newspaper owners and journalists engaged in **yellow journalism**. Those who adopted this approach to reporting intentionally sensationalized the news so that they could sell more newspapers and make higher profits. One prominent publisher who used this strategy was **William Randolph Hearst** (1863–1951). Hearst dominated the publishing industry for about 50 years. By using yellow journalism, he was able to sell millions of newspapers. During this time, he served in the U.S. House of Representatives.

He ran for mayor of New York City and governor of New York but lost in both races.

By the early 20th century, the use of radio as a means of communication had become more widespread in the United States. Warren Harding was the first president to have his voice transmitted on the radio in 1922. This technological advancement allowed leaders to directly communicate with citizens, something that President Franklin D. Roosevelt did effectively in the 1930s with his fireside chats. Shortly after he was inaugurated in 1933, Roosevelt gave a series of speeches from the White House directly to the homes of Americans who had radios. In his first address, just a few days after his inauguration, he attempted to appease concerns about the failing banks in the country. Later in the 20th century, arguably the most important technological invention in modern history was developed and widely disseminated in the United States: television.

Though television was invented in the 1920s, its use did not become widespread in America until the 1950s. The first televised national political conventions occurred in 1952. Television allowed citizens to actually watch their leaders and candidates in action. The impact of television on American politics was made apparent in the presidential debates of 1960. This was the first presidential election where the two major party candidates appeared together on television. In the first debate, Senator John F. Kennedy had a decisive victory over Vice President Richard Nixon. This debate illustrated the importance of appearances in the new era of American politics. During the debate Kennedy appeared confident, was tanned, and represented new youthful leadership. Nixon was perspiring, was pale and appeared to be nervous, and represented the politics of the past. In a very close election, at least in terms of the popular vote, some analysts contend that it was Kennedy's performance in the first debate that ultimately resulted in his electoral victory.

In the 1990s the internet commenced use in the United States in earnest. Bill Clinton was the first president to have a website for the White House and was the first president to use email. The capacity of the internet to provide information for citizens is unsurpassed in the history of the republic.

An important presumption in a democracy is the notion that people obtain the information they need to hold governmental leaders accountable from the mass media. A free and open press consists of journalists who seek to provide objective information about politics and public affairs in order to inform discerning adults so that they can form their own opinions about the issues of the day.

Historical Evolution of Interest Groups

As is the case with the mass media, citizens tend to be critical of interest groups as well. The existence of interest groups in a republic is necessary for democratic politics to be in existence. As James Madison detailed in *The Federalist* No. 10, interest groups link the people with their representatives. Madison envisioned a **pluralist democracy** where the people would have an indirect link to leaders who were empowered with making public policy through special interest groups, or "factions," as Madison referred to them. Madison argued that the larger the geographical region, the better chance that public policy would represent the diversity that exists in society. In the late 18th century, it was the perception of political theorists that democracy could work only in a small geographical setting. Here is what Madison wrote in late 1787:

> The other point of difference is, the greater number of citizens and extent of territory which may be brought within the compass of republican than of democratic government; and it is this circumstance principally which renders factious combinations less to be dreaded in the former than in the latter. The smaller the society, the fewer probably will be the distinct parties and interests composing it; the fewer the distinct parties and interests, the more frequently will a majority be found of the same party; and the smaller the number of individuals composing a majority, and the smaller the compass within which they are placed, the more easily will they concert and execute their plans of oppression. Extend the sphere, and you take in a greater variety of parties and interests; you make it less probable that a majority of the whole will have a common motive to invade the rights of other citizens; or if such a common motive exists, it will be more difficult for all who feel it to discover their own strength, and to act in unison with each other. Besides other impediments, it may be remarked that, where there is a consciousness of unjust or dishonorable purposes, communication is always checked by distrust in proportion to the number whose concurrence is necessary.[7]

In his eloquent manner, Madison highlighted the important role that interest groups perform in a democracy. In interest group politics, the collective wishes of the people are transmitted to public policy makers through interest group officials. Many citizens may not view interest groups as being vital to democratic politics; to Madison, however, unregulated interest groups, or factions, are quite essential to the cause of ensuring that no one group, or small number of groups, dominates policy making all the time.

Interest groups have a rich tradition in the American political experience. This historical reality was demonstrated by the French aristocrat Alexis de Tocqueville in 1835 and 1840 when his *Democracy in America* was published in two volumes. After traveling around the country, Tocqueville was clearly intrigued by the tendency of Americans to join numerous interest groups. In volume 2 he wrote:

> As soon as several of the inhabitants of the United States have conceived a sentiment or an idea that they want to produce in the world, they seek each other out; and when they have found each other, they unite. From then on, they are no longer isolated men, but a power one sees from afar, whose actions serve as an example; a power that speaks, and to which one listens. The first time I heard it said in the United States that a hundred thousand men publicly engaged not to make use of strong liquors, the thing appeared to me more amusing than serious, and at first I did not see well why such temperate citizens were not content to drink water with their families. In the end I understood that those hundred thousand Americans, frightened by the progress that drunkenness was making around them, wanted to provide their patronage to sobriety. They had acted precisely like a great lord who would dress himself very plainly in order to inspire the scorn of luxury in simple citizens. It is to be believed that if those hundred thousand men had lived in France, each of them would have addressed himself individually to the government, begging it to oversee the cabarets all over the realm.[8]

Tocqueville's observations are still widely intact today. Although Americans vote at low levels compared to citizens in other democracies, they have a high rate of participation when it comes to voluntarily joining interest groups. While this reality promotes the objective of public policy reflecting the inherent diversity that exists in society, it is also important to note that not all interest groups are equal. Some interest groups have had much more measurable success at affecting the creation of public policy than others. A prominent example of such a group today is the National Rifle Association, which has been effective at blocking efforts to pass gun control legislation at the state and federal levels of government for many years.

The existence of interest groups is protected by the First Amendment, which provides freedom of assembly. There were a number of groups in American history who favored independence from Great Britain in the 1770s. Throughout U.S. history, interest groups have formed in response to a myriad of social challenges. For example, antislavery groups formed decades before the Civil War started. Economic challenges in the late 19th and early 20th centuries resulted in the formation of various groups affiliated with labor, trade, and business organizations. Throughout the 1960s and 1970s, a number of groups formed because of social reform movements, including the struggle for civil rights, women's rights, the threatening menace of environmental degradation, as well as the consumer rights movement to combat the avarice of disreputable manufacturers.

A number of resources are available to interest groups in the attempt by lobbyists to influence public policy. The most obvious resource is people. The number of members who belong to an interest group can affect its ability to wield influence. A group that has millions of members will likely be in a more advantageous position to lobby effectively than a group that has only a few hundred. This simple reality is due to the fact that the size of the group affects its ability to raise money. Many interest groups charge members an annual fee; the larger the group, the more money it can raise in its quest to influence public policy. Another key resource for interest groups is their sheer expertise. Interest group officials provide information to policy makers within the traditional branches of government (legislative and executive), but they also disseminate knowledge to federal judges (through selected court cases), to journalists, and citizens alike.

Historical Evolution of Public Opinion

Before the 1930s there was no scientific way to measure public opinion in the United States. In the 1936 presidential election, Democrat Franklin Roosevelt was running for a second term against Republican challenger Alfred Landon. The editors of a popular magazine at the time, the *Literary Digest*, conducted a massive poll of about 2.4 million people and concluded that Landon would win by a landslide. George Gallup conducted a much smaller poll of about 50,000 and predicted that Roosevelt would win by a substantial margin. Roosevelt won all states except for Maine and Vermont. The editors of the *Literary Digest* had a high level of sampling error, which invalidated the results of their poll. Gallup understood the necessity of utilizing a **random sample** (a subset of Americans who participate in a survey through a process that guarantees all adults an equal chance of being chosen) of the population so that the results of the poll would replicate the nation as a whole with a relatively small error term. In short, those affiliated with the *Literary Digest* poll made the unfortunate mistake of sample bias in that its typically affluent subscribers were overly represented, which made it appear that Landon would win easily when in fact he did not. Due to this significant error, the magazine became defunct in 1938.[9]

Public opinion has always been important in American politics because the political decisions that citizens make are influenced by their political opinions. Opinions are not always based on concrete facts but are sometimes based on perceptions that may or may not be accurate. Political attitudes have always played an important role in the public affairs debate in the United States. A dividing line with regard to the proper role of the national government in the economy in particular has existed in this republic, even before political parties emerged. Some Americans have believed that it is more advantageous to have less involvement of the federal government in the domestic economy. Other Americans have concluded the opposite: that it is preferable to have more national involvement in the pursuance of a specific policy or political agenda. Throughout history some Americans have embraced the doctrine of states' rights while others have repudiated it. Although states' rights may mean something different now than it did 200 years ago, the philosophical divide concerning the appropriate realm of the national government still exists today.

Before the modern era, elections were the primary measure of public opinion. Elections remain an important gauge of public opinion, of course, and a great deal of money, time, and resources are allocated to public opinion polling today. Clearly, our leaders, journalists, and lobbyists believe that public opinion is important. What officials decide to do with the information they obtain—to give the people what they do or do not desire—is another matter altogether. At times, citizens are knowledgeable about given subjects and have a definitive opinion about them. At other times, citizens are ill-informed and do not have much of an opinion about a set of issues, particularly if they are not perceived to be important in nature. The variance can be considerable depending on the issues at hand.

Adult public opinion in the United States is measured routinely in three different ways: telephone interviews, mail surveys, and face-to-face interviews. Professional pollsters always use telephone interviews. Mail surveys are rejected by pollsters as a reasonable way to gauge public opinion, because many people do not bother to take the time to complete the survey and return it and either immediately throw it away or recycle it. Citizens who are inclined to complete the mail survey and return it are likely to have more formal education and earn a higher living than many Americans, thereby biasing the results of the survey. Face-to-face interviews are not used by Gallup and other pollsters simply because they are very expensive, and because they know that many citizens are fearful of allowing strangers into their homes. Thus, the only pragmatic approach to polling is via the telephone.

RDD (random digit dialing) sampling is the way that pollsters such as Gallup measure public opinion today. A computer randomly generates phone numbers with desired area codes to ensure that geographic diversity exists in the sample. Using RDD sampling allows pollsters to include respondents who may have an unlisted landline telephone number or cellular numbers. The interviewing process may be at least partly computerized. A number of polling firms utilize **computer-assisted telephone interviewing (CATI)** or robo-calls. A CATI system is utilized so that the polling organization will call random telephone numbers until a live person responds, who is then connected with a trained interviewer. As the respondent provides her or his answers, the interviewer enters the information into the computer system. Interviewers who do not enter the information correctly or go off the script can make the results of the poll less reliable.

As of 2019 there are approximately 255 million Americans in the voting age population (18 and older).[10] When done properly, so as to achieve a random sample of the population, only 1,000–1,500 people need to be interviewed to obtain a good idea about public opinion with a margin of error of plus or minus 2.5–3 percent. By way of illustration, a polling firm conducts a national poll to measure the approval rating of a president, and it is determined that 50 percent of the people approve of the president's job performance. The margin of error is plus or minus 3 percent. What this means is that if all 255 million people were polled, the president's approval rating would be between 47 and 53 percent 95 percent of the time. In short, the poll is very accurate at gauging popular approval of the president in question.

Yet pollsters can still make mistakes. The 1936 debacle by the editors of the *Literary Digest* is well documented. In 1948 several polling firms, including Gallup, incorrectly predicted that Republican Thomas

Dewey would easily defeat the Democratic incumbent, Harry Truman. Yet Truman's victory was one of the greatest upsets in presidential election history. Because he was so far ahead in the polls, Dewey ran a lackluster campaign that was focused on not making mistakes. Truman, on the other hand, ran an aggressive, populist campaign and traveled across the entire nation by train giving speeches and criticizing the Republican-controlled 80th Congress.[11] One of the most significant reasons why many pollsters erred in this election is because they stopped polling several weeks before the election. Many concluded that Dewey was going to win and there was no way Truman could keep the presidency. In addition, it appeared that support for Progressive Party candidate Henry Wallace had declined in the waning days of the campaign, and these voters defected to Truman on Election Day.[12]

In 1996, a different technological era than 1936 and 1948, the pollsters largely erred again. This time there were no headlines admonishing pollsters for predicting the wrong winner, for Democrat Bill Clinton was reelected over Republican Bob Dole by a comfortable margin. Yet many pollsters overestimated the size of Clinton's reelection victory.[13] Because many people assumed that Clinton would easily win by more than 10 percent of the popular vote, voter turnout may have been adversely affected, as this was the first presidential election going back to 1924 where turnout was lower than 50 percent of the voting age population.

The Mass Media, Interest Groups, and Public Opinion Today

Journalists, lobbyists, and citizens alike are central components for democratic political systems. Though adults tend to be critical of journalists and lobbyists in particular, we rely upon them to provide information to us on one hand and to link us with policy makers on the other. Most Americans rely heavily on television for the provision of their news, to the extent that newspaper subscriptions have declined over the past few decades. This is unfortunate, as the print media tend to provide more information and details about public policy issues. Television news stories tend to be very brief with very little substance. The discerning citizen today should take advantage of all modes of technology for the objective of gaining more knowledge about American politics. Thus, a combination of the internet, television, radio, as well as newspapers and other forms of print media maximizes the probability of gaining knowledge about current events in order to hold elected leaders accountable. In addition, citizens are encouraged to consume international reporting of

American politics (e.g., British Broadcasting Corporation). Finally, those who primarily rely on a single news source that has a particular ideological bent are advised to consume other sources as well, some of which may have the opposite ideological perspective.

Contrary to the perception of some people, it has not been proven that a definitive ideological bias exists when it comes to the reporting of the news. We know that some outlets have journalists who tout conservative values while others have reporters that promote liberal or progressive values. One important research finding with regard to the media is that journalists tend to set the political agenda for politicians in terms of the stories they choose to cover. Journalists tend to accentuate negativity in their reporting because people are more inclined to consume conflict and scandal than anything else. **Attack journalism** is a method of media coverage that focuses on political scandals and character assassinations, which results in negative ratings for political figures. It is also important to understand that there are two types of media coverage: **hard news** and **soft news**. Hard news is media coverage that focuses on facts and important issues that are timely and consequential. Soft news is media coverage that is designed to entertain or shock people, not to provide them with detailed information about substantive policy issues. It is often conducted through sensationalized reporting or by focusing on a politician's personality. Two other nuances regarding the mass media warrant more discussion. First, there is a tendency to rely on **horse race journalism** when it comes to elections. This approach involves media coverage that focuses on poll results, campaign fundraising, and stylistic issues rather than substantive differences between the political candidates on public policy issues. Finally, **leaking** is a practice that occurs when a government employee provides nonpublic information to a reporter with the specific goal of generating press coverage that is favorable to the leaker's objectives.

The producers of the news are not owned and operated by the government in the United States. In a democracy the government does not control the flow of information. However, the media are regulated by the federal government. The **Federal Communications Commission (FCC)** is an independent agency of the federal government that was created in 1934 to regulate radio stations in America and was later expanded to include television, wireless communications, and other broadcast media. One critical FCC regulation is the **equal time provision**, which stipulates that broadcast media are required to provide equal air time at equal rates to all candidates seeking public office. In this manner, a network cannot allow a candidate from one party to air commercials without allowing another candidate to do the same and at the same advertising fee.

Interest groups play a pivotal role in a pluralist democracy, as James Madison detailed in *The Federalist* No. 10. At times it appears that an **iron triangle** exists in the United States, in which three primary political players (congressional committees, executive branch agencies, and interest groups) create policies that are mutually beneficial to each player but perhaps harmful to the greater public good. At other times it appears that the United States is a diverse republic and that the country's public policy reflects, to some extent, the wishes of a diverse array of groups and institutions. One important reality is that citizens should be cognizant of the flow of money from special interest groups to political candidates. It is essential to be aware of what is happening regarding campaign contributions. Knowing who is contributing to whom will enhance citizens' understanding of American politics and increase their ability to hold elected leaders accountable for their actions or nonactions.

There are numerous other realities pertaining to interest group politics. One is the **free rider** problem. A free rider is a person who reaps the benefits of interest group activities but does not do any of the work or pay the membership fees. Another concern is interest group leaders who choose to engage in **astroturf lobbying**, a method of lobbying where it is made to appear as if a number of individuals decided to participate in a given cause in a grassroots, spontaneous manner when in fact the lobbying effort in question was orchestrated by interest group officials. **Grassroots lobbying** is a strategy that is reliant on the participation of interest group members at the local level. A protest is an example of grassroots lobbying. There are two main approaches to lobbying. An **inside strategy** is a traditional tactic adopted by interest group officials employed within Washington, D.C., in order to pursue their policy objectives. An **outside strategy** is a tactic employed by interest group leaders outside of Washington, D.C., in order to pursue their agenda.

Citizens tend to be very critical of the **revolving door** syndrome. As the term suggests, the revolving door refers to the movement of individuals back and forth from government positions to jobs with special interest groups or lobbying firms. The general perception is that politicians who engage in this behavior are using their office for personal economic gain and have little interest in promoting the greater common good. This general perception has been fueled by the growth in **political action committees (PACs)** since the 1970s. A PAC is an interest group or a division of a group that is authorized to raise money and contribute to political candidates or to spend money on advertisements in support of candidates. Federal law limits the amount of money that PACs can receive from donors and how much they can spend on election activities. Many citizens view the relationships between lobbyists and the elected members of Congress as suspect.

Political socialization is the process by which citizens' political opinions are influenced by other people, institutions, and the surrounding culture. Our political attitudes and beliefs are impacted, to some extent, by family members; institutions such as schools, churches, and civic organizations; peers, popular culture, and a host of other entities. Paramount to understanding public opinion in America is that citizens are intertwined and interconnected when it comes to the ability to wield political influence over each other. It would behoove all citizens to attempt to ascertain their own process of political socialization and identify how they were influenced and by whom in their own political evolution.

The relevance of public opinion in a democracy is obvious. Leaders need to know what the people know, what they prioritize by way of public policy, and how they perceive the issues of the day. What may be less apparent to some is the ideological polarization that exists in the United States. A diverse array of policy issues is currently in existence. Americans may be liberal on some issues, moderate on others, and take conservative stances on still other issues. **Conservatives** generally favor less federal intervention in public policy, especially in the domestic economy, and typically affiliate with the Republican Party. **Liberals** generally favor a more proactive federal government in order to pursue their objectives, and typically identify with the Democratic Party. Moderates are somewhere between the left and the right on a given set of issues. Both dominant ideologies contradict themselves when it comes to privacy issues. Conservatives generally support more federal involvement on such matters as abortion or same-sex marriage (i.e., they believe the federal government should ban such activities or let the states ban them). Contemporary liberals typically contend that the Constitution protects a woman's right to choose when it comes to abortion and the right of same-sex partners to get married legally. Therefore, there is no role for the government as it pertains to privacy.

The Importance of Citizenship in a Republic

The effective citizen today should seek to consume a mix of print media, television, radio, and internet news coverage. While there is nothing wrong with social media, citizens are discouraged from receiving their news from social media platforms. The accuracy of the news in question could be compromised, as was evidenced with Facebook in the 2016 presidential campaign, where thousands of advertisements were purchased by a Russian agency in order to distort and manipulate the political agenda in the United States. Citizens are encouraged to read national newspapers such as the *Washington Post* and the *New York Times* in addition to their state and local newspapers. Viewing a nightly television news broadcast such as PBS, CNN, ABC, NBC, or CBS is also prudent. Radio listeners are served well by National Public Radio in terms of journalistic accuracy and competence. The internet offers a wide range of opportunities for citizens to become more engaged in politics and public affairs. Part of the responsibility of being a citizen in a republic is to stay informed about the great issues of the day.

In 1788 James Madison presented his now classic treatise on checks and balances in *The Federalist* No. 51. In it, he declared:

> But what is government itself, but the greatest of all reflections on human nature? If men were angels, no government would be necessary. If angels were to govern men, neither external nor internal controls on government would be necessary. In framing a government which is to be administered by men over men, the great difficulty lies in this: you must first enable the government to control the governed; and in the next place oblige it to control itself.[14]

In an eloquent manner, Madison highlighted the importance of accountability in democratic systems of government. Accountability, manifested in the Constitution through separation of powers and checks and balances, ensures that no one branch of government exceeds its constitutional authority. But do recall that democratic governments all have one important thing in common: to be a democracy, a government must be accountable to its own citizens, as they are the ultimate sovereigns. In this chapter I have contended that the mass media, interest groups, and public opinion are all critical components of a democratic political system. All of these aspects of American politics help us to keep our own government accountable to us.

It is important to remember a quandary that exists in all democracies: should government leaders give the people what they desire, or should they do what they think is in the greater common good even though it may be unpopular? A prominent political scientist once described this dilemma in the following manner:

> More years ago than I care to remember, when I studied the writing of the Constitution in 11th-grade U.S. history, I naively asked my teacher, "Are the people we send to Congress supposed to do what we want them to do or are they supposed to do what they think is best?" I do not remember exactly what my teacher replied. I know that I did not get a satisfactory answer. I still do not have one.[15]

How should this question be answered? In my estimation, the best possible answer to this quandary is for each adult citizen to decide for herself or himself. An informed and proactive citizenry is well equipped to address this democratic dilemma and many others as well. While we will undoubtedly have different visions as to how democracy should be manifested, there should be considerable consensus on the premise that there are multiple actors in the American political system, and there is always ample room for journalists, lobbyists, and citizens to pursue the goal of a more effective democracy.

Knowledge Matters

One of my recommendations to win the ongoing war against poverty in the United States is to use science and data analysis to enhance citizens' collective knowledge about American politics and public affairs.[16] Public opinion, of course, should be consequential in a democracy. Yet the opinion of the citizens should be based on scientific knowledge, not simply ideology or anecdotal innuendo. In other words, one of the key reforms that is needed in this country is for all Americans to do a better job as citizens. This means that we need to know the state of current events. More important, we need to care about current policy issues. In so doing, all adult Americans will be better equipped to engage in reforming the status quo.

President Roosevelt envisioned a "thinking person's" government in 1935 when he created the Resettlement Administration (RA) via executive order. RA officials had three fundamental goals: (1) to restore land ownership through low-interest loans to farmers who had poor land, (2) to restore the productivity of ruined land through soil conservation and rebuilding projects, and (3) to resettle/relocate/rehabilitate/renew farm families whose agricultural livelihoods had been destroyed by the

Great Depression. Social scientists such as Edward Banfield, Robert Lynd, Gunnar Myrdal, Harold Lasswell, and Grant McConnell worked on this project as did artists and writers, including one of the great authors of the 20th century, John Steinbeck. The RA was an attempt of putting theory into practice. It was disbanded after two years, not because the premise of a thinking person's government was flawed but due to political differences.[17]

Policy makers and citizens alike should consider scientific findings as much as possible in terms of making judgments about the relative merits of policy ideas. More, not less, analysis by the experts should be undertaken when making important public policy decisions. Knowledge should always supplant partisan loyalty; it is important that officials address the policy needs of people, even when scientists are providing information that we do not want to consider.[18]

To be sure, reform is needed with regard to all aspects of American politics, including the key political actors in the United States. Journalists and lobbyists could be more effective in the performance of their tasks. Journalists should always seek to provide the people with the truth about politics, and it is incumbent upon them to inform citizens about what government officials are doing or not doing with regard to public problems. Likewise, lobbyists are challenged to represent all sectors of the diverse population. Yet all citizens would do well to understand that both journalists and lobbyists are crucial players in democratic systems. Most journalists do not seek to foment "fake news" for political purposes; most lobbyists are trying to promote the agenda of their respective interest groups. We should expect objective journalism on one hand and pluralism on the other, in that lobbyists have access to the traditional branches of government and can provide an indirect link between the people and their elected leaders in this republic, as Madison envisioned a long time ago.

Citizen Homework

Citizens can learn more about the three subject matters in this chapter, which are vital to democratic governance, by viewing the following three videos (each is about 30 minutes long):

"Understanding Media: The Inside Story" (https://www.learner. org/series/democracy-in-america/the-media-inside-story/).
"Interest Groups: Organizing to Influence" (https://

www.learner.org/series/democracy-in-america/
interest-groups-organizing-to-influence/).
"Public Opinion: Voice of the People" (https://
www.learner.org/series/democracy-in-america/
public-opinion-voice-of-the-people/).
"The Banking Crisis." President Franklin Roosevelt's First Fireside
Chat: March 12, 1933 (https://www.c-span.org/video/?298210-1/
president-franklin-roosevelts-fireside-chat). Listen to an audio
clip (about 13 minutes long) of President Roosevelt's explanation
of the banking crisis to the American people. Was he effective
in his quest to appease anxiety about banks during the Great
Depression?
The first presidential debate between Richard Nixon and John F.
Kennedy, September 26, 1960: https://www.jfklibrary.org/Asset-
Viewer/Archives/TNC-172.aspx. Watch a video of the first (of
four) presidential debates between the two major party candidates in the 1960 presidential election. It lasts about an hour.
Compare and contrast the appearances and performances of the
two candidates.

CHAPTER 5

Congress and Political Parties

No other issue was more important to the framers of the U.S. Constitution than the creation of Congress, for it was designed to be the closest to the people, in that the people could directly elect members of only one specific institution: the U.S. House of Representatives. State legislators were empowered with selecting U.S. senators, the president was selected directly by the Electoral College, and federal judges were appointed by the president and confirmed by the Senate with no direct role for citizens. In early 1788 James Madison offered this analysis of the proposed new House of Representatives in *The Federalist* No. 52:

> The term for which the representatives are to be elected falls under a second view which may be taken of this branch. In order to decide on the propriety of this article, two questions must be considered: first, whether biennial elections will, in this case, be safe; secondly, whether they be necessary or useful. First. As it is essential to liberty that the government in general should have a common interest with the people, so it is particularly essential that the branch of it under consideration should have an immediate dependence on, and an intimate sympathy with, the people. Frequent elections are unquestionably the only policy by which this dependence and sympathy can be effectually secured. But what particular degree of frequency may be absolutely necessary for the purpose, does not appear to be susceptible of any precise calculation, and must depend on a variety of circumstances with which it may be connected.[1]

In the context of the late 18th century, there had to be a direct link between the people and their new national government that was proposed under the Constitution. That link was the House of Representatives. With the passage of the Seventeenth Amendment, in 1913 the people were given the right to directly elect U.S. senators. As the framers envisioned the House, its members are capable, at least in theory, of entertaining new ideas, policy visions, and policy priorities every two years if the people collectively want to effect change.[2]

While the framers did not envision the relatively expedient evolution of **political parties** in America following the ratification and implementation of the new Constitution, parties have played an important role in politics and public affairs since the mid-1790s. Political parties are organized groups that seek to influence public policy making by electing their members to prominent government positions. Political parties perform a vital role in a republican form of government, for they provide citizens with definitive choices when they are operating effectively. In theory the people should know the fundamental philosophical beliefs of the various political parties, what they support, what they oppose, and how they would use power if they were afforded the opportunity to wield power by the electorate. Today there are two major political parties in the United States. The **Democratic Party** was founded in the late 1820s by supporters of Andrew Jackson. At that time Democrats embraced the doctrine of states' rights (a belief that the Constitution provided a limited mandate for the national government, where most policy issues were addressed at the state level). Democrats today typically believe in a proactive role for the national government in the economy and prioritize social equality over all other issues. At the same time, Democrats believe there should be no role for the government in privacy matters such as the abortion question or same-sex marriage. The **Republican Party** was founded in the 1850s, and one of its early adherents was Abraham Lincoln. Republicans at that time supported a more proactive national government on key issues such as slavery and infrastructure. Today Republicans believe in less national intervention in the domestic authority and more authority sent back to the states. The top priority for Republicans is the pursuit of individual freedom, which is defined by conservatives as meaning freedom from government intervention. At the same time, many Republicans believe there should be a strong role for the government in privacy matters—for example, restricting access to abortions via government intervention.

Citizens in America have always been confronted with a fundamental choice with regard to political parties. Since parties emerged in the United States during George Washington's administration, Americans have always had two major political parties. This does not mean that U.S. citizens have only two choices, as there are typically several minor (third) parties from which to select. But because the framers of the Constitution established a winner-take-all system for the House of Representatives, where the person with the most votes gets the job and the losers get nothing, even if this means the winner did not receive a simple majority of the total vote, Americans who vote for third-party candidates typically get nothing tangible in return for their vote. In other words, not many third-party candidates have been elected to the House or Senate, and no minor party candidate has been elected to the presidency. This prompts many Americans to either conform and vote for one of the major party candidates, and for some people it may even act as a deterrent to voting altogether. Some citizens think they are wasting their vote if they vote for a third-party candidate. Thus, while voting for a Socialist, Libertarian, Green, Natural Alliance, or other party candidate may be appealing, some citizens select a candidate from one of the major parties who is closest to them ideologically in lieu of casting a ballot for a third-party candidate. People who generally do not identify with either the Republican or Democratic Party call themselves **independents**. Independents are typically referred to as moderates or centrists.

Historical Evolution of Congress

The framers of the Constitution created Congress in Article I when they drafted the document in 1787. After weeks of debates, the framers adopted the Great (or Connecticut) Compromise. The Great Compromise was a political deal that was proposed by the Connecticut delegates in the Philadelphia Convention. The compromise resulted in the creation of a bicameral Congress. The lower chamber would be based on population and be called the House of Representatives; the upper chamber would have two legislators per state and be called the Senate. The Great Compromise was a blend of the Virginia Plan and the New Jersey Plan. The Virginia Plan was a series of proposals submitted by the Virginia delegates at the Philadelphia Convention that would strengthen the national government. During the debates concerning the creation of Congress, one proposal was to have a two-chamber Congress with each house based on population. The New Jersey Plan was a series of proposals submitted by the New Jersey delegates at the Philadelphia Convention in response to the Virginia Plan, which would preserve state power and maintain a weak national government. During the extensive debates on the creation of a legislative body, one proposal was to have a unicameral Congress with equal state representation regardless of population. From the Virginia Plan, the framers agreed to create a House of Representatives based on population. This meant that states with more people would have more political representation in the House. The framers decided to use the vision of the New Jersey Plan in creating the Senate, as each state was allocated two senators, regardless of the state's population. While the three most populated states at the time (Virginia, Massachusetts, and Pennsylvania) would have more delegates in the House than the smaller states, they would have the same number of senators as Delaware and Rhode Island, the least populated states.

The **enumerated powers** of Congress are delineated in Article I of the Constitution. The members of Congress were assigned a great deal of authority by the framers. Specifically, Congress has the power to make laws, to regulate commerce, to declare war, to lay and collect taxes, to coin and borrow money, to raise and support armies, and to make all laws that are necessary and proper to carry out its authority under the Constitution. In addition to enumerated powers, Congress also has **implied powers** (authority that is not specifically delineated in the federal Constitution but is suggested by the assignment of other enumerated powers).

It is important to understand that most of the work done in Congress does not take place on the floor of each respective chamber but in committees. The most important committees are **standing committees**. Just as the term suggests, standing committees are permanent committees that have more authority than any others in the U.S. Congress. There are 20 standing committees in the U.S. House and 16 in the U.S. Senate.[3] Since political power in the Congress is decentralized, each standing committee has several **subcommittees**. Subcommittees are committees within committees. Standing committees in the U.S. Congress typically create a number of subcommittees to divide the workload. While being a chair of a standing committee allows the chair of the committee to wield power in that particular policy area, power is also exercised by the chairs of the subcommittees as well. Typically, a member of Congress becomes a chair of a standing committee, or even a subcommittee, by meeting two criteria: she or he belongs to the majority party in that chamber and is the most senior member of the majority party on the committee at the time.

The framers created age, citizenship, and residency requirements for congressional service. House terms are two years whereas senators have six-year terms, as it was the intent of the framers to make the House closest to the people so that public opinion would be very important to House members when legislating. In the context of the late 18th century, the framers envisioned that members of the Senate would be less influenced by public opinion because they were selected by state legislators and because they had a longer term in office than House members or even the president. To them, the Senate would be a more deliberate body that would temper bills passed in the House if necessary. They viewed the Senate as being populated by statesmen who would be positioned to put the needs of the nation ahead of the perhaps provincial interests of the states they represented. Most members of Congress in the history of the country have been members of one of the two major political parties during their respective eras. Though this is not a constitutional or legal requirement, the importance of the political parties in Congress cannot be overemphasized.

The first session of Congress met in New York City in 1789. It then moved to Philadelphia in 1790 and then Washington, D.C., in 1800 and has been there ever since.[4] There were 65 members in the U.S. House and 26 senators (13 states) in the first session of Congress. Since 1959, when Alaska and Hawaii were admitted to the Union, there have been 100 U.S. senators. This number could increase if Puerto Rico, Washington, D.C., or a territory were elevated to statehood by Congress. Until 1929 the number of representatives has increased over time with the addition of more states. Currently, there are 435 voting members of the U.S. House. In 1929 the members of the House decided to cap the size of the House at its level following the 1910 census, and it has remained unchanged for a century.[5]

The most powerful member of the House has always been the **speaker**. The speaker is the presiding officer of the House and is elected by the majority party caucus. The rules of the House give the speaker a great deal of political power to control the flow of legislation in the House. Historically, the speaker has been the second most powerful elected official in the country behind the president. The first speaker of the House was Frederick Muhlenberg from Pennsylvania in 1789.[6] With the growth of the House in the 19th century, the position of **majority leader** was created. The majority leader is elected by the majority party caucus and is the person who sets the agenda for issues to be discussed on the floor and who oversees committee chairs in the House. The majority leader is the second highest position in the majority party. Before 1899 the majority leader had traditionally been the chair of the House Ways and Means Committee. This is the most powerful committee in the House, because the Constitution requires all bills of revenue to originate in the House and they do so in this important committee. The first elected majority leader in the House was Sereno Payne of New York in 1899.[7]

The most powerful position in the House for the minority party is called the **minority leader**. The minority leader is the person who directs the minority party and is elected by the minority party caucus. The minority leader is the minority counterpart to the speaker and is generally considered as the spokesperson of the loyal opposition to the majority party. The first elected minority leader was James Richardson of Tennessee in 1899. Before this time, the minority nominee for speaker was typically considered to be the leader of the minority party.[8]

Each majority party has had a whip since the late 19th century. The title "whip" comes from Great Britain. Since the late 18th century, the House of Commons has had party whips. It is the job of the whips to assist party leaders in managing their legislative program on the House floor.[9] The **House majority whip** is the person whose primary job is to ensure that fellow partisans support party positions when a floor vote is held. Today the whip is elected by the majority party caucus; it is the third highest position in the majority party. The **House minority whip** is the person who assists the minority leader in coordinating party strategy and ensuring that fellow partisans support party positions when a floor vote is taken. Today this leader is elected by the minority party caucus, and it is the second highest position in the minority party. The first House Republican whip was James Tawney of Minnesota in 1897.[10] The first House Democratic whip was Oscar Underwood from Alabama in 1899.[11]

The leadership structure in the Senate is different than it is in the House. While House rules afford the speaker a great deal of power, the leader in the Senate does not wield power to the same extent, for Senate rules protect the right of individual members to engage in extended debate on a given issue if they desire. The Senate has ceremonial leaders; under the Constitution, the vice president of the United States is also **president of the Senate**. Typically, however, the vice president does not preside over Senate debates unless a close vote is expected. The only power assigned to the vice president in the Constitution is the authority to cast a tie-breaking vote. Such votes are rare, however. The vice president can succeed a president in office if she or he dies in office or resigns the position.[12] In the absence of the president of the Senate (vice president) presiding over the Senate, that task is designated to the **president pro tempore of the Senate**. The president pro tempore is "president for a time" and is an elected position; by custom, the president pro tempore is the senator from the majority party with the longest record of continuous service.[13] Typically, the president pro tempore does not preside over the Senate in the absence of the vice president but assigns the duty to junior senators in the majority party on a rotational basis.

The substantive leaders in the Senate are the majority and minority leaders. The Senate majority leader is the chief spokesperson for the majority party and is elected by the majority caucus. The majority leader, in consultation with committee chairs and ranking members, schedules the business of the Senate. Similarly, the Senate minority leader is the chief spokesperson for the minority party and is elected by the minority caucus. The minority leader is responsible for coordinating the minority party's strategy in the Senate. The party floor leader positions in the Senate did not evolve until the early 20th century. The Democrats formally designated a floor leader in 1920 (Minority Leader Oscar Underwood of Alabama) and the Republicans later did so in 1925 (Majority Leader Charles Curtis of Kansas).[14]

A major difference between the Senate and the House has to do with how each chamber deals with debate on the floor. In the House the **Rules Committee** members determine how long the bill will be debated on the floor and how the bill may be amended. This committee is an extension of the power of the speaker, for the majority party controls this committee just like the other standing committees. The House, unlike the Senate, does not have the possibility of unlimited debate due to its size. The Senate, on the other hand, has a tradition dating back to the 19th century of extended debate if members take this prerogative. In 1841 the Democratic minority attempted to block a bank bill promoted by Senator Henry Clay. He threatened to change the rules of the Senate to allow the majority to close debate and hold a vote. Senator Thomas Hart Benton admonished Clay for trying to limit debate in the U.S. Senate.[15]

A **filibuster** is a legislative talkathon in the U.S. Senate. Filibusters are used by senators in the minority as a tactic to block a floor vote on a bill by continuing to hold the floor and speak until the senators in the majority on the bill back down and proceed to other issues. Although the word "filibuster" does not exist in the Constitution, extended debate is in conformance of the framers' wishes to ensure that the Senate cooled down the passions in the House. The longest filibuster in U.S. history was 24 hours and 18 minutes. Strom Thurmond conducted this filibuster in 1957 in opposition to the Civil Rights Act of 1957. Under Senate rules there is a way to end a filibuster, though not necessarily immediately. The procedure is known as **cloture**. Cloture is a Senate device where a petition is circulated to limit the amount of time debating a specific bill. Under Senate Rule 22, a filibuster ends when three-fifths of the Senate (60 senators) agree to do so. Even if cloture is invoked, up to 30 hours of additional debate can take place on the matter at hand. There was no way to end a filibuster in the 19th and early 20th centuries. Senators adopted Rule 22 in 1917 at the urging of President Woodrow Wilson. At that time, cloture could be invoked with a two-thirds majority vote. Today that would be 67 votes. In 1975 the members of the Senate reduced the number of votes required to invoke cloture from two-thirds to three-fifths (60 votes).[16]

Historical Evolution of Political Parties

When the framers wrote the Constitution, political parties did not exist in the United States. In the 1790s, however, parties emerged and they have been in existence ever since. Parties continue to be an important dividing line in national public policy debates. The first session of Congress began in 1789 when the new government commenced under the Constitution, which replaced the Articles of Confederation and Perpetual Union. Since House members are elected every two years, a new session of Congress begins after the House elections. In early 2019 the members of the 116th session of Congress were sworn into duty.

The first session of Congress resulted in a division between legislators who supported President George Washington and those who did not. Remember, there were no formal political parties when the nation began under the Constitution in 1789. By the end of the 18th century, however, two political parties formed in the United States: the **Federalist Party** and the **Democratic-Republican Party**. The Federalists organized around the philosophy of Alexander Hamilton. They believed in a strong national government and a broad interpretation of the Constitution. They also supported friendly relations with Great Britain. The Federalists organized in the early 1790s and lasted into the 1820s. The Democratic-Republican Party members embraced the states' rights philosophy of Thomas Jefferson and a strict interpretation of the Constitution. The Federalists thought that Congress should regulate all aspects of the American economy; Jefferson's followers thought that members of Congress could exercise the explicit (enumerated) powers assigned to the legislative branch under Article I and that all other powers should be properly exercised at the state level. Like the Federalists, the Democratic-Republican Party organized in the early 1790s and lasted until the late 1820s. Its members supported friendly relations with France as opposed to Great Britain.

What Americans today should realize is that political parties have always played an important role in American politics. The Democratic-Republican Party would later evolve into National Republicans in the early 19th century; shortly thereafter the Federalists would morph into Whigs. The **National Republican Party** organized as a result of political disputes between John Quincy Adams and Andrew Jackson. The Democratic-Republican Party split into the National Republican Party, which supported Adams and consisted of many former Federalists, and the Democratic Party of Andrew Jackson. Later in the 19th century, the National Republicans would cease to exist and the Democratic Party was created in the 1820s. Similar to the Democratic-Republicans, the National Republicans and then the Democrats attracted people who believed in the doctrine of states' rights. Instead of Thomas Jefferson, the leader of the Democratic Party was Andrew Jackson. Like the Federalists, the supporters of the **Whig Party** believed in a strong national government. The Whigs organized in the 1830s in opposition to the Democratic Party and Andrew Jackson and lasted into the 1850s when the Republican Party was formed. The Whigs supported the supremacy of Congress over the president and supported a program of modernization. By the late 1850s, the Whigs ceased to exist and a new Republican Party emerged, led by Abraham Lincoln in 1860.

At the time of the Civil War until the early 20th century, the Democratic Party attracted states' rights activists, especially in the South. They believed that the national government had a limited mandate under the Constitution and that states should be free to determine policy issues such as slavery. The Republican Party of Lincoln included citizens who believed in a stronger national government where members of Congress had a broad mandate under the Constitution to determine such issues as slavery and admitting states into the union.

The United States has had two major parties with the same labels, Republican and Democratic, ever since the Civil War. However, the Democratic Party evolved into the 20th century, especially under the leadership of President Franklin D. Roosevelt. The Democrats have generally favored more economic and environmental regulation as well as civil rights protections throughout the 20th and 21st centuries. The Republican Party is the more conservative of the major parties; contemporary Republicans, especially since Ronald Reagan's election in 1980, favor deregulated markets and less federal intervention in civil rights debates.

Elections matter in American history and politics. What the people choose to do, or not to do, is depicted in tables 5.1 and 5.2. Table 5.1 includes party divisions in the House since 1789 and table 5.2 covers the

Table 5.1. Party Divisions in the U.S. House of Representatives (1789–2021)

Session	Years	# of House Seats	Party Breakdown*
1	1789–1791	65	37 Pro-Administration/28 Anti-Administration
2	1791–1793	69	39 Pro-Administration/30 Anti-Administration
3	1793–1795	105	54 Anti-Administration/51 Pro-Administration
4	1795–1797	106	59 Democratic-Republicans/47 Federalists
5	1797–1799	106	57 Federalists/49 Democratic-Republicans
6	1799–1801	106	60 Federalists/46 Democratic-Republicans
7	1801–1803	106	68 Democratic-Republicans/38 Federalists
8	1803–1805	142	103 Democratic-Republicans/39 Federalists
9	1805–1807	142	114 Democratic-Republicans/28 Federalists
10	1807–1809	142	116 Democratic-Republicans/26 Federalists
11	1809–1811	142	92 Democratic-Republicans/50 Federalists
12	1811–1813	143	107 Democratic-Republicans/36 Federalists
13	1813–1815	182	114 Democratic-Republicans/68 Federalists
14	1815–1817	183	119 Democratic-Republicans/64 Federalists
15	1817–1819	185	146 Democratic-Republicans/39 Federalists
16	1819–1821	186	160 Democratic-Republicans/26 Federalists
17	1821–1823	187	155 Democratic-Republicans/32 Federalists
18	1823–1825	213	189 National Republicans/24 Federalists
19	1825–1827	213	109 National Republicans/104 Democrats
20	1827–1829	213	113 Democrats/100 National Republicans
21	1829–1831	213	136 Democrats/72 National Republicans
22	1831–1833	213	126 National Republicans/66 Democrats
23	1833–1835	240	143 National Republicans/63 Democrats
24	1835–1837	242	143 National Republicans/75 Democrats
25	1837–1839	242	128 Democrats/100 Whigs
26	1839–1841	242	125 Democrats/109 Whigs
27	1841–1843	242	142 Whigs/98 Democrats
28	1843–1845	223	147 Democrats/72 Whigs
29	1845–1847	228	142 Democrats/79 Whigs
30	1847–1849	230	116 Whigs/110 Democrats
31	1849–1851	233	113 Democrats/108 Whigs
32	1851–1853	233	127 Democrats/85 Whigs
33	1853–1855	234	157 Democrats/71 Whigs
34	1855–1857	234	100 Whigs/83 Democrats/51 Americans
35	1857–1859	237	132 Democrats/90 Republicans/14 Americans
36	1859–1861	238	116 Republicans/83 Democrats

Table 5.1.—*Continued*

Session	Years	# of House Seats	Party Breakdown*
37	1861–1863	183	108 Republicans/44 Democrats
38	1863–1865	184	85 Republicans/38 Democrats/18 Unionists
39	1865–1867	193	136 Republicans/38 Democrats
40	1867–1869	226	173 Republicans/47 Democrats
41	1869–1871	243	171 Republicans/67 Democrats
42	1871–1873	243	136 Republicans/104 Democrats
43	1873–1875	292	199 Republicans/88 Democrats
44	1875–1877	293	182 Democrats/103 Republicans
45	1877–1879	293	155 Democrats/136 Republicans
46	1879–1881	293	141 Democrats/132 Republicans
47	1881–1883	293	151 Republicans/128 Democrats
48	1883–1885	325	196 Democrats/117 Republicans
49	1885–1887	325	182 Democrats/141 Republicans
50	1887–1889	325	167 Democrats/152 Republicans
51	1889–1891	332	179 Republicans/152 Democrats
52	1891–1893	332	238 Democrats/86 Republicans
53	1893–1895	356	218 Democrats/124 Republicans
54	1895–1897	357	254 Republicans/93 Democrats
55	1897–1899	357	206 Republicans/124 Democrats
56	1899–1901	357	187 Republicans/161 Democrats
57	1901–1903	357	200 Republicans/151 Democrats
58	1903–1905	386	207 Republicans/176 Democrats
59	1905–1907	386	251 Republicans/135 Democrats
60	1907–1909	391	223 Republicans/167 Democrats
61	1909–1911	391	219 Republicans/172 Democrats
62	1911–1913	394	230 Democrats/162 Republicans
63	1913–1915	435	291 Democrats/134 Republicans
64	1915–1917	435	230 Democrats/196 Republicans
65	1917–1919	435	215 Republicans/214 Democrats
66	1919–1921	435	240 Republicans/192 Democrats
67	1921–1923	435	302 Republicans/131 Democrats
68	1923–1925	435	225 Republicans/207 Democrats
69	1925–1927	435	247 Republicans/183 Democrats
70	1927–1929	435	238 Republicans/194 Democrats
71	1929–1931	435	270 Republicans/164 Democrats
72	1931–1933	435	218 Republicans/216 Democrats
73	1933–1935	435	313 Democrats/117 Republicans
74	1935–1937	435	322 Democrats/103 Republicans
75	1937–1939	435	334 Democrats/88 Republicans
76	1939–1941	435	262 Democrats/169 Republicans
77	1941–1943	435	267 Democrats/162 Republicans
78	1943–1945	435	222 Democrats/209 Republicans
79	1945–1947	435	244 Democrats/189 Republicans
80	1947–1949	435	246 Republicans/188 Democrats
81	1949–1951	435	263 Democrats/171 Republicans

(*continues*)

Table 5.1.—*Continued*

Session	Years	# of House Seats	Party Breakdown*
82	1951–1953	435	235 Democrats/199 Republicans
83	1953–1955	435	221 Republicans/213 Democrats
84	1955–1957	435	232 Democrats/203 Republicans
85	1957–1959	435	232 Democrats/203 Republicans
86	1959–1961	436	282 Democrats/153 Republicans
87	1961–1963	437	264 Democrats/173 Republicans
88	1963–1965	435	258 Democrats/176 Republicans
89	1965–1967	435	295 Democrats/140 Republicans
90	1967–1969	435	248 Democrats/187 Republicans
91	1969–1971	435	243 Democrats/192 Republicans
92	1971–1973	435	255 Democrats/180 Republicans
93	1973–1975	435	243 Democrats/192 Republicans
94	1975–1977	435	291 Democrats/144 Republicans
95	1977–1979	435	292 Democrats/143 Republicans
96	1979–1981	435	278 Democrats/157 Republicans
97	1981–1983	435	243 Democrats/192 Republicans
98	1983–1985	435	269 Democrats/166 Republicans
99	1985–1987	435	254 Democrats/181 Republicans
100	1987–1989	435	258 Democrats/177 Republicans
101	1989–1991	435	260 Democrats/175 Republicans
102	1991–1993	435	267 Democrats/167 Republicans
103	1993–1995	435	258 Democrats/176 Republicans
104	1995–1997	435	230 Republicans/204 Democrats
105	1997–1999	435	226 Republicans/207 Democrats
106	1999–2001	435	223 Republicans/211 Democrats
107	2001–2003	435	220 Republicans/213 Democrats
108	2003–2005	435	229 Republicans/205 Democrats
109	2005–2007	435	233 Republicans/201 Democrats
110	2007–2009	435	233 Democrats/202 Republicans
111	2009–2011	435	257 Democrats/178 Republicans
112	2011–2013	435	242 Republicans/193 Democrats
113	2013–2015	435	234 Republicans/201 Democrats
114	2015–2017	435	247 Republicans/188 Democrats
115	2017–2019	435	241 Republicans/194 Democrats
116	2019–2021	435	235 Democrats/199 Republicans

Source: U.S. House of Representatives, "Party Divisions in the House of Representatives," http://history.house.gov/institution/Party-Divisions/Party-Divisions/

* The party breakdown figures are the House divisions as of the initial election results and do not reflect the changes in House membership that can occur through resignations, deaths, contested or special elections, or changes in political party affiliation after the elections in question. In addition, only major coalitions and/or political parties are reflected in the tallies unless otherwise noted.

Table 5.2. Party Divisions in the U.S. Senate (1789–2021)

Session	Years	# of Senate Seats	Party Breakdown*
1	1789–1791	26	18 Pro-Administration/8 Anti-Administration
2	1791–1793	30	16 Pro-Administration/13 Anti-Administration
3	1793–1795	30	16 Pro-Administration/14 Anti-Administration
4	1795–1797	32	21 Federalists/11 Democratic-Republicans
5	1797–1799	32	22 Federalists/10 Democratic-Republicans
6	1799–1801	32	22 Federalists/10 Democratic-Republicans
7	1801–1803	34	17 Democratic-Republicans/15 Federalists
8	1803–1805	34	25 Democratic-Republicans/9 Federalists
9	1805–1807	34	27 Democratic-Republicans/7 Federalists
10	1807–1809	34	28 Democratic-Republicans/6 Federalists
11	1809–1811	34	27 Democratic-Republicans/7 Federalists
12	1811–1813	36	30 Democratic-Republicans/6 Federalists
13	1813–1815	36	28 Democratic-Republicans/8 Federalists
14	1815–1817	38	26 Democratic-Republicans/12 Federalists
15	1817–1819	42	30 Democratic-Republicans/12 Federalists
16	1819–1821	46	37 Democratic-Republicans/9 Federalists
17	1821–1823	48	44 Democratic-Republicans/4 Federalists
18	1823–1825	48	44 National Republicans/3 Federalists
19	1825–1827	48	26 Democrats/22 National Republicans
20	1827–1829	48	27 Democrats/21 National Republicans
21	1829–1831	48	25 Democrats/23 National Republicans
22	1831–1833	48	24 Democrats/22 National Republicans
23	1833–1835	48	26 National Republicans/20 Democrats
24	1835–1837	52	26 Democrats/24 National Republicans
25	1837–1839	52	35 Democrats/17 Whigs
26	1839–1841	52	30 Democrats/22 Whigs
27	1841–1843	52	29 Whigs/22 Democrats
28	1843–1845	52	29 Whigs/23 Democrats
29	1845–1847	58	34 Democrats/22 Whigs
30	1847–1849	60	38 Democrats/21 Whigs
31	1849–1851	62	35 Democrats/25 Whigs
32	1851–1853	62	36 Democrats/23 Whigs
33	1853–1855	62	38 Democrats/22 Whigs
34	1855–1857	62	39 Democrats/21 Whigs
35	1857–1859	66	41 Democrats/20 Republicans
36	1859–1861	66	38 Democrats/26 Republicans
37	1861–1863	50**	31 Republicans/15 Democrats
38	1863–1865	52**	33 Republicans/10 Democrats/9 Unionists
39	1865–1867	54**	39 Republicans/11 Democrats/4 Unionists
40	1867–1869	68	57 Republicans/9 Democrats
41	1869–1871	74	62 Republicans/12 Democrats
42	1871–1873	74	56 Republicans/17 Democrats
43	1873–1875	74	47 Republicans/19 Democrats
44	1875–1877	76	46 Republicans/28 Democrats

(*continues*)

Table 5.2.—*Continued*

Session	Years	# of Senate Seats	Party Breakdown*
45	1877–1879	76	40 Republicans/35 Democrats
46	1879–1881	76	42 Democrats/33 Republicans
47	1881–1883	76	37 Democrats/37 Republicans
48	1883–1885	76	38 Republicans/36 Democrats
49	1885–1887	76	42 Republicans/34 Democrats
50	1887–1889	76	39 Republicans/37 Democrats
51	1889–1891	88	51 Republicans/37 Democrats
52	1891–1893	88	47 Republicans/39 Democrats
53	1893–1895	88	44 Democrats/40 Republicans
54	1895–1897	90	44 Republicans/40 Democrats
55	1897–1899	90	44 Republicans/34 Democrats
56	1899–1901	90	53 Republicans/26 Democrats
57	1901–1903	90	56 Republicans/32 Democrats
58	1903–1905	90	57 Republicans/33 Democrats
59	1905–1907	90	58 Republicans/32 Democrats
60	1907–1909	92	61 Republicans/31 Democrats
61	1909–1911	92	60 Republicans/32 Democrats
62	1911–1913	96	52 Republicans/44 Democrats
63	1913–1915	96	51 Democrats/44 Republicans
64	1915–1917	96	56 Democrats/40 Republicans
65	1917–1919	96	54 Democrats/42 Republicans
66	1919–1921	96	49 Republicans/47 Democrats
67	1921–1923	96	59 Republicans/37 Democrats
68	1923–1925	96	53 Republicans/42 Democrats
69	1925–1927	96	54 Republicans/41 Democrats
70	1927–1929	96	48 Republicans/46 Democrats
71	1929–1931	96	56 Republicans/39 Democrats
72	1931–1933	96	48 Republicans/47 Democrats
73	1933–1935	96	59 Democrats/36 Republicans
74	1935–1937	96	69 Democrats/25 Republicans
75	1937–1939	96	76 Democrats/16 Republicans
76	1939–1941	96	69 Democrats/23 Republicans
77	1941–1943	96	66 Democrats/28 Republicans
78	1943–1945	96	57 Democrats/38 Republicans
79	1945–1947	96	57 Democrats/38 Republicans
80	1947–1949	96	51 Republicans/45 Democrats
81	1949–1951	96	54 Democrats/42 Republicans
82	1951–1953	96	49 Democrats/47 Republicans
83	1953–1955	96	48 Republicans/47 Democrats
84	1955–1957	96	48 Democrats/47 Republicans
85	1957–1959	96	49 Democrats/47 Republicans
86	1959–1961	100	65 Democrats/35 Republicans
87	1961–1963	100	64 Democrats/36 Republicans
88	1963–1965	100	66 Democrats/34 Republicans

Table 5.2.—*Continued*

Session	Years	# of Senate Seats	Party Breakdown*
89	1965–1967	100	68 Democrats/32 Republicans
90	1967–1969	100	64 Democrats/36 Republicans
91	1969–1971	100	57 Democrats/43 Republicans
92	1971–1973	100	55 Democrats/45 Republicans
93	1973–1975	100	57 Democrats/43 Republicans
94	1975–1977	100	62 Democrats/38 Republicans
95	1977–1979	100	62 Democrats/38 Republicans
96	1979–1981	100	59 Democrats/41 Republicans
97	1981–1983	100	53 Republicans/47 Democrats
98	1983–1985	100	55 Republicans/45 Democrats
99	1985–1987	100	53 Republicans/47 Democrats
100	1987–1989	100	55 Democrats/45 Republicans
101	1989–1991	100	55 Democrats/45 Republicans
102	1991–1993	100	56 Democrats/44 Republicans
103	1993–1995	100	57 Democrats/43 Republicans
104	1995–1997	100	52 Republicans/48 Democrats
105	1997–1999	100	55 Republicans/45 Democrats
106	1999–2001	100	55 Republicans/45 Democrats
107	2001–2003	100	50 Republicans/50 Democrats
108	2003–2005	100	51 Republicans/49 Democrats
109	2005–2007	100	55 Republicans/45 Democrats
110	2007–2009	100	51 Democrats/49 Republicans
111	2009–2011	100	59 Democrats/41 Republicans
112	2011–2013	100	53 Democrats/47 Republicans
113	2013–2015	100	55 Democrats/45 Republicans
114	2015–2017	100	54 Republicans/46 Democrats
115	2017–2019	100	52 Republicans/48 Democrats
116	2019–2021	100	53 Republicans/47 Democrats

* The party breakdown figures are the Senate divisions as of the initial election results and do not reflect the changes in Senate membership that can occur through resignations, deaths, contested or special elections, or changes in political party affiliation after the elections in question. In addition, only major coalitions and/or political parties are reflected in the tallies unless otherwise noted. Where independents caucus with a major party, the senators are counted in the applicable major party.

** Due to the secession of the Southern states.

Source: U.S. Senate, "Party Divisions," https://www.senate.gov/history/partydiv.htm

Senate. In both cases, note that at times the people elect large majorities of one party over the other. Typically, however, this behavior is somewhat rare. Elections are tough competitions, and it is not unusual for Americans to give one party a slim majority over the other and then turn around two years later with the opposite result. As noted in chapter 3, the implications and consequences of elections are crucial. In the 21st century, citizens must embrace their important roles in democratic governance and register their choices accordingly by voting. A more engaged and participatory citizenry has the great potential of helping to resolve many of the vexing policy challenges of today.

Congress and Political Parties Today

With 435 members of Congress, 218 seats are required for majority party status. The House is much larger than the Senate, and debates are typically structured and limited accordingly. The Senate operates much differently than the House. The framers of the Constitution envisioned the Senate as the place where the great issues of the day would be debated at length. In the 19th century, filibusters began to be employed in the Senate. Since the framers believed that the Senate would be deliberative, the advent of the filibuster was seemingly compatible with the framers' vision of the chamber. Instead of ideologically driven bare majorities, the Senate requires greater consensus to pass legislation. Some contend that the desire of the framers to protect the rights of minorities is embodied in how the Senate operates to this day, as some bills require a filibuster-proof majority to pass (60 votes as opposed to a simple majority of 51 votes).

Today's political parties are not unlike the first political parties that were organized in the United States. Both initial parties organized around a central issue of federalism: how much power should the national government have in relation to the state governments? The contemporary Democratic Party attracts citizens who more readily embrace the philosophy of a strong national government. Those who identify with the Republican Party generally endorse the philosophy of less federal intervention and sending more power and policy issues to the state and local governments.

Members of Congress have three primary functions: lawmaking, representation of their constituents, and oversight of the executive branch of government. By definition, the most important aspect of being a senator or a representative is making laws that will make American society better. The legislative process includes four crucial stages for any bill proposal to become law: introduction, committee action, floor action, and enactment into law. Only a small percentage of bills that are introduced in Congress actually become law, and the roles played by party leaders in the House and Senate are instrumental in this process. The process of how a bill becomes a law is basically the same for the House and the Senate, with one significant difference: the role played by the members of the House Rules Committee is pivotal in terms of whether a bill passes in the House or not.

The framers required that for all bills to become law they must be passed in identical language in both chambers and that the president may either sign the bill, allow it to become law without a signature, or veto it. A bill can be introduced in the House or Senate only by the elected members of the respective chambers. A citizen can suggest a bill to a legislator but cannot propose one directly. The president has an indirect role in introducing bills. Today the president is considered the chief legislator, as the Office of Management and Budget routinely crafts legislation on behalf of the president and it can be proposed directly by an ally of the president in either the House or Senate.

Once a bill is proposed, it is referred to the appropriate standing committee(s). The rules of the House and Senate often give multiple committees jurisdiction over a policy area simultaneously. Technically, the speaker refers the bill to the appropriate committee(s) in the House and the presiding officer does the same in the Senate. Often, however, the referral is made by the House or Senate parliamentarian. The House speaker may set a time limit on the bill. Failure to act on a bill is akin to "killing" the bill.[17]

At the committee stage, comments about the bill's merit may be requested by executive branch officials, the bill can be assigned to a subcommittee by the chairperson, and hearings may be held on it. If a subcommittee works on the bill, its findings will be reported back to the standing committee. Once there is a vote in the full committee, the bill is reported to the parent chamber. When the members of a standing committee work on a bill, they will often hold a markup session, meaning they will literally mark up the bill line by line in order to enhance its chances for passage by the full chamber. A committee vote is a recommendation to the entire chamber; for example, if a bill passes out of a standing committee by a 15–4 margin, it is a recommendation to the entire chamber to support the bill as well.[18]

The basic legislative process is the same whether the bill is debated in the House or the Senate, with the most important difference being their role in how a bill becomes a law. Recall that when the bill is forwarded to the chamber floor, it is here that the members of the House Rules Committee attach a rule governing the terms of debate along with possible amendments. Senators protect their right to debate and have no such restriction. For the purpose of illustration, say that a bill governing climate change is being considered on the floor of the House.

A vote is taken in the House and the bill is passed. The bill is then sent to the Senate, unless it already has a similar measure under consideration. If the House and Senate pass a bill and there are differences between the two versions, a **conference committee** is formed. By definition a conference committee is a temporary committee that is created to negotiate differences between the House and Senate versions of a bill that have passed both chambers. The members are usually senior lawmakers of the standing committee that passed the bill in question in each chamber. The task of conference committee members is singular: to work out differences between the House and Senate versions of a bill so that one bill can be sent to the president. If the conference committee members are successful and do create one version out of the two bills that have passed in the House and Senate, the conference report must be approved again in the House and Senate if any part of the bill that pass earlier has been modified.[19]

The final stage is enactment into law. The bill that passed Congress is then sent to the president. The president has multiple options. The president can sign the bill and it can become law. The president can veto the bill by sending it back to Congress with a letter listing her or his reasons for issuing a veto. In turn, Congress can override the president's veto with a two-thirds majority vote in each chamber. The bill becomes law if the president decides to do nothing with it within ten business days while Congress is in session. A possible fourth option depends on when Congress is in session. If a president gets a bill and there are not ten working days left in the session of Congress, the president can take no action on it and the bill is effectively nullified. This is known as a **pocket veto**.[20]

It is important to understand that the process of how a bill becomes a law does not always work in the manner just described. In recent years there are times when members of Congress in both chambers express their frustration that important bills, especially revenue bills dealing with budgetary matters, have been passed with little input from most of the elected members of Congress. At times the top leaders of Congress and the president create bills, often in crisis mode, that have not evolved in the transparent manner delineated here. In such instances the members of Congress sometimes have only a short time to vote on a bill that may be several hundred pages long and incredibly complex. This manner of legislating is not inclusive and does not encourage diverse opinions and ideas about public policy.

The Importance of Citizenship in a Republic

It is important for citizens to understand the history behind the creation of Congress. The framers of the Constitution believed that in a republican form of government, Congress would be the predominant branch when it came to the crafting of public policy. It is no coincidence that Article I of the Constitution created Congress, as the framers envisioned legislative supremacy. Here is what James Madison said in *The Federalist* No. 51:

> In republican government, the legislative authority necessarily predominates. The remedy for this inconveniency is to divide the legislature into different branches; and to render them, by different modes of election and different principles of action, as little connected with each other as the nature of their common functions and their common dependence on the society will admit. It may even be necessary to guard against dangerous encroachments by still further precautions. As the weight of the legislative authority requires that it should be thus divided, the weakness of the executive may require, on the other hand, that it should be fortified.[21]

Because Congress was entrusted with so much political power, Madison believed that the House and Senate would be checks on each other's authority to safeguard against tyranny. The framers could not have envisioned the growth of the presidency as an institution during the 20th century. This is why they spent so much time during the Philadelphia Convention debating the creation of the new Congress. A great deal of authority was invested in this new Congress, and the framers sought to ensure that its members would be accountable to the people.

Citizens today need to pay close attention to what members of Congress do by way of public policy and also to what they choose not to do, or fail to enact, by way of legislation. Madison was an opponent of term limits, meaning a prescribed length of tenure for legislative service. He believed in the premise that legislative service can be improved with experience:

> No man can be a competent legislator who does not add to an upright intention and a sound judgment a certain degree of knowledge of the subjects on which he is to legislate. A part of this knowledge may

be acquired by means of information which lie within the compass of men in private as well as public stations. Another part can only be attained, or at least thoroughly attained, by actual experience in the station which requires the use of it. The period of service, ought, therefore, in all such cases, to bear some proportion to the extent of practical knowledge requisite to the due performance of the service.[22]

Madison is highlighting the importance of experience and knowledge in legislative service, though his premise has broad implications in many professions. It would be advantageous for citizens to be far more attentive to the work of the members of Congress than is presently the case. In this constitutional republic, we tend to focus a great deal on one person (the president) and are much less attentive to the 535 elected voting members of Congress. It would be beneficial to citizens, as well as the state of public policy in the United States, to maintain a constant watch over the members of Congress. If we think that the collective members of Congress are not especially effective at making citizens' lives better, then there are proactive measures that adults can take in the United States. A more informed, participatory, and enlightened citizenry will be better positioned to promote the cause of reform than a passive, reactive, and benighted one.

It is important for citizens to understand an important contradiction in American politics. As was discussed in chapter 3, Americans have a tendency to reelect House and Senate members at very high levels. Yet as an institution, Congress is usually very unpopular as measured by the Gallup Poll's standard question: "Do you approve or disapprove of the way Congress is handling its job?" This survey dates to the Watergate era. Outside of a significant crisis such as the September 11, 2001, terrorist attacks, the approval rating for Congress is usually very low. For the past several years, the approval rating of Congress as an institution typically has been below 20 percent.[23]

According to historians, Congress as an institution has never been very popular with the American public. This conclusion has certainly been corroborated since the Watergate era via public opinion polling. There is no singular remedy to making Congress a more effective institution. In the aftermath of the House check scandal in early 1992, several states passed referendums limiting the terms of federal legislators as a mechanism to make Congress more responsive to the public. (At that time in the U.S. House, over 300 current and former members of Congress overdrew their checking accounts at least once at the House bank.

There were no debit cards at this time.)[24] The term limits were immediately challenged on constitutional grounds, and the U.S. Supreme Court made a ruling on the issue in 1995 in *U.S. Term Limits, Inc. v. Thornton.* Writing for the Court's majority, Justice John Paul Stevens concluded:

> We are, however, firmly convinced that allowing the several States to adopt term limits for congressional service would effect a fundamental change in the constitutional framework. Any such change must come not by legislation adopted either by Congress or by an individual State, but rather—as have other important changes in the electoral process—through the Amendment procedures set forth in Article V. The Framers decided that the qualifications for service in the Congress of the United States be fixed in the Constitution and be uniform throughout the Nation. That decision reflects the Framers' understanding that Members of Congress are chosen by separate constituencies, but that they become, when elected, servants of the people of the United States. They are not merely delegates appointed by separate, sovereign States; they occupy offices that are integral and essential components of a single National Government. In the absence of a properly passed constitutional amendment, allowing individual States to craft their own qualifications for Congress would thus erode the structure envisioned by the Framers, a structure that was designed, in the words of the Preamble to our Constitution, to form a "more perfect Union."[25]

A fully engaged citizenry can make Congress a more attentive, responsive, and effective institution. A singular gimmick will undoubtedly not change much in the status quo. The onus is on "we the people" to make this republic, and country, a better place to live. Collectively, we have a responsibility to continue the work of our ancestors and strive to ensure that the best days for America lie in the future, not in the past.

Knowledge Matters

Political parties play a vital role in congressional politics and, more generally, in the life of the republic. Many citizens hold both major political parties in disdain, as evidenced by the reality that a sizable number of Americans identify as independents. But parties perform a vital link and cue for citizens in the political arena. Citizens are routinely accustomed to political parties fielding candidates in elections. But far more important is that citizens should expect party leaders and political candidates to share with the electorate their ideas about politics, public affairs, and the proper role of government in society. Consider this powerful conclusion offered by the 20th-century political scientist, E. E. Schattschneider:

> The rise of political parties is indubitably one of the principal distinguishing marks of modern government. The parties, in fact, have played a major role as *makers* of governments, more especially they have been the makers of democratic government. It should be stated flatly at the outset that this volume is devoted to the thesis that the political parties created democracy and that modern democracy is unthinkable save in terms of the parties. As a matter of fact, the condition of the parties is the best possible evidence of the nature of any regime. The most important distinction in modern political philosophy, the distinction between democracy and dictatorship, can be made best in terms of party politics. The parties are not therefore merely appendages of modern government; they are in the center of it and play a determinative and creative role in it.[26]

Schattschneider published his book in the early part of World War II; his premise is still invaluable. The existence of political parties in a democracy is a good thing. Through the varying ideas espoused by party candidates, citizens in a democracy are offered definitive choices about the direction of public policy. To be certain, all political players in the American political system could stand to reform and be more effective in the delivery of their tasks. There will always be a need for effective leadership, whether it pertains to the members of Congress or their respective political parties.

The members of Congress need to do some self-reflection. The abysmal approval rating of the institution is cause for consternation. Some members are more focused on raising money and winning elections than on actual governance. It seems to me that history will be kinder to legislators who contributed to the creation of policies that enhanced the lives of citizens and made society better. History will undoubtedly be less kind to legislators who may have been adept at winning elections, but when winning entails accepting campaign funds from unsavory sources and prompts citizens, especially young people, to disengage from politics, then the cost of winning is indeed excessive, self-serving, and downright hurtful.

Citizen Homework

All citizens should seek to empower themselves as much as possible. Every American adult can do more to make this democratic republic function better. An engaged and informed citizenry would be better equipped to hold elected members of Congress and the president more accountable for their actions. Here are some sources available on the internet that can enhance citizen knowledge of both Congress and political parties in general:

U.S. House of Representatives: https://www.house.gov. Information about the 435 voting members of the House, current legislative activity, committees, leadership, and the history of the House is available at this website.

U.S. Senate: https://www.senate.gov. Information about the 100 voting members of the Senate, committees, legislation and records, art and history, and additional references is available at this website.

How a bill becomes a law: http://www.annenbergclassroom.org/page/the-legislative-process-how-a-bill-becomes-a-federal-law. Watch a 19-minute video titled "The Legislative Process: How a Bill Becomes a Federal Law."

Republican Party: https://www.gop.com. Information about the Republican Party, its philosophy, and its policies are available at this website.

Democratic Party: https://www.democrats.org. Information about the Democratic Party, its philosophy, and its policies are available at this website.

CHAPTER 6

Presidency and the Executive Branch

The framers of the Constitution understood that one person, the president, would wield a great deal of power in their new proposed republic. While it was commonly understood that if the Constitution was ratified, George Washington would likely become the first president because of his stature in terms of public opinion and his leadership skills, this pending likelihood was undoubtedly a great comfort to the architects of the republic. But who would follow the legendary general? Obviously, the framers did not know the answer to this question, which made the selection of the president a highly significant issue for them. We know this because they took many votes on the issue of presidential selection when they broke into the Committee of the Whole at the Philadelphia Convention. A committee of the whole is all the members of a legislative assembly. By breaking into the committee mode, it meant that the framers could vote on measures that would not be binding, as a committee vote is a recommendation to the entire convention, which literally meant that the framers were making recommendations to themselves but could continue to debate the issue(s) at hand.[1]

The vision of the framers pertaining to presidential selection is available in *The Federalist* No. 69, written by Alexander Hamilton:

> That magistrate is to be elected for FOUR years; and is to be re-eligible as often as the people of the United States shall think him worthy of their confidence. In these circumstances there is a total dissimilitude between HIM and a king of Great Britain, who is an HE-REDITARY monarch, possessing the crown as a patrimony descend-

ible to his heirs forever; but there is a close analogy between HIM and a governor of New York, who is elected for THREE years, and is re-eligible without limitation or intermission. If we consider how much less time would be requisite for establishing a dangerous influence in a single State, than for establishing a like influence throughout the United States, we must conclude that a duration of FOUR years for the Chief Magistrate of the Union is a degree of permanency far less to be dreaded in that office, than a duration of THREE years for a corresponding office in a single State.[2]

In the original Constitution, the framers rejected term limits. Though George Washington established the two-term presidential precedent when he left office voluntarily in 1797, it would not be until the 20th century when a future president would serve longer than eight years (Franklin D. Roosevelt). Subsequently, the Constitution was amended in 1951 with the Twenty-second Amendment to limit presidential terms to two or a total of no more than ten years.

Hamilton and the framers envisioned a proactive presidency:

THERE is an idea, which is not without its advocates, that a vigorous Executive is inconsistent with the genius of republican government. The enlightened well-wishers to this species of government must at least hope that the supposition is destitute of foundation; since they can never admit its truth, without at the same time admitting the condemnation of their own principles. Energy in the Executive is a leading character in the definition of good government. It is essential to the protection of the community against foreign attacks; it is not less essential to the steady administration of the laws; to the protection of property against those irregular and high-handed combinations which sometimes interrupt the ordinary course of justice; to the security of liberty against the enterprises and assaults of ambition, of faction, and of anarchy. Every man the least conversant in Roman story, knows how often that republic was obliged to take refuge in the absolute power of a single man, under the formidable title of Dictator, as well against the intrigues of ambitious individuals who aspired to the tyranny, and the seditions of whole classes of the community whose conduct threatened the existence of all government, as against the invasions of external enemies who menaced the conquest and destruction of Rome.[3]

It was commonly understood in the late 18th century that a president would be the only elected official with a true national constituency. The energetic president that Hamilton wrote about would truly be the only official in the United States who would be challenged to promote the greater common good for all citizens, not just from a state or even simply part of a state. At that time in history, Americans tended to identify strongly with their state of residence as opposed to the greater United States of America. But a president would need to represent all citizens of a growing country, as the framers knew that a couple of states would likely be added to the Union soon, but they could not have known how much the new nation would expand and how long this process would ultimately take.

It is in this context that the framers created the presidency. They wanted a strong leader who would implement the laws passed by Congress and the powers invested in the institution under the Constitution. Yet unlike monarchies that existed at the time, presidents would be held accountable for their actions by the people and members of Congress. The vision that the framers had regarding presidential power would later be known as **Whig theory**, which was common in the country in the late 18th and 19th centuries. Under this view, the presidency as an institution was a limited one in that presidents could exercise the powers that were specifically assigned to them under the Constitution but nothing more. In the early 20th century, a new theory concerning presidential power, initially espoused by President Theodore Roosevelt, became more popular. **Stewardship theory** is a vision of the presidency that emphasized the fact that the president is the only public official in the country with a constituency of all citizens. Accordingly, presidents are stewards of the greater national good and should seek to make citizens lives better as long as the actions in question are not contrary to the federal Constitution or federal law.

Since the framers determined that the legislative branch would be the dominant policy-making institution in government, it is understandable that presidents of the past had a different vision of their job than the presidents of the modern era. Most 18th- and 19th-century presidents embraced Whig theory with the notable exceptions of Andrew Jackson and Abraham Lincoln in the 19th century. In the early 20th century, President Theodore Roosevelt articulated his stewardship theory of the presidency, but some of his successors still embraced Whig theory (William Howard Taft, Warren Harding, Calvin Coolidge, and Herbert Hoover). All presidents since Franklin D. Roosevelt, Republicans and

Democrats alike, have embraced the view of the presidency that Theodore Roosevelt espoused over a century ago.

Historical Evolution of the Presidency

The presidency and bureaucracy were created in Article II of the federal Constitution. The framers assigned the president the following formal (enumerated) powers: power to sign or veto legislation (if the president vetoes a bill, Congress can override the veto with a two-thirds majority vote in both chambers); power to faithfully execute the federal law; power to serve as commander in chief of the armed forces; power to pardon (except in cases of impeachment); power to make treaties with foreign countries (requires a two-thirds consent vote in the Senate); power to appoint cabinet secretaries, ambassadors, and all federal judges (with the consent of the Senate); power to fill vacancies when the Senate is in recess; power to give a State of the Union address; and a general foreign policy power to receive leaders from other countries on behalf of the nation. A president can be removed from office for "Treason, Bribery, or other high Crimes and Misdemeanors" under Article II, Section 4, of the Constitution.

According to political scientist Richard Neustadt, the most important presidential power is not listed in the Constitution. It is the **power to persuade**. An effective president must be adept at persuading members of Congress and the general public simultaneously to embrace his or her policy agenda. In a republican form of government, presidents are limited in their capacity to change public policy. By this measure, Franklin D. Roosevelt was the most effective president in the modern era, as he was able to persuade members of Congress to pass many major bills, especially during the early years of his presidency.[4] In fact, he set a standard for passing major bills in his first 100 days in office that is unlikely to be surpassed anytime soon, signing 15 major bills into law by the end of his 100th day in office.[5] Most recent presidents struggle to sign one or two major pieces of legislation in their first year in office.

The framers established three qualifications for a person to serve as president: citizenship, age, and residency, not unlike the members of Congress, though the standards are higher for the presidency than the Senate or House. A president must be a natural-born citizen, at least 35 years of age, and a resident of the United States for 14 years.

The framers had an extensive debate about how the president should be selected. Some of the framers wanted members of Congress to pick the president, others wanted direct election by a group of eligible voters. At that time, only white males who were old enough and had a sufficient amount of property were allowed to vote. Ultimately a compromise measure was created. The president would be directly selected by a simple majority of the Electoral College. The Electoral College would equal the number of representatives and senators allocated for each state (three more for the District of Columbia were added in 1961 via the Twenty-third Amendment). Today there are 538 total votes in the Electoral College; a simple majority required to win the presidency is 270 votes. If no candidate wins a simple majority, the House of Representatives determines the winner by state delegation. Consequently, if the House decided a presidential election today and all state delegations cast a vote, 26 votes would be needed to win a simple majority of 50.

When citizens vote for the president, they are not voting directly for the candidate of their choice. They are voting for a slate of electors who, in turn, are pledged to their candidate. Debates regarding the plausibility of the Electoral College and whether the Constitution should be amended to abolish it have occurred for over 200 years. In fact, there have been more than 700 proposed amendments in U.S. history to modify or abolish the Electoral College, more than any other subject of constitutional reform.[6] Whether the Electoral College should be abolished or not is a matter of preference. History, however, is clear about one thing: the creation of the Electoral College, which was heavily debated by the framers, was a political compromise in Philadelphia between those who wanted direct election by the people and those who wanted members of Congress to select a president. As political scientist Robert Dahl explains:

> Every solution seemed worse than the rest. The arrangement they finally cobbled together at the last minute was adopted more out of desperation, perhaps, than out of any great confidence in its success. So why did the delegates finally give their approval to the electoral college? Probably the best answer to our question would be: the Framers settled on an electoral college because they had run out of alternatives.[7]

Like most legislative assemblies, the framers compromised on the issue of selecting a president. Whether this compromise is reasonable in the context of the 21st century is an issue for citizens to ponder.

Because the framers did not envision the evolution of political parties, they assumed that most presidential elections would be determined in the U.S. House due to the inability of regional candidates to garner an Electoral College majority. Beyond George Washington, they assumed that candidates may be popular in their own geographic region but would be unable to muster a political following outside their respective areas. Thus, the House would routinely decide presidential election outcomes due to the inability of a candidate to secure at least a simple majority of the Electoral College. During the Philadelphia Convention, Virginian George Mason predicted that the House would decide 19 of 20 presidential elections (95 percent).[8] As history would have it, the House determined two presidential elections (1800 and 1824). This means that since the inception of the republic, the House has decided a grand total of 2 of 58 elections (3.4 percent). The third presidential election in U.S. history represented a fundamental change in presidential elections that the framers could not have predicted. In 1796 John Adams (Federalist) and Thomas Jefferson (Democratic-Republican) competed for the presidency, representing two organized political parties for the first time. The emergence of two major political parties allows voters to make a decisive choice rather than nominate several candidates who likely will not secure a simple majority of the electoral vote. Table 6.1 includes a list of all presidents, their political party affiliation, as well as the years they served in office.

Historical Evolution of the Executive Branch

As leader of the executive branch, the president is in charge of a vast federal bureaucracy. A **bureaucracy** is a system of federal civil servants and political appointees who are responsible for implementing decisions made by Congress and by the president. Perhaps the most recognizable part of the federal bureaucracy is the **cabinet**, which is a collection of 15 executive department heads whose primary task is to implement the president's agenda in their respective departments. The cabinet departments to date include Agriculture, Commerce, Defense, Education, Energy, Health and Human Services, Homeland Security, Housing and Urban Development, Interior, Justice, Labor, State, Transportation, Treasury, and Veterans Affairs. George Washington's initial cabinet in 1789 consisted of four people: secretary of state (Thomas Jefferson); secretary of the Treasury (Alexander Hamilton); secretary of War—now called Defense (Henry Knox); and the attorney general (Edmund Randolph). Typically, the four inner cabinet secretaries (State, Treasury, Defense,

Table 6.1. U.S. Presidents (1789–2020)

Number	Name	Dates in Office	Political Party
1	George Washington	1789–1797	None
2	John Adams	1797–1801	Federalist
3	Thomas Jefferson	1801–1809	Democratic-Republican
4	James Madison	1809–1817	Democratic-Republican
5	James Monroe	1817–1825	Democratic-Republican
6	John Quincy Adams	1825–1829	Democratic-Republican
7	Andrew Jackson	1829–1837	Democratic
8	Martin Van Buren	1837–1841	Democratic
9	William Henry Harrison	1841	Whig
10	John Tyler	1841–1845	Whig
11	James K. Polk	1845–1849	Democratic
12	Zachary Taylor	1849–1850	Whig
13	Millard Fillmore	1850–1853	Whig
14	Franklin Pierce	1853–1857	Democratic
15	James Buchanan	1857–1861	Democratic
16	Abraham Lincoln	1861–1865	Republican
17	Andrew Johnson	1865–1869	Democratic
18	Ulysses S. Grant	1869–1877	Republican
19	Rutherford B. Hayes	1877–1881	Republican
20	James Garfield	1881	Republican
21	Chester Arthur	1881–1885	Republican
22	Grover Cleveland	1885–1889	Democratic
23	Benjamin Harrison	1889–1893	Republican
24	Grover Cleveland	1893–1897	Republican
25	William McKinley	1897–1901	Republican
26	Theodore Roosevelt	1901–1909	Republican
27	William Howard Taft	1909–1913	Republican
28	Woodrow Wilson	1913–1921	Democratic
29	Warren Harding	1921–1923	Republican
30	Calvin Coolidge	1923–1929	Republican
31	Herbert Hoover	1929–1933	Republican
32	Franklin D. Roosevelt	1933–1945	Democratic
33	Harry Truman	1945–1953	Democratic
34	Dwight Eisenhower	1953–1961	Republican
35	John F. Kennedy	1961–1963	Democratic
36	Lyndon B. Johnson	1963–1969	Democratic
37	Richard Nixon	1969–1974	Republican
38	Gerald Ford	1974–1977	Republican
39	Jimmy Carter	1977–1981	Democratic
40	Ronald Reagan	1981–1989	Republican
41	George H. W. Bush	1989–1993	Republican
42	Bill Clinton	1993–2001	Democratic
43	George W. Bush	2001–2009	Republican
44	Barack Obama	2009–2017	Democratic
45	Donald Trump	2017–	Republican

Source: The White House, "Presidents," https://www.whitehouse.gov/1600/Presidents

and the attorney general) have more access to the president than the other cabinet secretaries due to the prominence of the policy areas that they address (foreign policy, domestic economy, national security, and law enforcement). The eleven remaining secretaries are generally considered outer cabinet positions.

Bureaucrats are responsible for administering programs created by Congress on a day-to-day basis. One of the most important activities undertaken by bureaucrats is the creation of **regulations**. A regulation is a rule or directive created and enforced by an authority established by Congress. Regulations have the effect of law even though they are not created directly by members of Congress. Regulations are created in pursuance of requirements established by Congress. Members of Congress often pass broad and somewhat ambiguous laws for the simple reason that it is easier to get legislators to vote in favor of bills that avoid being overly specific. Details are often deferred to the technical experts in the executive branch of government to figure out and address. Regulations are created through a process known as **rule making**. The regulation that is created allows bureaucrats to exercise control over individuals and corporations by restricting certain behavior.

When the republic began, the federal government was very small in size and scope, which reflected public opinion at the time and popular distrust of government in general but especially unelected officials. When George Washington was president in the late 18th century, the first census, in 1790, indicated that there were 4 million people in the country (Native Americans were excluded).[9] By 1792, when the federal government became fully operational after ratification of the Constitution, there were about 780 federal employees.[10] At the turn of the century in 1800, when John Adams was president, the number of people working for the federal government had increased to 3,000.[11] People received jobs in the federal government during this time due to the **spoils system**. The spoils system, also known as the patronage system, involves the practice of rewarding loyal partisan supporters with government jobs whether the appointees are qualified for the job or not. For the first 40 years of the republic, presidents generally hired civic-oriented elites like themselves to serve in government positions. This practice changed dramatically with the election of Andrew Jackson in 1828. Jackson vastly expanded the use of the spoils system during his tenure (1829–1837).

Political reformers attempted to highlight inherent problems with the spoils system. One of these problems was that some government workers were not competent in their jobs. Political loyalty had helped many to get jobs in the federal bureaucracy. This did not mean, however, that they had the professional background, knowledge, and skills to perform their tasks effectively. In other cases, political corruption was commonplace. Some government workers were using their jobs to enhance their own economic well-being and were not interested in serving the greater public good. Reformers were not successful at altering how the spoils system was used in national politics until a tragedy occurred. President James Garfield was shot in 1881 in his first year in office by a disappointed office seeker. Charles Guiteau, a writer and lawyer, perceived that he had helped Garfield secure the Republican nomination as well as the presidency. When Garfield did not give him a job in the federal bureaucracy, Guiteau decided to assassinate the president. He shot Garfield, who lingered for weeks before ultimately dying from his wounds. There was public pressure to address this unfortunate situation, which prompted members of Congress to act. In 1883 the **Pendleton Civil Service Act** was passed and signed into law. For the first time in history, a **civil service (merit) system** was established at the federal level. A civil service system is a model for managing a bureaucracy that relies on individuals who are selected for their positions based on competitive examinations or professional qualifications as opposed to political loyalty. The central premise of a civil service or merit system is to award government jobs based on qualifications and not on political support. A **civil servant** is an employee of a bureaucratic agency within the government. At first the merit system applied to only about 10 percent of the federal bureaucracy. Since the late 19th century, the civil service system has been revised and now applies to about 90 percent of the federal bureaucracy. The spoils system, however, is still subject to contention because most top-level cabinet and agency positions are political appointments made by the president.

The size and scope of the executive bureaucracy increased in 1939 when Congress authorized the creation of the **Executive Office of the President (EOP)** with the Reorganization Act of 1939.[12] The EOP is a group of policy-related offices that serve as support staff to the president. President Franklin D. Roosevelt issued Executive Order 8248 as a result of this law, and the EOP has existed ever since, though there are more offices in it now than when it was originally created.[13] In 1936 Roosevelt appointed a committee to recommend measures to reorganize the executive branch of government. The committee was chaired by Louis Brownlow and included political scientists Charles Merriam and Luther Gulick. The committee members recommended an overhaul of the executive branch in its report in 1937. The result of this report was the creation of the EOP.[14] The most famous recommendation was a simple one: "The President needs help."[15]

The Presidency and the Executive Branch Today

An important measure of presidential performance today stems from a question that dates back to the late 1930s and was created by the Gallup Poll: "Do you approve or disapprove of the way that _____ is handling his job as president?" This question is used to measure **presidential approval** rating, the percentage of Americans who believe that the president is doing an effective job in office. Popular approval of the president generally follows a few discernible patterns. Typically, new presidents start their terms with higher approval ratings that are destined to decline over time. Only two presidents since Harry Truman have left office more popular than when they started: Ronald Reagan and Bill Clinton. Contextually, however, they did not begin their terms with very high approval ratings compared to others. Indeed the ratings of many presidents have fluctuated through their tenure in office. When a crisis occurs, at least in the short term, presidential approval typically increases as Americans rally behind their president. However, if citizens do not think that a president handles a crisis effectively, the rating results are lower. See table 6.2

Table 6.2. Presidential Approval Ratings, from Harry Truman to Barack Obama

President	Dates in Office	Average Approval Rating during Presidency	Highest Approval Rating during Presidency	Lowest Approval Rating during Presidency
Harry Truman	1945–1953	45.4%	87%	22%
Dwight Eisenhower	1953–1961	65.0%	79%	48%
John Kennedy	1961–1963	70.1%	83%	56%
Lyndon Johnson	1963–1969	55.1%	79%	35%
Richard Nixon	1969–1974	49.0%	67%	24%
Gerald Ford	1974–1977	47.2%	71%	37%
Jimmy Carter	1977–1981	45.5%	75%	28%
Ronald Reagan	1981–1989	52.8%	68%	35%
George H.W. Bush	1989–1993	60.9%	89%	29%
Bill Clinton	1993–2001	55.1%	73%	37%
George W. Bush	2001–2009	49.4%	90%	25%
Barack Obama	2009–2017	47.9%	69%	38%

Source: Adapted from Gallup Poll, "Presidential Approval Ratings—Gallup Historical Statistics and Trends," https://news.gallup.com/poll/116677/presidential-approval-ratings-gallup-historical-statistics-trends.aspx for a list of presidents from Harry Truman through Barack Obama, their average approval rating during their presidencies, and their highest and lowest approval ratings during their time in office.

Presidential historians generally rank U.S. presidents on a number of factors such as public persuasion, crisis leadership, economic management, moral authority, international relations, administrative skills, relations with Congress, vision/setting an agenda, pursued equal justice for all, and performance within the context of the times. In a number of scholarly surveys since the end of World War II, scholars typically identify three presidents as the all-time great leaders in U.S. history: Abraham Lincoln, George Washington, and Franklin Roosevelt. Lincoln is typically ranked first, while second and third place rotate between Washington and Roosevelt. Lincoln receives accolades for keeping the nation intact during the Civil War and for the emancipation of the slaves. Washington led the country during America's second iteration with democracy. The first experiment failed badly. He started the two-term precedent and also outlined his foreign policy vision in his farewell address: to avoid entangling alliances with great European powers. This vision would later be called isolationism. Roosevelt had to address two major crises during his tenure: the Great Depression and World War II. Most scholarly surveys rank Theodore Roosevelt in fourth place and label him a near great president who lacked a major crisis during his presidency. The presidents who generally rank as failures include James Buchanan, Andrew Johnson, and Franklin Pierce.[16]

Besides their formal powers, presidents can create public policy through issuing **executive orders**. An executive order is a proclamation made by the president that changes government policy without congressional approval. Generally, presidents are limited to purely administrative matters when they issue executive orders, unless members of Congress have authorized a president to create policy on a given issue by passing legislation authorizing him or her to do so. Presidents sometimes engage in foreign policy making without congressional approval as well. An **executive agreement** is a negotiated arrangement between the executive branch of government and a foreign government that does not require endorsement by the members of the U.S. Senate as is necessary for formal treaties.

When presidents sign congressional bills, they sometimes issue a **signing statement**. A signing statement is made when the U.S. president signs a bill into law and issues a document that explains the president's interpretation of the law. When signing statements are issued, typically the president's interpretation of the law is different from the interpretation of the law by members of Congress, and the statement is designed to influence how the law will be implemented by bureaucrats.

Because Americans look to the president for leadership on behalf of the nation, and not so much the 535 voting members of Congress, presidents often use a strategy known as **going public** in order to pursue their policy agendas. Going public occurs when a president uses speeches and other forms of communication to appeal directly to citizens about issues that she or he would like members of Congress to address.

How much power do U.S. presidents have as the leader of the free world and oldest democracy on the planet? At times in U.S. history this has been a controversial issue. For example, some presidents during their tenure in office have invoked **executive privilege**. Executive privilege is the prerogative of the president to keep executive branch conversations and correspondence confidential from the legislative and judicial branches of government. In *U.S. v. Nixon* (1974) the Supreme Court justices determined that executive privilege is constitutional when pertaining to national security matters but not criminal investigations. This decision by the justices led to Nixon's resignation in the Watergate scandal.

Today there are about 2.7 million federal civil servants, almost 600,000 of whom are employed by the U.S. Postal Service. Another 1.4 million Americans are uniformed military employees.[17] Though this contradicts conventional wisdom, there are many more bureaucrats at the state and local levels than at the national level. The Department of Defense is the biggest cabinet department by far. The president has an entire bureaucracy at his or her disposal covering a wide range of policy areas in the Executive Office of the President. Traditionally, many of the president's closest advisers work in the Executive Office of the President. The **Office of Management and Budget (OMB)** is particularly prominent, as this is the office in the EOP whose officials create the annual federal budget on behalf of the president. Office personnel also review proposed rules and perform other tasks related to budgetary matters.

Oversight is a constitutional requirement of Congress to make sure that laws are implemented correctly by federal bureaucrats after they have been enacted. Generally, members of Congress attempt to hold executive branch officials accountable in one of two different ways: **fire alarm and police patrol oversight**. Fire alarm oversight occurs when members of Congress respond to complaints about the bureaucracy or implementation problems only when they arise rather than maintaining constant vigilance over the executive bureaucracy. Police patrol oversight exists when members of Congress constantly monitor the bureaucracy to make sure that laws are implemented correctly. Typically, the fire alarm approach is the most common. Members of Congress generally defer to executive branch officials unless a crisis occurs; then they actively intervene rather than oversee the executive branch in an ongoing and consistent manner. Police patrol oversight suggests a constant, ongoing oversight presence. While this approach may sound plausible, members of Congress generally do not embrace this manner of holding executive branch leaders accountable. Members of Congress actually spend a great deal of time with their lawmaking and representation functions, never mind the amount of time it takes to raise money in order to win reelection. These demands on their time generally render a typical result; many members of Congress dedicate only a small percentage of their time to the oversight function.

Citizens regularly impugn bureaucrats and believe that the federal government has created too much **red tape**, or excessively cumbersome or unnecessary regulations created by civil servants. Critics also believe that some bureaucrats succumb to **regulatory capture**, which is a situation where bureaucrats favor the interests of groups or corporations that they are supposed to regulate at the expense of the greater public good. It is important to understand that reform of the bureaucracy, just like reforming any other aspect of the political system, is a noteworthy objective. Officials at all levels of government can and should aspire to improve on the delivery of services to the citizenry. Yet it is also equally important to understand that programs and services created by legislators do not get implemented unless technical experts—also known as bureaucrats, civil servants, and public administrators—put them into effect.

The Importance of Citizenship in a Republic

The best thing citizens can do to understand the executive branch of government is to reflect on the Constitution. The United States is a constitutional republic, where political power is shared between and among institutions. The presidency is not all-powerful, though many citizens tend to perceive that presidents have more power than then they do under the Constitution. Recall in chapter 5 that the framers envisioned, and fully desired, legislative supremacy. They were fearful that one person with a great deal of power could become a tyrant, which helps to explain why they sought to limit presidential power with checks and balances. A hallmark for democratic governments is accountability, and the framers wanted the chief executive to be held accountable to the people so that there would be no monarchy in the New World. According to Alexander Hamilton in *The Federalist* No. 68, the way to safeguard against executive tyranny is to ensure that the people have an important role in presidential selection. In describing the Electoral College, Hamilton prophesied the following:

> The process of election affords a moral certainty, that the office of President will never fall to the lot of any man who is not in an eminent degree endowed with the requisite qualifications. Talents for low intrigue, and the little arts of popularity, may alone suffice to elevate a man to the first honors in a single State; but it will require other talents, and a different kind of merit, to establish him in the esteem and confidence of the whole Union, or of so considerable portion of it as would be necessary to make him a successful candidate for the distinguished office of President of the United States. It will not be too strong to say, that there will be a constant probability of seeing the station filled by characters pre-eminent for ability and virtue.[18]

Hamilton was advocating for the plausibility of a republican form of government. Even the president, who is an elected official with a great deal of political power, is accountable to the people. All citizens should reflect on a fundamental principle of republicanism: the ultimate sovereign in the United States is not the president, but the people of this country.

Applying Hamiltonian and Madisonian theory to the early part of this century, citizens have a fundamental duty to perform in democratic nations, meaning that all of us should actively participate not only in elections but also in the development and formulation of public policy. Collectively, Americans can do more with regard to electoral participation and to ensure that policies enacted by government officials are as effective as possible.

Consider the power to persuade. Because a president must collaborate with the members of Congress in order to get policies enacted, citizens must always be vigilant when electing a president. It is incumbent upon all candidates to share their ideas with the people. In other words, we should expect candidates to share their visions about how they can make citizens' lives better in this country. In addition, we must collectively make an informed judgment as it pertains to the power of persuasion. An effective president must be adept at persuading the people and the leaders in Congress that her or his policy agenda will be advantageous for the country. After all, elected presidents are not dictators, and they must rely on legislators to a considerable extent in order to make public policy.

The executive branch of government is important in a constitutional republic. All legislation and programs that are created by the members of Congress are put into effect by mostly career civil servants. These people typically have a good deal of discretion in terms of putting laws into effect, as members of Congress tend to be vague when creating legislation because less specificity typically enhances the chances for securing affirmative votes on proposed bills.

In 230 years of history under this republic, only 44 individuals have served as president. The average tenure for America's presidents is 5.2 years. Donald Trump is the 45th president, but recall that Grover Cleveland is credited with having two different administrations, being the only president in history to serve nonconsecutive terms. Cleveland was the 22nd president (1885–1889) and the 24th president (1893–1897). Thus, presidents do not have very long to establish legacies for their service. Members of Congress may serve for several decades in their capacities as legislators. Federal judges have lifetime tenure, but presidents enter the office knowing that their time in office is likely to be brief, at least when compared with the other institutions. Unelected civil servants tend to remain in their professions much longer than the chief executive.

When it comes to elections, those for president attract the most attention in America. Voter turnout is higher in a presidential election year than a midterm election, as was discussed earlier. But note the amount of improvement that is possible in presidential elections. Americans have not exceeded 60 percent in turnout of the voting age population since 1968. Just barely more than half of adults have bothered to participate in recent presidential elections. Citizens must embrace their duty and opt to educate themselves about the candidates, their vision of the institution, and what they will do if elected. Upon doing so, Americans can register their choices accordingly and a renaissance in citizen participation can be witnessed so that the United States can join the community of other Western democracies, where voter turnout is typically much higher. The policy challenges facing Americans, and peers across the entire globe, are very serious and require immediate attention. The optimum approach to confronting difficult times is inclusive, where citizens, of their own volition, decide that political participation is a fundamental component of problem recognition and solving.

Knowledge Matters

On the subject of citizenship, a former president, Theodore Roosevelt, had much to offer by way of insight. In a speech in Asheville, North Carolina, on September 9, 1902, he declared:

> For a citizen to be worth anything, what you need is character, and into character many elements enter. In the first place, decency and honesty; if a man isn't honest, isn't decent, then the brighter he is, the more dangerous he is to his community.[19]

Roosevelt had a point in associating character with citizenship. He also provided an important revelation for the people who were in the audience: "You are the government, you and I, and the government will do well or ill according as we."[20] The "government" is not an abstract entity. It consists of human beings who have flaws. Our collective challenge is to establish a fully functional, effective government that addresses the needs of citizens in an effective, equitable, and efficient manner.

Reviewing Article II of the Constitution is helpful to the citizen who yearns to learn more about presidential power. However, the interpretation of the Constitution has evolved over time on this issue. The framers intended for the president to be energetic, as Hamilton described. But at the same time, they imagined legislative supremacy in terms of policy making at the national level. Roosevelt was a visionary in this regard. He foresaw a much more proactive presidency than many of his contemporaries in the early 20th century:

> The most important factor in getting the right spirit in my Administration, next to the insistence upon courage, honesty, and a genuine democracy of desire to serve the plain people, was my insistence upon the theory that the executive power was limited only by specific restrictions and prohibitions appearing in the Constitution or imposed by the Congress under its Constitutional powers. My view was that every executive officer, and above all every executive officer in high position, was a steward of the people bound actively and affirmatively to do all he could for the people, and not to content himself with

the negative merit of keeping his talents undamaged in a napkin. I declined to adopt the view that what was imperatively necessary for the Nation could not be done by the President unless he could find some specific authorization to do it. My belief was that it was not only his right but his duty to do anything that the needs of the Nation demanded unless such action was forbidden by the Constitution or by the laws. Under this interpretation of executive power I did and caused to be done many things not previously done by the President and the heads of the departments. I did not usurp power, but I did greatly broaden the use of executive power. In other words, I acted for the public welfare, I acted for the common well-being of all our people, whenever and in whatever manner was necessary, unless prevented by direct constitutional or legislative prohibition. I did not care a rap for the mere form and show of power; I cared immensely for the use that could be made of the substance.[21]

Any exercise of executive power, whether by the president, secretary of state, director of the Environmental Protection Agency, or some other executive branch official, should be in pursuit of promoting the general welfare of the people. The exercise of political power for the right reasons is highly plausible. The pursuit of power for self-aggrandizement, to punish one's critics, or to cover-up an illegal action is not appropriate and is in violation of the Constitution; such behavior by any executive branch official should prompt a thorough investigation by the members of Congress.

Citizen Homework

The presidency as an institution is of central importance in American politics. Citizens should know more about their presidents and what they are empowered to do through the Constitution and by congressional statutes. In a presidential campaign, Americans should seek more information about the candidates and their specific public policy views regarding the issues that are important to them.

Presidential historians: https://www.c-span.org/presidentsurvey 2017/. Learn more about how presidential historians rank all U.S. presidents and the criteria they utilize to judge them. Compare these surveys with Gallup polls of the general public and determine where citizens and scholars have common ground and where they diverge when it comes to assessing presidential effectiveness.

C-SPAN American Presidents Series: https://www.c-span.org/series/?presidents. Information about all U.S. presidents can be extracted from this website.

Basic information about presidential power: https://www.youtube.com/watch?v=5l02sK5LovI. Watch a seven-minute video titled "Presidential Power: Crash Course Government and Politics #11."

Basic information about the U.S. federal bureaucracy: https://www.youtube.com/watch?v=I8EQAnKntLs. Watch a seven-minute video titled "Bureaucracy Basics: Crash Course Government and Politics #15."

Learn about how presidents actually govern in conjunction with their White House advisers and federal bureaucrats: https://www.youtube.com/watch?v=5vnuFJSMYkY. Watch a nine-minute video titled "How Presidents Govern: Crash Course Government and Politics #14."

CHAPTER 7

Supreme Court and Federal Judiciary

In order to seek relief in American federal courts, litigants must have **standing**, which is a requirement that those who file cases must be harmed by a law or action in order to sue. A **plaintiff** is the person or party who initially brings a case to court. The **defendant** is the person or parties against whom a case is filed. Under the Articles of Confederation and Perpetual Union, there were no federal courts. State judges interpreted the meaning of federal law, typically in a manner that was self-serving to the state in question. Accordingly, the framers understood the need to create federal courts.

The Supreme Court of the United States was created by the framers of the Constitution in Article III:

> The judicial Power of the United States, shall be vested in one supreme Court, and in such inferior Courts as the Congress may from time to time ordain and establish. The Judges, both at the supreme and inferior Courts, shall hold their Offices during good Behaviour.

While the framers made the Supreme Court the highest tribunal in the country, they assigned the members of Congress the authority to establish the size of the Court as well as the responsibility of creating all lower federal courts.

In *The Federalist* No. 78, Alexander Hamilton explained to Americans that the Supreme Court would be a policy-making institution like Congress and the presidency but that it would be the weakest of the three branches at the national level:

Whoever attentively considers the different departments of power must perceive, that, in a government in which they are separated from each other, the judiciary, from the nature of its functions, will always be the least dangerous to the political rights of the Constitution; because it will be least in a capacity to annoy or injure them. The Executive not only dispenses the honors, but holds the sword of the community. The legislature not only commands the purse, but prescribes the rules by which the duties and rights of every citizen are to be regulated. The judiciary, on the contrary, has no influence over either the sword or the purse; no direction either of the strength or of the wealth of the society; and can take no active resolution whatever. It may truly be said to have neither FORCE nor WILL, but merely judgment; and must ultimately depend upon the aid of the executive arm even for the efficacy of its judgments.[1]

Hamilton highlighted how the framers of the Constitution created two types of policy-making institutions at the federal level: proactive and reactive. By design, the two traditional institutions of government, Congress and the presidency, are proactive because they can make public policy anytime the political will to do so exists. The same does not hold true regarding the Supreme Court. It is a reactive, or passive, institution because the justices can engage in public policy making only through the guise of a specific court case. In other words, the justices must wait for a case to come to them to even have the opportunity to engage in policy making. While the members of Congress have the power to pass a federal budget and regulate all aspects of the domestic economy, and while the president is the commander in chief of the armed forces, the justices have the power to interpret the meaning of the law. Interpreting the meaning of the federal Constitution and federal law can result in some critical policy decisions, however. It is important for citizens to understand that the federal courts, and especially the Supreme Court, are very important in terms of public policy making in the United States. Yet as Hamilton instructed Americans a long time ago, the judiciary is a policy-making institution but must be understood in an appropriate context. Although some extraordinary cases have been decided by the justices with a significant impact on society, most of the time the federal judiciary is still the weakest of the three institutions, just as the framers envisioned it.

The framers gave the Supreme Court two types of jurisdiction under Article III. Almost all cases arrive at the Supreme Court based on its **appellate jurisdiction**. This means that the case must be adjudicated by a lower court first. The Supreme Court has **original jurisdiction** in two instances: when ambassadors or states are a party to the suit. Under original jurisdiction, the Supreme Court is the only court to hear the case; such cases are extremely rare, thus highlighting the importance of the federal court structure.

The Supreme Court has operated in several places since it was established in 1790. Initially the justices convened in the Merchants Exchange Building in New York City. When the new nation's capital moved to Philadelphia in 1790, the justices moved with it. Chambers were established in the Pennsylvania State House (Independence Hall) and later in city hall. When the federal government moved again in 1800, so did the justices. There was no provision for a Supreme Court building at that time, so the justices were afforded space by the members of Congress. During the War of 1812, the justices had to work in a private house after the British set fire to the Capitol. After that war the justices returned to the Capitol and met from 1819 to 1860 in a chamber now restored as the "Old Supreme Court Chamber." From 1860 to 1935 the justices met in what is now known as the "Old Senate Chamber." It was Chief Justice William Howard Taft (the former president) who persuaded the members of Congress that the Court should have its own permanent home. Construction began in 1932, the building was completed in 1935, and the justices have been located at this venue ever since.[2]

It is important to note that the Supreme Court is the least democratic of the three branches of government. The framers ultimately decided that the president would select all federal judges, and the Senate had the power to confirm all nominees. The framers determined that, if approved by the Senate, lifetime tenure was needed so that federal judges could operate independently of the two traditional branches of government. The people have no direct say when it comes to federal judges. Citizens can attempt to lobby presidents and members of the Senate, but these methods are indirect at best and the tenure for federal judges is life, which in most cases is much longer than a Senate, presidential, or House term.

Since the members of Congress passed the Judiciary Act of 1925, appealing cases to the Supreme Court has been markedly different.

Before that time the justices were obligated to make a ruling on numerous appeals. For almost the last century, however, the justices have had almost complete control over the Court's docket. Most litigants appealing to the Supreme Court apply for a **writ of certiorari** to the justices, which is effectively an application for judicial review.[3] Under the **rule of four**, four of the nine justices must grant judicial review for a case to be placed on the docket. In recent years, the justices will issue about 70–80 decisions per term out of more than 8,000 applications for judicial review. If the justices do not accept a case for judicial review, they are invoking stare decisis, which means they examine past precedents and follow the legal rule that was established in the earlier cases.

If a case is placed on the Court's docket, **oral arguments** are scheduled. This gives the attorneys for each side the opportunity to summarize their cases and the justices time to ask questions. It is typically scheduled for one hour (a half hour for each side), but the justices can extend the time frame for oral arguments at their discretion.

By statute the Court begins a new session on the first Monday in October. The **October term** typically lasts until late June or early July of the following year. Then the justices recess for the summer. Each of the associate justices may hire up to four law clerks per year. The chief justice may have up to five. All federal judges typically have at least one law clerk.

Opinion writing for Supreme Court cases is an essential exercise. Determining which justice will write the **majority opinion** (a written opinion that explains the rationale for the winning side) or **dissenting opinion** (a written opinion filed by a judge who disagrees with the majority or plurality opinion and explains her or his arguments) is predicated on the principle of seniority. Whatever side the chief justice may endorse, he or she has the authority to assign writing the opinion to a colleague. By way of illustration, the chief justice may be on the winning side of a 6–3 vote. In such case, he or she will assign the majority opinion. The most senior justice on the losing side in terms of tenure on the Court would assign the dissenting opinion. All nine of the justices are free to write separately if they so desire. The most powerful decision the Supreme Court can render is a 9–0 unanimous decision written by the chief justice with no separate opinions. Such unanimity was witnessed in the famous segregation case of *Brown v. Board of Education of Topeka, KS* (1954). A **concurring opinion** is one that is filed by a judge who agrees with the majority or plurality opinion in a case but for different reasons than those specified in the court's opinion.

There is no explicit reference to **judicial review** in Article III. Judicial review is the power of Supreme Court justices to strike down a law passed by Congress or an action taken by the president if they believe that the law or action is unconstitutional. Hamilton shared his views about judicial review in *The Federalist* No. 78:

> If it be said that the legislative body are themselves the constitutional judges of their own powers, and that the construction they put upon them is conclusive upon the other departments, it may be answered, that this cannot be the natural presumption, where it is not to be collected from any particular provisions in the Constitution. It is not otherwise to be supposed, that the Constitution could intend to enable the representatives of the people to substitute their WILL to that of their constituents. It is far more rational to suppose, that the courts were designed to be an intermediate body between the people and the legislature, in order, among other things, to keep the latter within the limits assigned to their authority. The interpretation of the laws is the proper and peculiar province of the courts. A constitution is, in fact, and must be regarded by the judges, as a fundamental law. It therefore belongs to them to ascertain its meaning, as well as the meaning of any particular act proceeding from the legislative body. If there should happen to be an irreconcilable variance between the two, that which has the superior obligation and validity ought, of course, to be preferred; or, in other words, the Constitution ought to be preferred to the statute, the intention of the people to the intention of their agents.[4]

Later in the early part of the nineteenth century, judicial review would become more explicit in the American political tradition. The principle of judicial review was formally established in the Supreme Court case of ***Marbury v. Madison*** (1803).[5] In the presidential election of 1800, Thomas Jefferson defeated the incumbent, John Adams. Before Jefferson took office on March 4, 1801, members of Congress passed the Judiciary Act of 1801, which created new courts and judges. John Adams signed the bill into law on February 13, 1801, less than three weeks before he left office. Since the Federalist Party lost control of the presidency and both chambers of Congress, the **lame duck** Federalists sought to entrench themselves in the judiciary, which infuriated Jefferson. Lame ducks are officials who are completing the rest of their terms but will not continue their service once their terms have expired.[6]

All of the judicial nominations submitted by Adams were approved by the U.S. Senate, but the appointments in question would not be valid until their commissions were delivered by the U.S. secretary of state. At the time, the hastily confirmed appointees were known as the "midnight judges."[7] Time expired for the Adams administration, and the commissions for William Marbury and a few others were not delivered. When Jefferson became president on March 4, 1801, he forbade the delivery of the remaining judicial commissions. Marbury sued Jefferson's secretary of state, James Madison, in order to obtain his commission. The case went directly to the Supreme Court.[8]

The Supreme Court justices heard this case first because of Section 13 of the Judiciary Act of 1789. Section 13 authorizes the Supreme Court justices to hear all cases directly if they involve officers of the federal government. Since Madison was the secretary of state, the case went directly to the justices. Unfortunately for Marbury, it should not have done so. The Supreme Court justices, through Chief Justice John Marshall, determined that the Court did not have the jurisdiction to order Madison to deliver Marbury's commission. In his opinion, Marshall declared:

> It is emphatically the province and duty of the judicial department to say what the law is. Those who apply the rule to particular cases, must of necessity expound and interpret that rule. If two laws conflict with each other, the courts must decide on the operation of each. So if a law be in opposition to the constitution; if both the law and the constitution apply to a particular case, so that the court must either decide that case conformably to the law, disregarding the constitution; or conformably to the constitution, disregarding the law; the court must determine which of these conflicting rules governs the case. This is of the very essence of judicial duty.[9]

Marshall and the other justices established judicial review in this case. They concluded that they could not order Madison to deliver Marbury's commission because the justices did not have the authority to do so. They lacked the legal power to compel Madison to deliver Marbury's commission despite his being appointed by a president and confirmed by the Senate, which is the proper procedure. But Section 13 of the Judiciary Act of 1789 purported to give the Supreme Court authority that it did not have under the Constitution. In Article III the Court's original jurisdiction included only cases involving states or ambassadors. The dispute over Marbury's judicial commission should not have been adjudicated in the Supreme Court; the case should have originated in a lower federal court first. While Marbury never received his job, Marshall and the justices invoked the power of judicial review. The justices struck down Section 13 as unconstitutional because it sought to expand the Court's original jurisdiction authority. A statute cannot contradict the federal Constitution. If members of Congress wish to expand the Court's jurisdiction, a constitutional amendment is the only remedy. The **supremacy clause** of the Constitution stipulates that the federal Constitution is the supreme law of the land. Section 13, even though it was passed by the first session of Congress and signed by the first president, contradicted the Constitution. Thus, judicial review has been practiced by the Supreme Court for almost 220 years.

Historical Evolution of the Federal Judiciary

Since the framers assigned the duty of creating lower federal courts to the members of Congress, the first session of Congress created lower federal courts initially in the Judiciary Act of 1789. In this law the members of Congress mandated that the Supreme Court would have one chief justice and five associate justices, and they also created the first federal district courts.[10] **District courts** are trial-level courts in the federal judiciary that handle most federal cases. Such courts have a fact-finding mission. The members of Congress, however, changed the number of justices on the High Court several times in the 19th century. In 1807 the number of justices increased to seven. In 1837 it was further increased to nine, and in 1863 it increased again to ten. In 1866 the members of Congress shrank the number of justices to seven but then in 1869 increased the size of the Court back to nine. It has remained at nine ever since.[11]

To this day, district courts are still the general trial courts in the federal judiciary. Trial courts have original jurisdiction, and most cases in the federal system start at the district court level. Since trial courts have a primary fact-finding mission, upon ascertaining the facts, district court judges apply existing constitutional or statutory law to the case and render a decision. Both **civil** and **criminal cases** are tried in the district courts. A civil case is a legal dispute between two or more parties. Civil cases typically result in monetary damages or orders to do or not do something. Criminal cases are more onerous than civil cases in that they involve crimes against the state or society in general. People convicted of violating criminal law could spend time in jail for their actions and lose their freedom accordingly.

A comprehensive group of appellate courts did not exist for a century in the United States. There were no circuit courts of appeal until 1891. Instead, the Supreme Court justices had to "ride circuit." Under this practice, the Supreme Court justices not only had to do their job on the nation's highest tribunal, but they were also assigned to various circuits where they had to preside over trial level cases with other judges. They did this for much of the 19th century, a time when travel was particularly challenging.[12]

Circuit courts of appeal are first-level appellate courts in the federal judiciary. Circuit courts of appeal review the decisions of the district courts and are typically staffed by three judges, who do not use a jury. These courts were officially created by the Judiciary Act of 1891, commonly known as the Evarts Act. The creation of the circuit courts of appeal gave the Supreme Court justices much more discretion regarding their selection of cases and reduced their case burden as well.[13]

The Supreme Court and Federal Judiciary Today

The basic structure of the federal courts is a three-tiered system. Litigation in the federal system begins with the district courts. Each state has at least one district court, and there are 94 of them across the nation. To date, the members of Congress have created a total of 677 district court judgeships. A litigant who loses at the district court level can appeal to the assigned circuit court of appeals. There are 13 circuit courts in the United States, with a total of 179 judgeships. It is the duty of the circuit court judges to determine if the law was applied properly at the district court level. Since the circuit courts of appeal are first-level appellate courts, the Supreme Court is a second-level appellate court.[14]

Appointments to the federal courts, and especially the Supreme Court, can be contentious and render extensive debate. Presidential appointments to the federal judiciary can establish a legacy for any president, since they entail lifetime tenure. Any president who appoints several hundred judges will continue to wield influence in the federal judiciary long after he or she departs the White House.

Controversy regarding judicial appointments typically stems from differing visions about how the Constitution should be interpreted and the proper role of federal judges in American politics. A person's **judicial philosophy** is central to understanding the work of federal judges. Judicial philosophy involves one's underlying set of ideas and beliefs about constitutional interpretation, which helps to shape how judges rule on specific cases. There are two primary judicial philosophies today: **judicial activism** and **judicial restraint**. Activist judges are typically considered to be liberal while restrainist judges are generally labeled as conservative.

Judicial activists endorse a broad interpretation of the Constitution. They generally contend that Americans have more civil liberties than those expressly granted in the Constitution. Many who embrace this philosophy believe that a number of liberties are implied by the sheer existence of liberties already extended, such as the right to privacy. Though there is no amendment that guarantees an explicit right to privacy, activists contend that privacy is implied by the First, Fourth, Fifth, Ninth, and Fourteenth Amendments. Activists also believe that it is appropriate for federal judges to engage in policy making as long as the Constitution warrants it. The fundamental reason why some people embrace the philosophy of judicial activism is the belief in a "**living Constitution**." Adherents to this philosophy maintain that the framers of the Constitution meant it to be a base foundation to apply to society as it evolved. In other words, they believe the framers wished for democracy to expand over time in ways they could not have imagined in 1787. Those who believe the Constitution is a living document profess that constitutional interpretation should take contemporary attitudes, values, and circumstances into account, especially if the outcome expands democracy in the United States. Subscribers to this philosophy believe that federal judges should not simply scrutinize the plain text of the Constitution or congressional statutes. This approach to constitutional interpretation suggests that the framers of the Constitution did not intend for the Constitution to be a static document and would evolve in meaning over the passage of time, especially if this evolution had the effect of making the country more democratic.[15]

As the term suggests, judicial restrainists believe that federal judges should avoid making public policy in their decisions. Instead, they should defer policy making to the two traditional branches of government. To them, the Constitution should be interpreted narrowly: liberties exist if they are delineated in the Constitution. A right to privacy should not come to fruition through judicial interpretation but through a formal constitutional amendment. Restrainists tend to embrace the theory of **original intent**. To them, the work of the framers, or Congress through the amendments, should not be altered. In other words, if possible, federal judges should seek to discern and apply the intent of either the framers when the original Constitution was written in 1787 or the members of Congress when amendments were added and apply those intentions to the case before them. It is not always possible to identify original intent if historical evidence does not exist pertaining to a specific matter. The appropriate methodology for constitutional changes is the amendment procedure, not constitutional interpretation by federal judges.

Citizens tend to know little about American politics and public affairs, though they generally know more about the presidency and Congress than they do about the Supreme Court. A list of the current justices, as well as all who have served on the Supreme Court throughout history, is available in table 7.1. To date, only 113 people have served as justices since 1790. A few have served as both an associate justice as well as chief justice.

Table 7.1. Chief Justices and Associate Justices of the U.S. Supreme Court (1789–2020)

Chief Justices

Number	Name	Appointed by President	Years of Service
1	John Jay	George Washington	1789–95
2	John Rutledge	George Washington	1795
3	Oliver Ellsworth	George Washington	1796–1800
4	John Marshall	John Adams	1801–1835
5	Roger Taney	Andrew Jackson	1836–1864
6	Salmon Chase	Abraham Lincoln	1864–1873
7	Morrison Waite	Ulysses S. Grant	1874–1888
8	Melville Fuller	Grover Cleveland	1888–1910
9	Edward White	William H. Taft	1910–1921
10	William H. Taft	Warren Harding	1921–1930
11	Charles Evans Hughes	Herbert Hoover	1930–1941
12	Harlan Stone	Franklin D. Roosevelt	1941–1946
13	Fred Vinson	Harry Truman	1946–1953
14	Earl Warren	Dwight Eisenhower	1953–1969
15	Warren Burger	Richard Nixon	1969–1986
16	William Rehnquist	Ronald Reagan	1986–2005
17	John Roberts	George W. Bush	2005–

Associate Justices

Number	Name	Appointed by President	Years of Service
1	John Rutledge	George Washington	1790–1791
2	William Cushing	George Washington	1790–1810
3	James Wilson	George Washington	1789–1798
4	John Blair	George Washington	1790–1795
5	James Iredell	George Washington	1790–1799
6	Thomas Johnson	George Washington	1792–1793
7	William Paterson	George Washington	1793–1806
8	Samuel Chase	George Washington	1796–1811
9	Bushrod Washington	John Adams	1798–1829
10	Alfred Moore	John Adams	1800–1804
11	William Johnson	Thomas Jefferson	1804–1834

Table 7.1.—*Continued*

Associate Justices

Number	Name	Appointed by President	Years of Service
12	Brockholst Livingston	Thomas Jefferson	1807–1823
13	Thomas Todd	Thomas Jefferson	1807–1826
14	Gabriel Duvall	James Madison	1811–1835
15	Joseph Story	James Madison	1812–1845
16	Smith Thompson	James Monroe	1823–1843
17	Robert Trimble	John Quincy Adams	1826–1828
18	John McLean	Andrew Jackson	1830–1861
19	Henry Baldwin	Andrew Jackson	1830–1844
20	James Wayne	Andrew Jackson	1835–1867
21	Philip Barbour	Andrew Jackson	1836–1841
22	John Catron	Andrew Jackson	1837–1865
23	John McKinley	Martin Van Buren	1838–1852
24	Peter Daniel	Martin Van Buren	1842–1860
25	Samuel Nelson	John Tyler	1845–1872
26	Levi Woodbury	James K. Polk	1845–1851
27	Robert Grier	James K. Polk	1846–1870
28	Benjamin Curtis	Millard Fillmore	1851–1857
29	John Campbell	Franklin Pierce	1853–1861
30	Nathan Clifford	James Buchanan	1858–1881
31	Noah Swayne	Abraham Lincoln	1862–1881
32	Samuel Miller	Abraham Lincoln	1862–1890
33	David Davis	Abraham Lincoln	1862–1877
34	Stephen Field	Abraham Lincoln	1863–1897
35	William Strong	Ulysses S. Grant	1870–1880
36	Joseph Bradley	Ulysses S. Grant	1870–1892
37	Ward Hunt	Ulysses S. Grant	1873–1882
38	John Marshall Harlan I	Rutherford B. Hayes	1877–1911
39	William Woods	Rutherford B. Hayes	1881–1887
40	Stanley Matthews	James Garfield	1881–1889
41	Horace Gray	Chester Arthur	1882–1902
42	Samuel Blatchford	Chester Arthur	1882–1893
43	Lucius Lamar	Grover Cleveland	1888–1893
44	David Brewer	Benjamin Harrison	1890–1910
45	Henry Brown	Benjamin Harrison	1891–1906
46	George Shiras	Benjamin Harrison	1892–1903
47	Howell Jackson	Benjamin Harrison	1893–1895
48	Edward White	Grover Cleveland	1894–1910*
49	Rufus Peckham	Grover Cleveland	1896–1909
50	Joseph McKenna	William McKinley	1898–1925
51	Oliver Wendell Holmes	Theodore Roosevelt	1902–1932
52	William Day	Theodore Roosevelt	1903–1922
53	William Moody	Theodore Roosevelt	1906–1910
54	Horace Lurton	William H. Taft	1910–1914
55	Charles Evans Hughes	William H. Taft	1910–1916
56	Willis Van Devanter	William H. Taft	1911–1937
57	Joseph Lamar	William H. Taft	1911–1916

Table 7.1.—*Continued*

Associate Justices

Number	Name	Appointed by President	Years of Service
58	Mahlon Pitney	William H. Taft	1912–1922
59	James McReynolds	Woodrow Wilson	1914–1941
60	Louis Brandeis	Woodrow Wilson	1916–1939
61	John Clarke	Woodrow Wilson	1916–1922
62	George Sutherland	Warren Harding	1922–1938
63	Pierce Butler	Warren Harding	1923–1939
64	Edward Sanford	Warren Harding	1923–1930
65	Harlan Stone	Calvin Coolidge	1925–1941*
66	Owen Roberts	Herbert Hoover	1930–1945
67	Benjamin Cardozo	Herbert Hoover	1932–1938
68	Hugo Black	Franklin D. Roosevelt	1937–1971
69	Stanley Reed	Franklin D. Roosevelt	1938–1957
70	Felix Frankfurter	Franklin D. Roosevelt	1939–1962
71	William Douglas	Franklin D. Roosevelt	1939–1975
72	Frank Murphy	Franklin D. Roosevelt	1940–1949
73	James Byrnes	Franklin D. Roosevelt	1941–1942
74	Robert Jackson	Franklin D. Roosevelt	1941–1954
75	Wiley Rutledge	Franklin D. Roosevelt	1943–1949
76	Harold Burton	Harry Truman	1945–1958
77	Tom Clark	Harry Truman	1949–1967
78	Sherman Minton	Harry Truman	1949–1956
79	John Marshall Harlan II	Dwight Eisenhower	1955–1971
80	William Brennan	Dwight Eisenhower	1956–1990
81	Charles Whittaker	Dwight Eisenhower	1957–1962
82	Potter Stewart	Dwight Eisenhower	1958–1981
83	Bryon White	John F. Kennedy	1962–1993
84	Arthur Goldberg	John F. Kennedy	1962–1965
85	Abe Fortas	Lyndon B. Johnson	1965–1969
86	Thurgood Marshall	Lyndon B. Johnson	1967–1991
87	Harry Blackmun	Richard Nixon	1970–1994
88	Lewis Powell	Richard Nixon	1972–1987
89	William Rehnquist	Richard Nixon	1972–1986*
90	John Paul Stevens	Gerald Ford	1975–2010
91	Sandra Day O'Connor	Ronald Reagan	1981–2006
92	Antonin Scalia	Ronald Reagan	1986–2016
93	Anthony Kennedy	Ronald Reagan	1988–2018
94	David Souter	George H. W. Bush	1990–2009
95	Clarence Thomas	George H. W. Bush	1991–
96	Ruth Bader Ginsburg	Bill Clinton	1993–
97	Stephen Breyer	Bill Clinton	1994–
98	Samuel Alito	George W. Bush	2006–
99	Sonia Sotomayor	Barack Obama	2009–
100	Elena Kagan	Barack Obama	2010–
101	Neil Gorsuch	Donald Trump	2017–
102	Brett Kavanaugh	Donald Trump	2018–

* Elevated to chief justice.

Source: U.S. Supreme Court, "Justices: 1789 to Present," https://www.supremecourt.gov/about/members_text.aspx

Most court cases in the United States are state cases. In fact, state courts address 95 percent of all cases in the United States.[16] Because of a high volume of cases in both venues, **plea bargaining** is likely to continue to be prevalent in the U.S. justice system. A plea bargain is an agreement achieved between the prosecution and the defense to settle a case before it goes to trial and a verdict is announced. In civil law a plea bargain usually involves an admission of guilt and an agreement of monetary damages. In criminal law a plea bargain usually involves an admission of guilt in exchange for a reduced charge or sentence.

Although interest group officials cannot lobby federal judges directly, they often do have a mechanism for sharing their views with them indirectly. This process is known as an amicus curiae brief, the Latin term meaning "friend of the court." An interested group or person may file a brief to a court case that shares relevant information about the case in order to assist judges with reaching a decision. At the Supreme Court level, the current record for amicus briefs in one case is 148, which occurred in *Obergefell v. Hodges* (2015).

The Importance of Citizenship in a Republic

The way to optimize the effectiveness of a representative democracy is to enhance citizens' knowledge about their own government. A more inquisitive and knowledgeable citizenry will understand the complexities of American politics better, especially in the judicial arena. In 2018 C-SPAN/PSB conducted a survey about citizen knowledge of the Supreme Court. Only 48 percent of the adult population could name one of the nine justices on the most powerful tribunal in the country. Ruth Bader Ginsburg was the best-known justice at 25 percent; the justice who was least recognizable to citizens was Stephen Breyer (2 percent), despite the fact that he has been serving on the Court since 1994.[17] Thus, we can all do more to be attentive to the Supreme Court and the other federal courts, as the decisions rendered in the federal judiciary can have profound implications for adults and children alike in the United States.

It is important to remember some of Hamilton's prophecies when it comes to federal judges. Appointing a federal judge for life is an important and solemn power bestowed upon presidents. They should do extensive homework before submitting names to the U.S. Senate. In turn, U.S. senators should scrutinize all nominees very carefully. Hamilton offered the following counsel on this matter:

To avoid an arbitrary discretion in the courts, it is indispensable that they should be bound down by strict rules and precedents, which serve to define and point out their duty in every particular case that comes before them; and it will readily be conceived from the variety of controversies which grow out of the folly and wickedness of mankind, that the records of those precedents must unavoidably swell to a considerable bulk, and must demand long and laborious study to acquire a competent knowledge of them. Hence it is, that there can be but few men in the society who will have sufficient skill in the laws to qualify them for the stations of judges. And making the proper deductions for the ordinary depravity of human nature, the number must be still smaller of those who unite the requisite integrity with the requisite knowledge. These considerations apprise us, that the government can have no great option between fit character; and that a temporary duration in office, which would naturally discourage such characters from quitting a lucrative line of practice to accept a seat on the bench, would have a tendency to throw the administration of justice into hands less able, and less well qualified, to conduct it with utility and dignity. In the present circumstances of this country, and in those in which it is likely to be for a long time to come, the disadvantages on this score would be greater than they may at first sight appear; but it must be confessed, that they are far inferior to those which present themselves under the other aspects of the subject.[18]

All federal judges should be expected to have a high level of knowledge about the law. As Hamilton indicated, they should also have a high level of character and integrity, which are crucial components of the legal profession, then and now.

Hamilton advocated for the knowledge of legal **precedents**, which are cases decided earlier that deal with issues similar to those of the present case. It is the business of the judge and the attorneys involved to be fully cognizant of precedents. This does not mean that judges today should always be bound by precedents, but they must at least be aware of them and the legal rules that were established in the cases in question.[19]

Hamilton surmised that lifetime behavior would be advantageous for two reasons: it would promote judicial independence of the other branches of government, and it would help attract talent in the federal judiciary. Hamilton contended that skilled legal practitioners would be more inclined to leave a lucrative position for the federal courts only if they were given lifetime tenure; a fixed term would discourage them for fear of losing their job after only a few years.

Citizens must also realize that the Supreme Court and the lower federal courts are political institutions. Like members of the legislative and executive branches, federal judges are typically partisan (presidents generally appoint fellow partisans to judicial vacancies the vast majority of the time). They have views about politics, the proper role of government, and constitutional interpretation. Consequently, being attentive to the judicial branch of government is part of effective citizenship. Elections have consequences and one of them is the impact they have on the federal judiciary. While judicial politics has always been contentious during the history of the republic, one recent illustration is a reminder that conflicts over the judiciary can be particularly challenging when the perceived political stakes are high.

Democratic president Barack Obama nominated Judge Merrick Garland to the Supreme Court to fill the vacancy left after Justice Antonin Scalia's death in 2016. At the time, Garland was chief judge of the D.C. Circuit Court of Appeals, the nation's second most powerful federal court and sometimes called the "little Supreme Court." Garland had been a member of the D.C. Circuit Court of Appeals since 1997, when he was confirmed by a 76–23 vote upon President Bill Clinton's nomination. Several of the Republican senators who voted to oppose his nomination indicated that they did so not because of Garland and his constitutional views but because they did not think the D.C. circuit needed 11 seats. Garland was a former law clerk for Supreme Court Justice William Brennan and received the highest rating from the American Bar Association. After 293 days his nomination was returned to Obama and was effectively rejected without any Senate action on January 3, 2017, when the 114th session of Congress adjourned forever.[20]

Senate Majority Leader Mitch McConnell (R-Kentucky) had indicated in 2016 that a Supreme Court selection should not be made during a presidential election with a lame duck president. Garland's appointment languished as a result of McConnell's decision, and no hearings were held on his nomination. Although meetings with senators from both major political parties are the norm with Supreme Court nominations, most Republican senators refused to meet with Garland. In 2019 McConnell said he would work to confirm an appointment made by fellow Republican Donald Trump if a vacancy occurs in 2020.[21] Supreme Court nominations are considered to be of paramount importance to U.S. senators, as one selection can literally change the ideological balance of power on the Court on many significant policy issues. The case of Merrick Garland in 2016 illuminates this political situation.

The U.S. Senate has the constitutional duty of confirming or rejecting all federal judicial nominations made by the president. The process can be prickly, as is illustrated in table 7.2, which includes the Senate votes for the current Supreme Court justices. There have always been contentious Senate confirmation votes of Supreme Court nominees, as well as appointees to other federal judgeships, throughout U.S. history. Yet most nominees have been confirmed quite easily. When there was a good deal of controversy regarding the appointment, either the nominee withdrew or was rejected by the Senate. For example, Robert Bork was selected by President Ronald Reagan to fill the vacancy created by the retiring Lewis Powell in 1987. Because Bork was perceived by many senators to be too extreme in his constitutional beliefs, he was formally rejected by a 58–42 vote. Bear in mind that many confirmation votes in the late 18th, 19th, and even 20th centuries were done by voice vote, so no official vote tally exists.

The Senate as an institution has evolved in recent years when it comes to confirming federal judicial appointments. While Supreme Court vacancies are somewhat rare in history, it is also important for citizens to understand why senators and presidents take the matter of lower court judges so seriously as well. Because the Supreme Court justices accept so very few cases every year through the rule of four, this means that the courts of last resort for most federal litigants are the circuit courts of appeal. They have become more active policy makers in recent decades for the simple reason that the Supreme Court justices are content with

Table 7.2. U.S. Senate Confirmation Votes of U.S. Supreme Court Justices (2020)

Nominee	President in Office	Senate Vote	Date
Chief Justice John Roberts	George W. Bush	78–22	September 29, 2005
Clarence Thomas	George H. W. Bush	52–48	October 15, 1991
Ruth Bader Ginsburg	Bill Clinton	96–3	August 3, 1993
Stephen Breyer	Bill Clinton	87–9	July 29, 1994
Samuel Alito	George W. Bush	58–42	January 31, 2006
Sonia Sotomayor	Barack Obama	68–31	August 6, 2009
Elena Kagan	Barack Obama	63–37	August 5, 2010
Neil Gorsuch	Donald Trump	54–45	April 7, 2017
Brett Kavanaugh	Donald Trump	50–48	October 6, 2018

Source: U.S. Senate, "Supreme Court Nominations: Present–1789," https://www.senate.gov/pagelayout/reference/nominations/Nominations.htm

resolving fewer than 100 cases each year. In a way, many legal issues are deferred to the courts of appeal by the justices of the High Court.

Acrimony has clearly been witnessed as it pertains to judicial nominations to the circuit courts of appeal and district courts for the past several years. Ironically, one could argue that leaders in both major political parties have behaved in the exact same manner when it comes to changing the Senate's customs and practices. Recall from chapter 5 that 60 votes are needed to break a filibuster when it comes to legislation. In 2013 the Democrats had majority status, and through Majority Leader Harry Reid (D-Nevada) the rules were altered with regard to lower federal court nominations and cabinet secretaries. The Democrats invoked the **nuclear option**, meaning the rules governing judicial nominations to the circuit courts and district courts (as well as cabinet secretaries) were changed so that nominees could be approved by a simple majority (51) rather than the 60 votes needed to end a traditional filibuster. The Democrats grew weary of the Republicans blocking President Obama's judicial nominees.[22]

In 2017 the Republicans had majority status in the Senate, and Majority Leader McConnell and his fellow Republicans changed the Senate filibuster rules for Supreme Court nominees. In 2013 McConnell was opposed to the Democratic move to invoke the nuclear option for lower court nominees. He retaliated four years later, which is why Neil Gorsuch was confirmed with 54 votes, as the Democrats were going to filibuster his nomination. The same thing happened in 2018 with Brett Kavanaugh, who would have been filibustered by the Democrats were it not for the nuclear option. Kavanaugh was confirmed with 50 votes (two senators did not vote).[23]

The Senate custom known as **senatorial courtesy** may be an artifact of past times. Senatorial courtesy was a custom, not a rule, whereby some nominations for federal positions, including lower court judgeships, were endorsed by fellow senators only if there was no objection to them by the senators from the appointee's state, especially the senior senator from the president's party (if applicable). When the Senate was arguably more bipartisan and consensus-building in its operation, such customs were perpetuated regardless of the political party in power at the time. To the citizens of this republic, it is necessary to understand the federal judiciary as a political institution not unlike the other branches of government. At the same time, as Hamilton shared a long time ago, its primary role is fundamentally different from the legislative and executive branches of government.

Why is it important for citizens to understand the federal judiciary, especially the Supreme Court? It is of fundamental importance because crucial legal disputes have the potential to be decided by a simple majority of nine people who have lifetime tenure.

One way for a president to establish a legacy after she or he leaves office is to make numerous lifetime appointments to the federal judiciary. This has always been true in American history, and the dispute that William Marbury brought to the Supreme Court in the early 19th century attests to this reality. While there have been only 17 chief justices in U.S. history, there have been more than 100 associate justices. Franklin D. Roosevelt, who was president longer than anyone else in history, appointed one chief justice and eight associate justices. Excluding George Washington, as he was the first president and made all the appointments accordingly, several presidents in history made multiple appointments during their tenure in office. As of this writing, 28 Supreme Court justices in history have served more than 25 years on the Court (9,125 days). Thus, presidents can be long out of office for decades but still have influence through their Supreme Court selections (as well as other levels of the federal judiciary). The current record holder for service on the Supreme Court is William Douglas at 13,358 days; he was appointed by Roosevelt in 1939 and had served over 36 years when Gerald Ford appointed his replacement in 1975.

Even though many Supreme Court cases may not have wide impact on society as a whole, clearly some decisions have broad implications for millions of citizens. Remember, it was the justices who determined that segregation was constitutional in 1896 but then later reversed themselves in 1954. The members of Congress did not end segregation in American society, nor did a president. It was the unelected members of the Supreme Court.

The justices extended the right to privacy to include at least first trimester abortions in 1973. Under the constitutional belief that they were safeguarding constitutional liberties and guarantees, the justices have also upheld same-sex marriage and the Affordable Care Act in recent years. Some decisions have wide reverberations all across the country in terms of their impact on society.

Supreme Court justices do not have to be overly attentive to public opinion, as they have lifetime tenure once confirmed by the Senate. The framers promoted the concept of an independent judiciary, based on their belief that the most undemocratic branch at the national level should be in charge of constitutional interpretation. At times, safeguarding civil liberties can be particularly unpopular, especially if overtly racist groups are allowed to express their opinions in public. But that is exactly what federal judges are supposed to do: interpret the Constitution in an independent manner. Yet it is important to know that at the present time, only half the population approves of how the Supreme Court justices are handling their job.[24] Such poll results suggest that many Americans not only perceive the justices to be excessively partisan but also question the Court's independence in the American democracy.

Citizen Homework

Here are some sources on the internet that can enhance fundamental knowledge about the Supreme Court and judicial politics in general:

U.S. Supreme Court: https://www.supremecourt.gov/. Information about the justices, history of the Court, cases, opinions, and oral arguments is available at this website.

Oyez Project: https://www.oyez.org/. This is a free law project with collaboration from the Cornell University Legal Information Institute, Chicago-Kent College of Law, and Justia.com. Case summaries can be secured at this website, along with illustrated decision information about the cases, information about the justices, and a panoramic tour of the Supreme Court building, including the chambers of the justices.

C-SPAN Supreme Court Survey (March 2017): https://static.c-span.org/assets/documents/scotusSurvey/CSPAN%20PSB%20Supreme%20Court%20Survey%20COMPREHENSIVE%20AGENDA%20sent%2003%2013%2017.pdf. Find out how much citizens know about the current Supreme Court. Almost 60 percent of American adults cannot identify even one of the nine Supreme Court justices. The most recognizable justice was identified by only 16 percent of the adult population.

American Courts: https://www.youtube.com/watch?v=IGyx5UEwgtA. Watch a seven-minute video titled "Structure of the Court System." Information about state and federal courts is available at this website.

Federal Judiciary Center: https://www.fjc.gov/. The Federal Judiciary Center was created by Congress in 1967. This website contains information about the federal courts, how the center educates judges and their staff about the law, the history of the federal judiciary, and international judicial relations.

CHAPTER 8

Social, Economic, and Foreign Policy

Public policy is what government officials choose to do or not to do about existing public problems. Public policies tend to be manifested through laws or rules. It is important to consider and analyze not only what policies are enacted by government officials but also what policies are not selected and to ascertain the implications of both situations on the general population. **Social policy** is an area of public policy that is focused on maintaining or improving the quality of life of citizens in the United States. **Economic policy** is an area of public policy that covers decisions regarding taxation, spending levels, the money supply, interest rates, and a plethora of other issues related to the domestic economy. **Foreign policy** is an area of public policy that is focused on the strategy of government officials in dealing with other nation-states. Public policy is ultimately what leaders do or fail to do to address problems in society. Many citizens, for very good reason, tend to examine public policy outcomes when ascertaining whether leaders are doing a good job or not. Perhaps most important, it is essential to analyze the ideas that are behind the public policy choices. One of the most important things to discern in a political campaign is the set of ideas of the various candidates that lead them to advocate or reject certain public policy options. Citizens should always expect candidates to share their ideas and vision of public policy. It is a substantive way to judge candidates and their likelihood of making society better if elected.

A number of political scholars describe the policy process in six distinct stages.[1] The first stage is often called agenda setting or problem recognition. To create a public policy, officials need to first be aware that a problem exists. Upon doing so, policy formulation is the next stage. During policy formulation, policy makers create several options to address the problem. In the third phase, policy adoption, they select the option they believe would be most plausible to address the problem at hand. The fourth stage is policy implementation, where officials put the policy of choice into effect. The first four stages are prospective; the last two are retrospective. The fifth stage is evaluation. Policy makers determine to what extent the policy achieved its stated goals and objectives. The last stage is termination. While many policies and programs can exist for decades and even generations, they are typically modified and adjusted throughout their existence, so the original policy is terminated and adjusted in the manner that policy makers choose.

It is important for citizens to understand two fundamental facts about American politics. First, American politics is enormously complicated. Policies are not created by a singular source. In addition, America is a federal republic, so policies are enacted at the national, state, and local levels of government. Policies can be created by legislative bodies, chief executives, judges, public administrators, or the people through a popular referendum. It is challenging for citizens to determine which entities of the political system are responsible for the policies in question. Nevertheless, it is the collective business of citizens to know and figure out policy successes or policy failures from their own perspective.

Second, politics is inherently conflictual. There is virtually always conflict in democratic systems of government, because people are free to express their own opinions, even if they are unpopular with the majority. Sometimes people lament the fact that, for example, Democrats and Republicans disagree on many issues, and conflict arises as a result. The conflict should be considered positively, for it reflects a diversity of opinion in society and the freedom of the people to voice their opinions without fear of reprisal. What we should expect as citizens, especially with our elected leaders, is a reasonable approach to managing the conflict that exists in society so that policies are enacted to address the needs of the general public. The framers of the Constitution, by way of example, had a diversity of opinions when they drafted the Constitution in the late 18th century. The delegates who served in Philadelphia were participants in a legislative assembly. As such, not one of them left Philadelphia supporting every single aspect of the Constitution. They compromised on numerous political measures in order to create a new structure of governance. Even James Madison, an important contributor to be sure, did not get consent from all of his colleagues for all of his proposals. When the votes do not exist to secure passage, elected officials must often be compelled to engage in the art of political compromise. In other words, even though a politician may not get everything she or he wants in a particular proposal, by forging compromises with opponents, she or he may still end up getting a significant portion of what was sought and therefore must decide whether compromising is advantageous or not. Sometimes compromises are not possible, particularly when officials believe that their core fundamental values and principles are at stake. At other times, compromises are possible if the political players involved decide that compromising would be in the best interests of the people.

Historical Evolution of Social Policy

Social policy has always existed in U.S. history, but the role of the federal government in society has changed a great deal in the 20th century. In the late 18th and 19th centuries, churches, families, and private charities largely attended to the needs of the impoverished and disadvantaged. This started to change after the Civil War. Federal officials started to provide financial support for Civil War veterans and their families. In the late 19th and early 20th centuries, war pensions and support for veterans' widows was the highest singular expenditure at the federal level, followed by interest on the national debt (which increased dramatically during the Civil War).[2]

When the stock market crashed in October 1929, plunging the nation into the **Great Depression**, a dire situation existed in the United States. Though there was no official measure of poverty at that time, many historians believe that half the country's people were living in poverty. Unemployment was around 25 percent when Franklin Roosevelt assumed the presidency. The Great Depression was the worst economic downturn in the history of the industrialized world; it lasted for about 10 years, many investors lost all their money, and countless banks failed all across the country.[3] This sobering circumstance became a primary focal point for the administration in 1933, and Roosevelt was able to persuade members of Congress to implement his **New Deal.** The New Deal was an array of public policies espoused by Roosevelt from the beginning of his presidency through 1935 to promote economic recovery and social welfare during the Great Depression. Some of his New Deal programs included the Agricultural Adjustment Administration, the National Recovery Administration and Public Works Administration, the Federal Emergency Relief Administration, Civilian Works Administration and Civilian Conservation Corps, and the Social Security Act.[4] Besides winning the presidency in a landslide over Herbert Hoover in 1932, New Deal Democrats won a decisive majority in both chambers of Congress as well. A primary component of Roosevelt's social policy agenda was getting members of Congress to pass Aid to Dependent Children (ADC), which was the precursor of a long-standing federal social policy for the impoverished, Aid to Families with Dependent Children (AFDC), a program that lasted until 1996. Since the passage of the New Deal, the role of the federal government in social policy has changed forever. While future Congresses and presidents would seek to scale back the New Deal in various ways, one thing has remained constant since the 1930s: the federal government has played an instrumental role in social policy for the past 80 years and will likely continue to do so.[5]

One of the most fundamental changes that occurred during the New Deal was the creation of the **Social Security** program. Social Security is a federal entitlement program created in 1935 that provides cash benefits to current retirees based on social insurance payroll taxes paid by all current workers over the course of their entire work careers. By law, this program is "pay as you go," meaning that working Americans pay taxes to support current retirees. Under the social contract of the program, in return for paying taxes for one's entire career, retirees are promised that they will receive benefits when they end their working lives and that their benefits will be paid by the next generation of workers. **Entitlements** are programs created by members of Congress that provide benefits to all Americans who meet the requirements specified by law. Social Security and Medicare are prominent entitlement programs in the contemporary era.

About thirty years after the initial New Deal agenda, a second major expansion of the federal government's role in social policy took place as part of President Lyndon Johnson's (1963–1969) vision of a **Great Society**, his social agenda designed to improve the quality of life in the United States through government intervention. Besides the expansion of civil and voting rights in 1964 and 1965, Johnson made his War on Poverty an important part of the Great Society. Central to his vision of eliminating poverty in the United States was the creation of two new programs in 1965: **Medicare** and **Medicaid**. Medicare is a federal entitlement program that provides health care coverage for citizens 65 and older through hospital care (Part A) and medical care (Part B); a prescription drug benefit (Part D) was added later. Medicaid is a federal entitlement program that is funded by both the federal and state governments that provides health care coverage for low-income citizens.[6]

During his presidency, Johnson persuaded members of Congress to create a myriad of new programs in the health, education, and housing sectors (e.g., Head Start, Office of Economic Opportunity, the Jobs Corps, Elementary and Secondary Education Act of 1965, Child Nutrition Act of 1966, and the creation of the Department of Housing and Urban Development). Johnson sought to reduce the ravages of poverty during his tenure. We now refer to his vision as a means to reduce the official **federal poverty level**, which today is an annual measure of income issued by officials in the Department of Health and Human Services (HHS). Citizens who earn less money than the measure in terms of total household income are defined as living in poverty. Those who earn more than the measure are defined as not living in poverty. It is a dichotomous measure as such. The HHS measure in 2020 for a family of four living in the 48 contiguous states is $26,200.[7]

Efforts in the Johnson era to mitigate the implications of poverty were undermined by the Vietnam War. The funding required for the war made it exceedingly difficult for federal lawmakers to keep funding Johnson's social agenda and the war effort simultaneously. Since that time, some presidents have sought to cut the welfare state in a significant manner, especially Ronald Reagan, George W. Bush, and Donald Trump. A good portion of the social safety net, however, remains intact and suggests that Americans endorse the notion of federal intervention in the social policy arena, at least at some discernible level.

Historical Evolution of Economic Policy

Much of the focus of this chapter is on **fiscal policy**, which involves decisions made by government officials on taxing and spending issues. **Monetary policy** entails decisions about how to influence the domestic economy through controlling the flow of money and by setting interest rates. Monetary policy is conducted by the officials at the **Federal Reserve Board**, an independent regulatory agency created by Congress in 1913 that establishes monetary policy in the United States and operates as the nation's central bank.

The evolution of economic policy in the United States is somewhat parallel to that of social policy. From the beginning of the republic until 1933 when Franklin Roosevelt was inaugurated as president, the dominant economic philosophy was laissez-faire capitalism. The federal government during this extended time period was a relatively small operation in size and scope. Americans embraced Adam Smith's philosophy that he articulated in *The Wealth of Nations* (1776) that the national government should be small and have little regulation in the domestic economy. The dominant belief was that the market would cure itself if needed and that too much government interference would impede the expansion of the economy. The Great Depression suggested to many, including Roosevelt, that the federal government could be the lead player in getting the economy back in balance and in a position to expand again.

Roosevelt embraced the philosophy of **Keynesian economics** when he was president. John Maynard Keynes (1883–1946) was a British economist who believed that national governmental leaders should use economic policy, including taxing and spending decisions, to maintain a stable economy. Roosevelt operationalized Keynesianism during his tenure as presidency; his New Deal was based on the premise that the federal government, through short-term deficit spending, was the proper vehicle to lift the nation out of the Great Depression. As discussed in chapter 6, the size and scope of the federal government increased a great deal compared with previous time periods. The Keynesian philosophy remained popular in both major political parties after Roosevelt's death in 1945, as embodied in Republican president Richard Nixon's famous quote in 1971: "We are all Keynesians now."[8]

It was not until the election of Ronald Reagan as president in 1980 that a major change occurred in economic philosophy on the part of national leaders. Reagan was an advocate of **supply-side economics**, commonly referred to as Reaganomics during his tenure as president. Supply-side economics was a theory espoused by conservative economists predicated on the assumption that lowering tax rates, especially for the wealthy, would stimulate the economy by encouraging citizens to consume more goods and services. In turn, economic growth would occur, which would eventually offset the loss of revenue from the tax cuts. Reagan was also a firm believer in **deregulation**, the process of removing regulations on specific industries in order to promote economic prosperity. Since 1981 there has not been a dominant economic theory embraced by leaders in both major political parties. While Democrats and Republicans and liberals and conservatives all support the notion of economic growth, their ideas about how prosperity should occur and what role the federal government should have in promoting it are poles apart.

In the modern era, liberals generally support a broad and active role for the federal government in expanding the U.S. economy and providing equality for all citizens. Conversely, conservatives tend to embrace less regulation and their conception of more individual freedom. For some time, adherents to both major political parties tended to be supporters of a small and limited national government; the Great Depression, however, affected American society in a profound manner. Ever since, citizens expect federal leaders to provide assistance in times of need. Liberals generally are trying to preserve the welfare state that has already been created; conservatives may support cuts in social policy spending, but they are not currently trying to eliminate programs such as Social Security and Medicare.

Historical Evolution of Foreign Policy

George Washington had a profound impact on the development of U.S. foreign policy well into the 20th century. In his farewell address in late 1796, he warned Americans about the inherent dangers of taking sides in European conflicts, especially by forging alliances with either the British or the French. He offered this foreign policy advice to his contemporaries:

> It is our true policy to steer clear of permanent alliances with any portion of the foreign world; so far, I mean, as we are now at liberty to do it; for let me not be understood as capable of patronizing infidelity to existing arrangements. I hold the maxim no less applicable to public than to private affairs, that honesty is always the best policy. I repeat it, therefore, let those engagements be observed in their genuine sense. But, in my opinion, it is unnecessary and would be unwise to extend them.[9]

This policy of avoiding entangling alliances would later be called **isolationism**. Isolationism is a foreign policy idea that a country should avoid involving itself in international affairs. Rather, leaders should be mainly focused on domestic policy issues. This was the dominant approach to U.S. foreign policy until the Japanese attacked Pearl Harbor in 1941, which prompted U.S. involvement in World War II.

After the war, **containment** became the dominant approach to foreign policy in the United States. The main premise of containment was that the United States, through diplomatic, economic, and militaristic strategies, actively sought to prevent the Soviet Union from expanding its communist ideology across the world. The United States and Soviet Union existed in a bipolar world between the West (democracies led by the United States) and the East (communist countries led by the Soviet

Union). It was the policy of the United States to contain the spread of communism in the world, which eventually led to the Korean War and later the Vietnam War. American policy makers during the Cold War subscribed to two important theories: **mutually assured destruction** and the **domino theory**. Mutually assured destruction was an idea that was prominent during the Cold War, when two military superpowers existed (the United States and Soviet Union). Both nations possessed a large cache of nuclear weapons and could destroy the earth in an exchange of nuclear weapons. The premise of this theory is that it would be very unlikely that any superpower would attack the other, because the world would be annihilated. The domino theory was a premise predicated on the belief that if one country became influenced by the communist ideology of the Soviet Union, surrounding nations would also succumb to a communist takeover. This theory was prominent during the Vietnam War era. The **Cold War** lasted from 1945 to about 1991 and is a term used to describe the tension between the United States and the former Soviet Union. The Cold War featured an arms race between the West, led by the United States, and the East, led by the Soviet Union.

When the Cold War ended and the Soviet Union collapsed, President George H. W. Bush declared that a new world order existed. In a speech in September 1990, he declared:

> We stand today at a unique and extraordinary moment. The crisis in the Persian Gulf, as grave as it is, also offers a rare opportunity to move toward an historic period of cooperation. Out of these troubled times, our fifth objective—a new world order—can emerge: a new era—freer from the threat of terror, stronger in the pursuit of justice, and more secure in the quest for peace. An era in which the nations of the world, East and West, North and South, can prosper and live in harmony. A hundred generations have searched for this elusive path to peace, while a thousand wars raged across the span of human endeavor. Today that new world is struggling to be born, a world quite different from the one we've known. A world where the rule of law supplants the rule of the jungle. A world in which nations recognize the shared responsibility for freedom and justice. A world where the strong respect the rights of the weak. This is the vision that I shared with President Gorbachev in Helsinki. He and other leaders from Europe, the Gulf, and around the world understand that how we manage this crisis today could shape the future for generations to come.[10]

After the demise of the Soviet Union, the United States remained the lone superpower in the world, but the threats to global peace existed due to the spread of nuclear weapons and international terrorism. Bush envisioned a global opportunity for peace in the aftermath of the decline of communism and the end of the Cold War. Unfortunately, events such as the first Persian Gulf War demonstrated that the world remained volatile in spite of the fact that the Soviet Union ceased to exist.

Social, Economic, and Foreign Policy Today

Social insurance taxes help to fund the two largest entitlements in the United States today: Social Security and Medicare. In 2020 the Social Security tax is 6.2 percent for the first $137,700 of one's income. The 6.2 percent tax is matched by a worker's employer (self-employed people pay the entire 12.4 percent tax). Medicare has no cap; wage earners pay the Medicare tax for the entire calendar year. It is currently 1.45 percent. As of January 2013, individuals with an income over $200,000 or married couples filing jointly with an income over $250,000 pay an additional 0.9 percent in Medicare taxes. Thus, the social insurance tax is effectively 7.65 percent for most Americans (15.3 percent for those who are self-employed).[11] The great challenge to federal officials today in fiscal policy is how to keep fully funding popular entitlements, such as Social Security and Medicare, when the **baby boom** generation retires. Baby boomers are Americans born in the post–World War II era from 1946 to 1964. Over the next generation, baby boomers will be retiring from their jobs in historically large numbers, thus putting a financial strain on the Social Security and Medicare systems. This comes in the context of a challenging annual **federal budget**, recurring annual **budget deficits,** and a growing **national debt**. By law, the federal government has an annual budget. The **fiscal year**, or financial year, is used by governments for accounting and budget purposes. The fiscal year for the U.S. federal government runs from October 1 through September 30. Thus, fiscal year 2020 for federal officials will run from October 1, 2019 through September 30, 2020. The federal budget is the amount of money spent at the federal level in a given fiscal year. The budget is not a singular entity; on an annual level a budget is created if members of Congress pass a dozen appropriations bills and they are all signed by the president. Since the Watergate era, it is common for a fiscal year to expire without an agreement between the president and Congress on a budget. When a budget agreement does not occur, typically a **continuing resolution** is passed. A continuing resolution is an appropriation bill passed by members of Congress that provides funding for specific programs or services. Typically, continuing resolutions are adopted in order to keep the government open when fiscal years end and members of Congress and the president have not agreed on a new budget. They typically keep funding for various agencies at existing levels for a few weeks or a few months, until officials in the two traditional branches of government can come to some consensus on fiscal policy.

A **balanced budget** is a spending bill for a given fiscal year in which a government's expenditures are equal to its revenue. For example, if federal officials spent $4 trillion in a given fiscal year and secured $4 trillion in revenue for the same fiscal year, there would be a balanced budget at the federal level. A budget deficit is the amount of money by which governmental spending exceeds its revenue in a given fiscal year. For example, if federal officials spent $4 trillion in a given fiscal year and secured $3 trillion in revenue for the same fiscal year, there would be a budget deficit of $1 trillion for that year. Since 1969, budget deficits have been the norm. The only balanced federal budgets, resulting in a budget surplus (when revenue exceeds spending), since that time occurred in fiscal year 1998, 1999, 2000, and 2001.

The highest budget deficit in U.S. history in one year is $1.4 trillion in fiscal year 2009, during an economic recession, though this record is likely to be eclipsed due, in part, to the coronavirus pandemic. Experts estimate that trillion-dollar deficits will likely resume over the next few years.[12] The national debt (the total amount of money borrowed by federal officials, including interest on the debt, from 1789 to the present) exceeded $23.4 trillion as of March 2020.[13]

Members of Congress and the president have another important budgetary challenge at present. About two-thirds of the annual federal budget is defined as **mandatory spending**. Mandatory spending refers to expenditures that are required by law through entitlements. Unless, for example, the rules of programs such as Social Security and Medicare are changed by members of Congress, benefits are automatically sent to citizens who qualify under federal law because they are entitled to the benefits in question. With the interest on the national debt included, this leaves only one-third of the budget for **discretionary spending**. Discretionary spending includes expenditures in the federal budget that can be cut if members of Congress wish to do so without changing existing law. Bear in mind, however, that although discretionary spending is about one-third of the current federal budget, it does not cover entitlements or interest on the national debt, but it does cover national defense and a wide variety of other policy needs. In 1970 only 31 percent of the budget was spent on mandatory programs. Over the next decade, discretionary spending is projected to only be 20 percent of total federal spending.[14]

There are a great number of social policy challenges at the present time. To many scientists the most fundamental issue of our time is **climate change**. Climate change is the warming of global temperatures in a measurable manner that was initially documented in the late 20th century and continues in the 21st century. Scientists believe that climate change is caused by human beings burning fossil fuels and increasing the amount of carbon dioxide in the atmosphere. Climate change is also known as "global warming." It is generally feared that failure to reverse the effects of climate change could result in substantial damage to the environment, human health, and the global economy.

Another controversial issue in another policy realm, education, and in other policy issues is **privatization**. Privatization is the process of transferring the management of government programs from a public bureaucracy to a private company. Conservatives tend to advocate for privatization of public services while liberals generally oppose it. Undoubtedly the most divisive issue related to privatization in K-12 public education has to do with **school vouchers**. Vouchers are a public policy advocated by conservatives where taxpayers' money is sent directly to parents who qualify through a means test to allow them to send their children to private (including parochial) schools rather than public schools. Conservatives tout vouchers as an expansion of school choice; liberals view vouchers as a violation of the separation of church and state under the Establishment Clause of the First Amendment. Liberals tend to be staunch supporters of traditional public schools and believe that more funding is needed to address school funding disparities, especially in urban schools in poor neighborhoods.

The school choice movement has been growing in recent years, particularly with the expansion of **charter schools**. Charter schools are non-traditional public schools of choice that exist in 43 states at the present time. Such schools are funded at taxpayers' expense but operate in an independent manner from traditional public schools in that they are not bound by the same regulations that apply to traditional public schools. Created typically by teachers, parents, or community groups, charter schools are bound by the charter with a local or national body, which generally is predicated on a promise of improving the standardized test scores for the students enrolled in the school in a given time period. Charter schools are an example of the contemporary privatization movement: traditional schools are run by school board members who run in democratic elections; charter schools are often operated by private, for-profit companies.[15]

American policy makers must confront economic challenges through policy making and the creation of regulations. Recent national leaders have been faced with a recurring dilemma: Can the U.S economy be expanded, resulting in job growth, while promoting environmental protection? Are the two goals mutually exclusive or can both be pursued in earnest successfully? An important decision, especially for U.S. presidents, continues to be, what can be done about climate change? How will these policies affect the U.S. economy? Can the United States reduce its dependency on fossil fuels to address its energy needs? What are the policy implications of using renewable sources of energy? In addition, the United States has higher rates of poverty and income inequality than most industrialized nations. What, if anything, should be done to alleviate these situations?

Ideas about fiscal policy issues tend to be largely a function of ideology. For example, while people generally do not like to pay taxes, the revenue is needed to run the country and provide an array of services to citizens. Conservatives generally favor a **regressive tax** while liberals generally support a **progressive tax**. A regressive tax takes a higher percentage of income of less affluent citizens and a smaller percentage of income of more affluent citizens. Examples of a regressive tax include a state sales tax and social insurance payroll taxes. A progressive tax takes a higher percentage from more affluent wage earners and a lower percentage from less affluent wage earners. The current federal tax code is an example of a progressive tax system. Liberals generally would like to preserve the current nature of the federal tax system while many conservatives favor a type of **flat tax** (i.e., all income above a designated level would be taxed at the same percentage, whether a taxpayer made $70,000 or several million or more).

The context of the world changed after the demise of the Soviet Union in that there is only one superpower in the traditional sense of the term (military and economic power). Listed in table 8.1 are the top 15 nations in the world in terms of military spending in 2018. U.S. officials spent $649 billion, and the country closest to the United States in terms of spending was China at $250 billion. No other country allocated more than $70 billion to national defense.

Gross Domestic Product (GDP) has traditionally been a measure of economic power. Table 8.2 lists all 16 nations that exceeded $1 trillion in GDP for 2018. The United States had a GDP of $20.5 trillion. Once again, China was second at $13.6 trillion. No other country had a GDP in excess of $5 trillion. Bear in mind that as of 2019 estimates, China had a population of 1.39 billion and the United States had 331 million.[16]

The philosophy of **internationalism** has dominated U.S. foreign policy making during the post–World War II era, at least until the Trump administration with its "America first" agenda. Internationalism is a foreign policy idea predicated upon a belief that a country should be involved in the affairs of other nations, not only for self-interest but also due to moral obligation. Many foreign policy analysts refer to **globalization** in the 21st century, which is the process of interacting and integrating with people from other countries through trade, travel, culture, investment, and information technology. Those advocating this type of approach to foreign policy making typically espouse **diplomacy**, which is foreign policy making through representatives who engage in negotiations with representatives from other countries in a peaceful manner.

A significant change in U.S. foreign policy occurred in the aftermath of the terrorist attacks of September 11, 2001. The **doctrine of preemp-**

Table 8.1. Top 15 Nations in Military Spending (2018)

Rank	Nation	Total Military Spending (in U.S. Billions)
1	United States	649
2	China	250
3	Saudi Arabia	67.6
4	India	66.5
5	France	63.8
6	Russia	61.4
7	United Kingdom	50.0
8	Germany	49.5
9	Japan	46.6
10	South Korea	43.1
11	Italy	27.8
11	Brazil	27.8
13	Australia	26.7
14	Canada	21.6
15	Turkey	19.0

Source: "Trends in World Military Expenditure, 2018," Stockholm International Peace Research Institute, April 2019, https://www.sipri.org/sites/default/files/2019-04/fs_1904_milex_2018.pdf

tion (the Bush Doctrine) was articulated by President George W. Bush in advance of the Iraq War. He claimed that the United States had the right to engage in a preemptive military strike if intelligence revealed threats to its national security. Whether future presidents endorse this policy approach is unknown. In early 1961 President Dwight D. Eisenhower issued a profound warning in his farewell address. He told Americans to beware of the military-industrial complex and to be vigilant in the careful and often tenuous balance between the preservation of democracy on one hand and providing national security on the other:

> This conjunction of an immense military establishment and a large arms industry is new in the American experience. The total influence—economic, political, even spiritual—is felt in every city, every State house, every office of the Federal government. We recognize the imperative need for this development. Yet we must not fail to comprehend its grave implications. Our toil, resources and livelihood are all involved; so is the very structure of our society. In the councils of government, we must guard against the acquisition of unwarranted influence, whether sought or unsought, by the military-

Table 8.2. Top 16 Nations in Gross Domestic Product (2018)

Rank	Nation	Gross Domestic Product (in U.S. Trillions)
1	United States	20,544,343
2	China	13,608,152
3	Japan	4,971,323
4	Germany	3,947,620
5	United Kingdom	2,855,297
6	France	2,777,535
7	India	2,718,732
8	Italy	2,083,864
9	Brazil	1,868,626
10	Canada	1,713,342
11	Russia	1,657,555
11	South Korea	1,619,424
13	Australia	1,433,904
14	Spain	1,419,042
15	Mexico	1,220,699
16	Indonesia	1,042,173

Source: "Gross Domestic Product, 2018," World Bank, https://databank. worldbank.org/data/download/GDP.pdf

industrial complex. The potential for the disastrous rise of misplaced power exists and will persist. We must never let the weight of this combination endanger our liberties or democratic processes. We should take nothing for granted. Only an alert and knowledgeable citizenry can compel the proper meshing of the huge industrial and military machinery of defense with our peaceful methods and goals, so that security and liberty may prosper together.[17]

It is up to citizens to hold our leaders accountable and to make sure that government officials provide security while simultaneously ensuring democracy and freedom. Eisenhower's challenge remains highly relevant in the contemporary era.

The Importance of Citizenship in a Republic

When it comes to public policy debates, citizens have much to offer. The more we know about substantive issues, the less susceptible we are to political manipulation from a variety of sources. Remember that a key benchmark for democracy is accountability. The framers of the Constitution painstakingly established separation of powers and checks and balances to ensure that no one branch of government exceeded its constitutional authority. In a democracy, however, government officials are ultimately accountable to the will of the people. Citizenship is generally not taught in a singular place in the course of one's life. Yet as long as Americans live, they are citizens in a democratic republic. It is a necessary part of the human condition to engage in the responsibilities, duties, and rights of citizenship. With all the serious public policy challenges that exist in U.S. and global politics today, we simply must be more attentive to politics and public affairs. It is not uncommon to hear, somewhat on a regular basis, that the next presidential election may be the most important in one's lifetime. Such rhetoric is typically not hyperbolic; all elections are crucial, for the nature and course of democracy are contingent on their results.

The Constitution is much more democratic today in practice than in the late 18th century when it was written. The rights of citizenship have been extended through the nation's history, often due to prolonged political struggle. Given the history of the United States, there is every reason to believe that democracy will flourish in ways we cannot presently identify. Conceptually, most Americans would embrace this notion. With rights come responsibilities. I challenge the current generation to attempt what our predecessors have embraced throughout U.S. history. The best thing we can do as citizens, parents, family members, friends, and patriots is to leave this world in better shape than it was when we were born. This is truly the mission of citizenship.

Social, economic, and foreign policy are of crucial importance in a republic like the United States. Because the United States is the sole superpower on the planet, public policies made by U.S. leaders impact not only Americans but citizens across the world too. As many scientists and policy analysts have documented, Americans consume far more natural resources and live much less sustainably than any other industrialized nation on earth. What we consume by way of energy, food, and water and what we throw away impacts the rest of the world. According to one study, America makes up 5 percent of the global population but creates 50 percent of the solid waste in the world.[18] Our collective decision making, whether we are aware of it or not, or whether we have a sufficient selection of policy choices provided by elected officials or not, affects the rest of the world in a profound manner. This is just one illustration of a broader point about the power of citizens in this superpower republic.

More education, knowledge, awareness, compassion, and empathy on the part of citizens in this country can lead to social, political, and economic reforms. Collectively, citizens will have to determine the direction of public policy making in the United States. As an individual, I may have my own ideas, values, preferences, and priorities, but others may view the world in a much different manner. However, in our demographically diverse country, the policies that are created by leaders who are elected to represent the people directly should reflect that diversity, which continues to be a source of great strength and pride.

Knowledge Matters

Basic truths about the federal budget will be helpful for all citizens in truly understanding the fiscal realities of the day. About two-thirds of the budget is already allocated from one year to the next when accounting for entitlements and interest on the debt. Entitlements entail legal financial obligations that have been made by members of Congress to citizens. Presumably, the only way to garner substantial savings in entitlement spending is to cut benefits, which is something citizens generally oppose. While some advocate defaulting on the debt, most economists contend that it would have a crippling effect on the U.S. economy. Since 1789 the U.S. government has honored its financial commitments to its creditors by paying the interest on the debt. Undoubtedly, policy makers should continue to honor the financial obligations of the nation from both past and current sessions of Congress.

While it is easy to cast blame on Congress and presidents for the national debt situation of the country, citizens have to take some ownership of it as well. One approach to achieving a balanced budget is to cut spending and increase taxes, perhaps simultaneously. Citizens generally do not support cuts in benefits and services, nor do they typically embrace increases in taxes. Many members of Congress in general, but particularly in an election year, will be hesitant to engage in decision making that is viewed as austere by the general public. Americans typically believe they are taxed at higher rates compared to their counterparts across the free world, which is not the case at all.

Context matters in politics. Americans presently face a number of policy challenges, whether we choose to accept this or not. The gap between rich and poor in this country is at a historic level, the middle class is shrinking, and the proportion of people living in poverty is much higher here than in other industrialized democracies. About 50 million people in the United States have no health insurance, live in poverty, and have limited opportunities at best. Part of the reason why citizens express their frustration with the government is that they see officials creating policies that are indifferent to their needs, such as tax cuts targeted to the wealthy, the inability or unwillingness of Congress to raise the minimum wage, and the influence of big money in the political system, to name just a few.[19]

For those citizens who may be frustrated with the status quo, indifference will not make things better. All citizens, regardless of their views on public policy, should equip themselves with a more fundamental understanding of American politics and policy and be willing to engage actively in the political process. A knowledgeable citizenry, dedicated to making this republic more democratic and public policy making more responsive to the diverse population, will yield some very positive results and establish a strong precedent for citizen activism in the United States.

In the pursuit of more knowledge about U.S. politics and policy, it would benefit all of us to learn more about the world in which we live. Violent behavior persists in this country and all across the world. The great hope in foreign affairs is that at some point citizens in all nation-states can live in relative peace and avoid military confrontations with one another. Diplomacy is undoubtedly instrumental in the pursuit of this noteworthy objective. The global community is positioned to pursue and maintain a state of peace if all people begin to care to know more about the diverse world in which we inhabit and at least attempt to understand, and respect, our differences of opinion on a wide variety of issues.

Citizen Homework

All citizens should be well versed in social, economic, and foreign policy to hold elected leaders accountable. A wealth of information is available on the internet that will assist interested and proactive citizens in their quest to know more about the American democracy. Here are a few examples:

The debt to the penny from 1790–2019: https://www.treasurydirect. gov/govt/reports/pd/histdebt/histdebt.htm. The debt to the penny as of today: https://treasurydirect.gov/NP/debt/current. Most citizens blame past and current members of Congress and presidents for the ascendancy of the debt in U.S. history. These are the people who have the power to vote on federal budgets. Have citizens contributed to the increase of the debt? Why or why not?

Federal poverty level: https://aspe.hhs.gov/poverty-guidelines. Many citizens are not aware of the current measure of poverty in the United States. Is it too low, about right, or too high? What are the implications of the current federal poverty level?

Learn more about mandatory versus discretionary spending: https://www.nationalpriorities.org/budget-basics/ federal-budget-101/spending/.

Learn more about military spending across the world: https://www. sipri.org/databases/milex. How does the United States compare with the rest of the world?

Basic information about foreign policy: https://www.youtube.com/ watch?v=PMhIQNkO_Y0. Watch a 10-minute video titled "Foreign Policy: Crash Course Government and Politics #50."

Epilogue

While it may seem daunting and even audacious to ponder changing the status quo, history is replete with examples where courageous citizens have accepted the challenge of their times and, because of their activism, not only enhanced society but also made this republic more democratic.

Think of the feminists who gathered in Seneca Falls, New York, at Wesleyan Chapel on July 19 and 20, 1848. The First Women's Rights Convention was attended by 300 people, mostly residents from that area. On the first day, only women were allowed to partake in the meeting. The second day of the convention was open to men as well.[1] At the end of this meeting, 100 people signed the Declaration of Sentiments (68 women and 32 men).[2] The attendees of this event had many grievances. **Elizabeth Cady Stanton** (1815–1902) was one of the organizers of the meeting.[3] She began the gathering by declaring:

> We are assembled to protest against a form of government, existing without the consent of the governed—to declare our right to be free as man is free, to be represented in the government which we are taxed to support, to have such disgraceful laws as give man the power to chastise and imprison his wife, to take the wages which she earns, the property which she inherits, and, in case of separation, the children of her love.[4]

This convention came at a time when women could not exercise the franchise, nor did they have any legal rights in practical terms. The event is often referred to as the beginning of the women's suffrage movement.

Stanton was the primary author of the Declaration of Sentiments. She relied on the Declaration of Independence as her justification, offering the following powerful statement:

> We hold these truths to be self-evident; that all men and women are created equal; that they are endowed by their Creator with certain inalienable rights; that among these are life, liberty, and the pursuit of happiness; that to secure these rights governments are instituted, deriving their just powers from the consent of the governed. Whenever any form of Government becomes destructive of these ends, it is the right of those who suffer from it to refuse allegiance to it, and to insist upon the institution of a new government, laying its foundation on such principles, and organizing its powers in such form as to them shall seem most likely to effect their safety and happiness. Prudence, indeed, will dictate that governments long established should not be changed for light and transient causes; and accordingly, all experience hath shown that mankind are more disposed to suffer, while evils are sufferable, than to right themselves, by abolishing the forms to which they are accustomed. But when a long train of abuses and usurpations, pursuing invariably the same object, evinces a design to reduce them under absolute despotism, it is their duty to throw off such government, and to provide new guards for their future security. Such has been the patient sufferance of the women under this government, and such is now the necessity which constrains them to demand the equal station to which they are entitled.[5]

In spite of overwhelming opposition, Stanton and her colleagues kept trying to advance the cause of fairness and equality to all citizens. They were focused, committed, and dedicated to gender equality. They did not experience much success for decades. Most reform movements are similar in this regard (e.g., civil rights, labor, environmental preservation, public health, and consumer product safety). Citizens should be prepared to be diligent, vigilant, and unwavering in their pursuit of a more vibrant democracy. Such a laudable goal is well worth our collective efforts.

The knowledge presented in this book is designed and intended to help equip people to embrace their roles as citizens in a republic. The intent is not to advocate for a specific political party or political ideology. Determining one's party or ideological choice is a personal decision. I have attempted to provide a framework of analysis; how people use the information is entirely up to them. I have made a fundamental assumption throughout the work: a representative democracy works best when citizens are actively engaged in the political and public policy process. A stable and sustained democracy continues in perpetuity if citizens choose to make their own government more effective. Democracy is in peril with citizen indifference, cynicism, and ignorance.[6]

The framers of the Constitution in the late 18th century started a work in progress in the 13 colonies—a republican form of government. They understood that by its very nature, a republic is a task that is never finished. The challenge they issued was to make democracy work, regardless of the circumstances in the nation at a given point in time. It is our duty as citizens to embrace and confront the challenge that was issued in the 1780s and create a more functional democracy for children and adults alike today and into the future. It is a noble calling and one that must be addressed by our peers today and those who will follow us.

Notes

PREFACE

1. Theodore Roosevelt, "The Duties of American Citizenship," speech delivered at Buffalo, New York, January 26, 1883. Gilder Lehrman Center for the Study of Slavery, Resistance, and Abolition, Yale University. https://glc.yale.edu/duties-american-citizenship

INTRODUCTION

1. "The Indian Citizenship Act," History.com, February 9, 2010, https://www.history.com/this-day-in-history/the-indian-citizenship-act

2. Center for Civic Education, "Constitutional Democracy," http://www.civiced.org/lesson-plans/constitutional-democracy

3. Charles E. Merriam, *The Making of Citizens: A Comparative Study of Methods of Civic Training* (Chicago: University of Chicago Press, 1931), 362.

4. "Guide to the Charles E. Merriam Papers, 1893–1957," University of Chicago Library, https://www.lib.uchicago.edu/e/scrc/findingaids/view.php?eadid=ICU.SPCL.MERRIAMCE

5. "Charles E. Merriam: Political Science, 1874–1953," University of Chicago Library, https://www.lib.uchicago.edu/projects/centcat/fac/facch15_01.html

6. "Civics Knowledge Predicts Willingness to Protect Supreme Court," University of Pennsylvania, Annenberg Public Policy Center, https://www.annenbergpublicpolicycenter.org/civics-knowledge-survey-willingness-protect-supreme-court

7. David M. Ricci, *Good Citizenship in America* (Cambridge: Cambridge University Press, 2004), 3.

8. National Council for the Social Studies, "Creating Effective Citizens: A Position Statement of National Council for the Social Studies," n.d. [2018], http://www.socialstudies.org/sites/default/files/publications/se/6505/650511.html

9. Michael Walzer, "Civility and Civic Virtue in Contemporary America," *Social Research* 41, no. 4 (1974): 593–611.

10. Caltech/MIT Voting Technology Project, "Reports," https://www.vote.caltech.edu/reports

11. Gallup Poll, "Satisfaction with the United States," Gallup, n.d., https://news.gallup.com/poll/1669/general-mood-country.aspx

12. Jennifer L. Hochschild and Katherine Levine Einstein, *Do Facts Matter? Information and Misinformation in American Politics* (Norman: University of Oklahoma Press, 2015), 14.

13. Jennifer L. Hochschild and Katherine Levine Einstein, "Do Facts Matter? Information and Misinformation in American Politics," *Political Science Quarterly* 130, no. 4 (2016): 624.

14. American Presidency Project, "John F. Kennedy: Inaugural Address—January 20, 1961," http://www.presidency.ucsb.edu/ws/index.php?pid=8032

15. Alexis de Tocqueville, *Democracy in America* (1835; Chicago: University of Chicago Press, 2000).

CHAPTER 1

1. Michael S. Kochin and Michael Taylor, *An Independent Empire: Diplomacy and War in the Making of the United States* (Ann Arbor: University of Michigan Press, 2020), 7–16.

2. Library of Congress, "The American Revolution, 1763–1783," n.d. [2018], http://www.loc.gov/teachers/classroommaterials/presentationsandactivities/presentations/timeline/amrev/

3. National Constitution Center, "On This Day: Congress Officially Creates the U.S. Army," September 29, 2019, https://constitutioncenter.org/blog/on-this-day-congress-officially-creates-the-u-s-army

4. Frank E. Manuel and Fritzie P. Manuel, *James Bowdoin and the Patriot Philosophers* (Philadelphia: American Philosophical Society, 2004), 204–36.

5. Library of Congress, "James Madison and the Federal Constitutional Convention of 1787," n.d. [2018], https://www.loc.gov/collections/james-madison-papers/articles-and-essays/james-madison-and-the-federal-constitutional-convention-of-1787/

6. Mary Sarah Bilder, *Madison's Hand: Revising the Constitutional Convention* (Cambridge, MA: Harvard University Press, 2015).

7. Max Farrand, *The Records of the Federal Convention of 1787*, 3 vols. (New Haven: Yale University Press, 1911).

8. "The Delegates Who Didn't Sign the Constitution," ConstitutionFacts.com, https://www.constitutionfacts.com/us-constitution-amendments/those-who-didnt-sign-the-constitution/

9. U.S. National Archives and Records Administration, "Garrison's Constitution: The Covenant with Death and How It Was Made," https://www.archives.gov/publications/prologue/2000/winter/garrisons-constitution-1.html

10. Morton Grodzins, *The American System: A New View of Government in the United States* (Chicago: Rand McNally, 1966), 25–41.

11. "New Deal," History.com, October 29, 2009, https://www.history.com/topics/great-depression/new-deal

12. *West Coast Hotel Company v. Parrish*, 300 U.S. 379 (1937).

13. Daniel E. Ho and Kevin M. Quinn, "Did a Switch in Time Save Nine?" *Journal of Legal History* 2, no. 1 (2010): 69–113.

14. "Roosevelt Announces 'Court-Packing' Plan," This Day in History: February 5, 1937, History.com, February 9, 2010, https://www.history.com/this-day-in-history/roosevelt-announces-court-packing-plan; and Federal Judicial Center, "FDR's 'Court-Packing' Plan (February 5, 1937)," https://www.fjc.gov/history/timeline/fdrs-court-packing-plan

15. Anne Stauffer, Justin Theal, and Brakeyshia Samms, "Federal Funds Hover at a Third of State Revenue," Pew Charitable Trusts, October 8, 2019, https://www.pewtrusts.org/en/research-and-analysis/articles/2019/10/08/federal-funds-hover-at-a-third-of-state-revenue

16. National Conference of State Legislatures, "NCSL Fiscal Brief: State Balanced Budget Provisions," October 2010, http://www.ncsl.org/research/fiscal-policy/state-balanced-budget-requirements-provisions-and.aspx. It should be noted that Vermonters expect that the state budget will be balanced by the legislature and governor nevertheless.

17. "Americans Are Poorly Informed about Basic Constitutional Provisions," University of Pennsylvania, Annenberg Public Policy Center, September 12, 2017, https://www.annenbergpublicpolicycenter.org/americans-are-poorly-informed-about-basic-constitutional-provisions/

18. Sandra Day O'Connor and Lee H. Hamilton, "A Democracy without Civics?" *Christian Science Monitor*, September 18, 2008, https://www.csmonitor.com/Commentary/Opinion/2008/0918/p09s01-coop.html

19. Franklin's speech was read by James Wilson. Farrand, *Records of the Federal Convention of 1787*, 2: 641–43.

20. Oliver Wendell Holmes, "The Path of the Law," *Harvard Law Review* 10, no. 8 (1897): 469.

CHAPTER 2

1. Gerald Rosenberg, "Much Ado about Nothing? The Emptiness of Rights' Claims in the Twenty-First Century United States," *Studies in Law, Politics, and Society* 48 (Special Issue) (2009): 1–41.

2. Cornell University Law School, Legal Information Institute, "Second Amendment," https://www.law.cornell.edu/wex/second_amendment

3. *Schenck v. United States*, 249 U.S. 47 (1919).

4. U.S. National Archives and Records Administration, "Pennsylvania Assembly: Reply to the Governor, 11 November 1755," *Founders Online*, https://founders.archives.gov/documents/Franklin/01-06-02-0107

5. History.com, "Patriot Act," History.com, December 19, 2017, https://www.history.com/topics/21st-century/patriot-act

6. *Plessy v. Ferguson*, 163 U.S. 537 (1896).

7. Brian L. Fife, *Desegregation in American Schools: Comparative Intervention Strategies* (New York: Praeger, 1992).

8. Brian L. Fife, "The Supreme Court and School Desegregation since 1896," *Equity and Excellence in Education* 29, no. 2 (1996): 46–55.

9. *Milliken v. Bradley*, 418 U.S. 717 (1974).

10. Martin Luther King Jr., "I Have a Dream," Speech, August 28, 1963, Washington, DC. See Gilder Lehrman Institute of American History, https://www.gilderlehrman.org/sites/default/files/inline-pdfs/king.dreamspeech.excerpts.pdf

11. Christopher Klein, "The State Where Women Voted Long before the 19th Amendment," History.com, August 26, 2015, https://www.history.com/news/the-state-where-women-voted-long-before-the-19th-amendment; and National Constitution Center, "Centuries of Citizenship: A Constitutional Timeline," n.d. [2018], https://constitutioncenter.org/timeline/html/cw08_12159.html

12. *Bradwell v. Illinois*, 83 U.S. 130 (1873).

13. U.S. Department of Labor, Bureau of Labor Statistics, "Highlights of Women's Earnings in 2017," https://www.bls.gov/opub/reports/womens-earnings/2017/home.htm

14. U.S. National Park Service, "Stonewall National Monument," https://www.nps.gov/places/stonewall-national-monument.htm

15. "Trail of Tears," History.com, November 9, 2009, https://www.history.com/topics/native-american-history/trail-of-tears

16. "Congress Enacts the Indian Citizenship Act," This Day in History: June 2, 1924, History.com, February 9, 2010, https://www.history.com/this-day-in-history/the-indian-citizenship-act

17. "Chinese Exclusion Act," History.com, August 24, 2018, https://www.history.com/topics/immigration/chinese-exclusion-act-1882

18. "FDR Orders Japanese Americans into Internment Camps," This Day in History: February 19, 1942, History.com, https://www.history.com/this-day-in-history/roosevelt-signs-executive-order-9066

19. Samuel D. Warren and Louis D. Brandeis, "The Right to Privacy," *Harvard Law Review* 4, no. 5 (1890): 193–220.

20. *Grutter v. Bollinger*, 539 U.S. 306 (2003).

21. Jane A. Grant, *The New American Social Compact: Rights and Responsibilities in the Twenty-First Century* (Lanham, MD: Rowman & Littlefield, 2008), 155.

22. Tocqueville, *Democracy in America*, 482–84.

23. Robert N. Bellah, Richard Madsen, William M. Sullivan, Ann Swidler, and Steven M. Tipton, *Habits of the Heart: Individualism and Commitment in American Life* (Berkeley: University of California Press, 1985); Robert D. Putnam, "Bowling Alone: America's Declining Social Capital," *Journal of Democracy* 6, no. 1 (1995): 65–78; Robert D. Putnam, *Bowling Alone: The Collapse and Revival of American Community* (New York: Simon & Schuster, 2000); and William E. Hudson, *American Democracy in Peril: Eight Challenges to America's Future*, 8th ed. (Thousand Oaks, CA: CQ Press, 2017).

24. Brian L. Fife, *Winning the War on Poverty: Applying the Lessons of History to the Present* (Santa Barbara, CA: Praeger, 2018), 115–49.

25. Helena Silverstein, *Unleashing Rights: Law, Meaning, and the Animal Rights Movement* (Ann Arbor: University of Michigan Press, 1996), 17.

26. Jeffrey M. Jones, "U.S. Preference for Stricter Gun Laws Highest since 1993," Gallup, March 14, 2018, https://news.gallup.com/poll/229562/preference-stricter-gun-laws-highest-1993.aspx

27. *Texas v. Johnson*, 491 U.S. 397 (1989).

28. *Texas v. Johnson* (1989).

29. *Texas v. Johnson* (1989).

30. *Texas v. Johnson* (1989).

31. Scott Bomboy, "Justice Antonin Scalia Rails again about Flag-Burning 'Weir-does,'" National Constitution Center, August 28, 2019, https://constitutioncenter. org/blog/justice-antonin-scalia-rails-again-about-flag-burning-weirdoes/

CHAPTER 3

1. Gallup Poll, "Confidence in Institutions," n.d., https://news.gallup.com/ poll/1597/confidence-institutions.aspx

2. Gallup Poll, "Confidence in Institutions." Results tabulated by author based on the Gallup Poll data.

3. Brian L. Fife, *Reforming the Electoral Process in America: Toward More Democracy in the 21st Century* (Santa Barbara, CA: Praeger, 2010), 31.

4. African American Registry, "February 8, 1898: 'Grandfather Clause' Enacted," https://aaregistry.org/story/grandfather-clause-enacted

5. *Guinn v. United States*, 238 U.S. 347 (1915).

6. "Literacy Tests and the Right to Vote," Connecticut History.org, https://con necticuthistory.org/literacy-tests-and-the-right-to-vote

7. "Voting Rights Act of 1965," History.com, November 9, 2009, https://www.his tory.com/topics/black-history/voting-rights-act

8. "Poll Taxes," Smithsonian Institution, National Museum of American History, http://americanhistory.si.edu/democracy-exhibition/vote-voice/keeping-vote/ state-rules-federal-rules/poll-taxes

9. *Harper v. Virginia Board of Elections*, 383 U.S. 663 (1966).

10. "Smith v. Allwright: White Primaries," *Texas Politics Project*, http://texaspolitics. utexas.edu/archive/html/vce/features/0503_01/smith.html

11. *Smith v. Allwright*, 321 U.S. 649 (1944).

12. "Ku Klux Klan," History.com, October 29, 2009, https://www.history.com/ topics/reconstruction/ku-klux-klan

13. Christopher Klein, "The State Where Women Voted Long before the 19th Amendment," History.com, https://www.history.com/news/the-state-where-women-voted-long-before-the-19th-amendment

14. U.S. National Archives and Record Administration, "Electoral College," https://www.archives.gov/federal-register/electoral-college/roles.html

15. Federal Election Commission, "Contribution Limits for 2019–2020," https:// www.fec.gov/resources/cms-content/documents/contribution_limits_chart_2019-2020.pdf

16. Federal Election Commission, "Making Independent Expenditures," https:// www.fec.gov/help-candidates-and-committees/making-independent-expenditures/

17. "*Citizens United v. FEC*," History.com, March 26, 2018, https://www.history. com/topics/united-states-constitution/citizens-united

18. PEW Charitable Trusts, "Why Are Millions of Citizens Not Registered to Vote?" https://www.pewtrusts.org/en/research-and-analysis/issue-briefs/2017/06/ why-are-millions-of-citizens-not-registered-to-vote

19. National Conference of State Legislatures, "Same Day Voter Registration,"

October 2010, http://www.ncsl.org/research/elections-and-campaigns/same-day-registration.aspx#_Toc522006760

20. New England Historical Society, "The First Town Meeting Still Going in Six States," http://www.newenglandhistoricalsociety.com/oldest-town-meeting-6-states

21. "Laws Governing Recall," Ballotpedia, n.d. [2019], https://ballotpedia.org/Laws_governing_recall

22. "States with Initiative or Referendum," Ballotpedia, 2019, https://ballotpedia.org/States_with_initiative_or_referendum

23. National Conference of State Legislatures, "Initiative, Referendum, and Recall," September 20, 2012, http://ncsl.org/research/elections-and-campaigns/initiative-referendum-and-recall-overview.aspx

24. Fife, *Winning the War on Poverty*, 174.

25. U.S. Department of Homeland Security, U.S. Citizenship and Immigration Services, "Citizenship Rights and Responsibilities," https://www.uscis.gov/citizenship/learners/citizenship-rights-and-responsibilities

26. *Palm Beach County Canvassing Board v. Harris*, 772 So. 2d 1220 (Fla. 2000).

27. Brennan Center for Justice, New York University Law School, "New Voting Restrictions in America," October 1, 2019, https://www.brennancenter.org/new-voting-restrictions-america

28. Aaron Blake, "A New Study Suggests Fake News Might Have Won Donald Trump the 2016 Election," *Washington Post*, April 3, 2018, https://www.washingtonpost.com/news/the-fix/wp/2018/04/03/a-new-study-suggests-fake-news-might-have-won-donald-trump-the-2016-election/

CHAPTER 4

1. Thomas Jefferson-Monticello, "Extract from Thomas Jefferson to Edward Carrington," http://tjrs.monticello.org/letter/1289

2. "Trump Tags US Media as Nation's 'Biggest Enemy' after Summit," Associated Press, https://apnews.com/f9614436c6364903af7f513ab72f8ddf

3. Megan Brenan, "Nurses Keep Healthy Lead as Most Honest, Ethical Profession," Gallup, December 26, 2017, https://news.gallup.com/poll/224639/nurses-keep-healthy-lead-honest-ethical-profession.aspx

4. "American Newspapers, 1800–1860: City Newspapers," University of Illinois, https://www.library.illinois.edu/hpnl/tutorials/antebellum-newspapers-city/

5. Samuel Finley Breese Morse, *First Telegraphic Message—May 24, 1844*, Library of Congress, https://www.loc.gov/item/mmorse000107

6. Daniel Walker Howe, "What Hath God Wrought," *American Heritage* 59, no. 4 (2010), https://www.americanheritage.com/what-hath-god-wrought

7. Avalon Project: Documents in Law, History and Diplomacy, "The Federalist Papers: No. 10," November 23, 1787, http://avalon.law.yale.edu/18th_century/fed10.asp

8. Tocqueville, *Democracy in America*, 492.

9. Frank Newport, "75 Years Ago, the First Gallup Poll," Gallup, https://news.gallup.com/opinion/polling-matters/169682/years-ago-first-gallup-poll.aspx

10. U.S. Elections Project, "Voter Turnout," http://www.electproject.org/home/voter-turnout

11. Elizabeth Nix, "'Dewey Defeats Truman': The Election Upset behind the Photo," History.com, https://www.history.com/news/dewey-defeats-truman-election-headline-gaffe

12. Steve Crabtree, "Gallup Brain: Strom Thurmond and the 1948 Election," Gallup, December 17, 2002, https://news.gallup.com/poll/7444/gallup-brain-strom-thurmond-1948-election.aspx

13. Warren J. Mitofsky, "Was 1996 a Worse Year for Polls Than 1948?" *Public Opinion Quarterly* 62, no. 2 (1998): 230–49.

14. Avalon Project: Documents in Law, History and Diplomacy, "The Federalist Papers: No. 51," February 8, 1788, http://avalon.law.yale.edu/18th_century/fed51.asp

15. Kay Lehman Schlozman, "Vox Populi: Public Opinion and the Democratic Dilemma, June 1, 2003," Brookings, June 1, 2003, https://www.brookings.edu/articles/vox-populi-public-opinion-and-the-democratic-dilemma/

16. Fife, *Winning the War on Poverty*, 190–91.

17. Louis C. Gawthrop, *Public Service and Democracy: Ethical Imperatives for the 21st Century* (New York: Chatham House, 1998), 102–23.

18. Richard K. Laird, *The Politics of Knowledge: When Loyalty Minimizes Learning* (Lanham, MD: Lexington Books, 2019).

CHAPTER 5

1. Avalon Project: Documents in Law, History and Diplomacy, "The Federalist Papers: No. 52," February 8, 1788, http://avalon.law.yale.edu/18th_century/fed52.asp

2. U.S. House of Representatives, "History of the House," https://www.house.gov/the-house-explained/history-of-the-house

3. U.S. House of Representatives, "Committees," https://www.house.gov/committees; and U.S. Senate, "Committees," https://www.senate.gov/committees/index.htm

4. U.S. House of Representatives, "The House Explained," https://www.house.gov/the-house-explained

5. U.S. House of Representatives, "The Permanent Apportionment Act of 1929," https://history.house.gov/Historical-Highlights/1901-1950/The-Permanent-Apportionment-Act-of-1929/

6. U.S. House of Representatives, "List of Speakers of the House," https://history.house.gov/People/Office/Speakers-List/

7. U.S. House of Representatives, "Majority Leaders of the House (1899 to present)," https://history.house.gov/People/Office/Majority-Leaders/

8. U.S. House of Representatives, "Minority Leaders of the House (1899 to present)," https://history.house.gov/People/Office/Minority-Leaders/

9. U.S. House of Representatives, "Democratic Whips (1899 to Present)," https://history.house.gov/People/Office/Democratic-Whips/

10. U.S. House of Representatives, "Republican Whips (1897 to Present)," https://history.house.gov/People/Office/Republican-Whips/

11. U.S. House of Representatives, "Democratic Whips (1899 to Present)."

12. U.S. Senate, "The President of the Senate's Role in the Legislative Process," https://www.senate.gov/general/Features/Part_1_VP.htm

13. U.S. Senate, "President Pro Tempore," https://www.senate.gov/reference/Index/President_Pro_Tempore.htm

14. U.S. Senate, "Majority and Minority Leaders," https://www.senate.gov/artandhistory/history/common/briefing/Majority_Minority_Leaders.htm

15. U.S. Senate, "Filibuster and Cloture," https://www.senate.gov/artandhistory/history/common/briefing/Filibuster_Cloture.htm

16. U.S. Senate, "Filibuster and Cloture."

17. "Government 101: How a Bill Becomes Law," *Vote Smart*, https://votesmart.org/education/how-a-bill-becomes-law#.XO2d-IhKiM8

18. "Government 101: How a Bill Becomes Law."

19. "Government 101: How a Bill Becomes Law."

20. "Government 101: How a Bill Becomes Law."

21. Avalon Project: Documents in Law, History and Diplomacy, "The Federalist Papers: No. 51," http://avalon.law.yale.edu/18th_century/fed51.asp

22. Avalon Project: Documents in Law, History and Diplomacy, "The Federalist Papers: No. 51."

23. Gallup Poll, "Congress and the Public," Gallup, n.d., https://news.gallup.com/poll/1600/congress-public.aspx

24. Clifford Krauss, "The House Bank; Committee Names All Who Overdrew at the House Bank," *New York Times*, April 17, 1992, https://www.nytimes.com/1992/04/17/us/the-house-bank-committee-names-all-who-overdrew-at-the-house-bank.html

25. *U.S. Term Limits, Inc. v. Thornton*, 514 U.S. 779 (1995).

26. E. E. Schattschneider, *Party Government* (1942; New Brunswick, NJ: Transaction, 2009), 1.

CHAPTER 6

1. Brian L. Fife, *Reforming the Electoral Process in America: Toward More Democracy in the 21st Century* (Santa Barbara, CA: Praeger, 2010), 71–85.

2. Avalon Project: Documents in Law, History and Diplomacy, "The Federalist Papers: No. 69," March 14, 1788, https://avalon.law.yale.edu/18th_century/fed69.asp

3. Avalon Project: Documents in Law, History and Diplomacy, "The Federalist Papers: No. 70," March 18, 1788, https://avalon.law.yale.edu/18th_century/fed70.asp

4. Richard E. Neustadt, *Presidential Power and the Modern Presidents: The Politics of Leadership from Roosevelt to Reagan* (New York: Free Press, 1980).

5. Sarah Pruitt, "Fast Facts on the 'First 100 Days,'" History.com, April 27, 2017, https://www.history.com/news/fast-facts-on-the-first-100-days

6. "Past Attempts at Reform," Fairvote.org, https://www.fairvote.org/past_attempts_at_reform

7. Robert A. Dahl, *How Democratic Is the American Constitution?* 2nd ed. (New Haven: Yale University Press, 2003), 74.

8. "Why Do We Still Let the Electoral College Pick Our President?" *Stanford News*, August 20, 2012, https://news.stanford.edu/2012/08/20/rakove-electoral-col lege-082012/; and F. H. Buckley, "The Efficient Secret: How America Nearly Adopted a Parliamentary System, and Why It Should Have Done So," *British Journal of American Legal Studies* 1 (2012): 386.

9. U.S. Census Bureau, "History: 1790 Overview," https://www.census.gov/his tory/www/through_the_decades/overview/1790.html

10. Congressional Research Service, *History of Civil Service Merit Systems of the U.S. and Selected Foreign Countries* (Washington, DC: U.S. Government Printing Office, December 31, 1976).

11. Congressional Budget Office, *The Federal Work Force: Its Size, Cost, and Activities* (Washington, DC: Government Printing Office, March, 1977).

12. Public Law 76-19, "Reorganization Act of 1939," April 3, 1939, https://www.loc. gov/law/help/statutes-at-large/76th-congress/session-1/c76s1ch36.pdf

13. American Presidency Project, "Executive Order 8248: Reorganizing the Executive Office of the President," https://www.presidency.ucsb.edu/documents/ executive-order-8248-reorganizing-the-executive-office-the-president

14. "Report of the President's Committee on Administrative Management (The Brownlow Committee Report, 1937)," Teaching American History.org, https://teach ingamericanhistory.org/library/document/report-of-the-presidents-committee-on-administrative-management-the-brownlow-committee-report/

15. President's Committee on Administrative Management, *Report of the President's Committee on Administrative Management* (Washington, DC: Government Printing Office, 1937), 5.

16. "Presidential Historians Survey: 2017," C-SPAN, https://www.c-span.org/ presidentsurvey2017/

17. Congressional Research Service, "Federal Workforce Statistics Sources: OPM and OMB," March 25, 2020, https://crsreports.congress.gov/product/pdf/R/ R43590

18. Avalon Project: Documents in Law, History and Diplomacy, "The Federalist Papers: No. 68," March 14, 1788, http://avalon.law.yale.edu/18th_century/fed68. asp

19. Thomas Calder, "Asheville Archives: President Theodore Roosevelt Arrives in the Mountains," *Mountain Xpress*, September 18, 2018, https://mountainx.com/ news/asheville-archives-president-theodore-roosevelt-arrives-in-the-mountains/

20. Calder, "Asheville Archives: President Theodore Roosevelt Arrives in the Mountains."

21. Theodore Roosevelt, *Theodore Roosevelt: An Autobiography* (New York: Macmil lan, 1913), 371–72.

CHAPTER 7

1. Avalon Project: Documents in Law, History and Diplomacy, "The Federalist Papers: No. 78," May 28, 1788, http://avalon.law.yale.edu/18th_century/fed78.asp

2. U.S. Supreme Court, "Building History," https://www.supremecourt.gov/ about/buildinghistory.aspx

3. Federal Judicial Center, "Landmark Legislation: The Judges' Bill," https://www.fjc.gov/history/legislation/landmark-legislation-judges-bill-0

4. Avalon Project: Documents in Law, History and Diplomacy, "The Federalist Papers: No. 78."

5. *Marbury v. Madison*, 5 U.S. 137 (1803).

6. Federal Judicial Center, "Landmark Legislation: Judiciary Act of 1801," https://www.fjc.gov/history/legislation/landmark-legislation-judiciary-act-1801

7. Federal Judicial Center, "Landmark Legislation: Judiciary Act of 1801."

8. *Marbury v. Madison* (1803).

9. *Marbury v. Madison* (1803).

10. Avalon Project: Documents in Law, History and Diplomacy, "The Judiciary Act: September 24, 1789," https://avalon.law.yale.edu/18th_century/judiciary_act.asp

11. Elizabeth Nix, "7 Things You Might Not Know about the U.S. Supreme Court," History.com, October 8, 2013, https://www.history.com/news/7-things-you-might-not-know-about-the-u-s-supreme-court

12. Federal Judicial Center, "Circuit Riding (September 24, 1789)," https://www.fjc.gov/history/timeline/circuit-riding

13. U.S. Courts, "The Evarts Act: Creating Modern Appellate Courts," https://www.uscourts.gov/educational-resources/educational-activities/evarts-act-creating-modern-appellate-courts

14. U.S. Department of Justice, "Introduction to the Federal Court System," https://www.justice.gov/usao/justice-101/federal-courts; and U.S. Courts, "Authorized Judgeships," https://www.uscourts.gov/judges-judgeships/authorized-judgeships

15. Thurgood Marshall, "Reflections on the Bicentennial of the United States Constitution," *Harvard Law Review* 101, no. 1 (1987): 1–5.

16. Brennan Center for Justice, "Promote Fair Courts," 2019, https://www.brennancenter.org/issues/fair-courts

17. "Supreme Court Survey 2018," C-SPAN/PSB, August 2018, https://www.c-span.org/scotussurvey2018/

18. Avalon Project: Documents in Law, History and Diplomacy, "The Federalist Papers: No. 78."

19. Holmes, "Path of the Law," 457–78.

20. "Merrick Garland," Ballotpedia, 2019, https://ballotpedia.org/Merrick_Garland

21. Ted Barrett, "In Reversal from 2016, McConnell Says He Would Fill a Potential Supreme Court Vacancy in 2020," CNN.com, May 29, 2019, https://www.cnn.com/2019/05/28/politics/mitch-mcconnell-supreme-court-2020/index.html

22. Colby Itkowitz, "Sen. Klobuchar: Democrats Shouldn't Have Gone 'Nuclear' on Judicial Nominees," *Washington Post*, September 2, 2018, https://www.washingtonpost.com/politics/2018/09/02/sen-klobuchar-democrats-shouldnt-have-gone-nuclear-judicial-nominees/?utm_term=.c3f911bbef2e

23. Jane C. Timm, "McConnell Went 'Nuclear' to Confirm Gorsuch, but Democrats Changed Filibuster Rules First," NBC News, June 28, 2018, https://www.nbcnews.com/politics/donald-trump/mcconnell-went-nuclear-confirm-gorsuch-democrats-changed-senate-filibuster-rules-n887271

24. Gallup Poll, "Supreme Court," Gallup, September 4, 2019, https://news.gal lup.com/poll/4732/supreme-court.aspx

CHAPTER 8

1. Garry D. Brewer and Peter deLeon, *The Foundations of Policy Analysis* (Home-wood, IL: Dorsey Press, 1983); and Christopher M. Weible, Tanya Heikkila, Peter deLeon, and Paul A. Sabatier, "Understanding and Influencing the Policy Process," *Policy Sciences* 4, no. 1 (2012): 1–21.

2. Theda Skocpol, *Protecting Soldiers and Mothers: The Political Origins of Social Policy in the United States* (Cambridge, MA: Harvard University Press, 1992).

3. "Great Depression History," History.com, October 29, 2009, https://www.his tory.com/topics/great-depression/great-depression-history

4. Pruitt, "Fast Facts on the 'First 100 Days.'"

5. Fife, *Winning the War on Poverty*, 40–83.

6. Public Law 89-97, "Social Security Amendments of 1965," July 30, 1965, https:// www.govinfo.gov/content/pkg/STATUTE-79/pdf/STATUTE-79-Pg286.pdf

7. U.S. Department of Health and Human Services, "2020 Poverty Guidelines," https://aspe.hhs.gov/2020-poverty-guidelines

8. C. R., "A Keynes for All Seasons: Keynes Was Much More Empirical in His Think-ing Than Even Keynesian Economists Are Willing to Admit," *The Economist*, Novem-ber 6, 2013, https://www.economist.com/free-exchange/2013/11/26/a-keynes-for-all-seasons

9. Avalon Project: Documents in Law, History and Diplomacy, "Washington's Farewell Address: 1796," https://avalon.law.yale.edu/18th_century/washing.asp

10. American Presidency Project, "George Bush: Address Before a Joint Session of the Congress on the Persian Gulf Crisis and the Federal Budget Deficit, September 11, 1990," https://www.presidency.ucsb.edu/documents/address-before-joint-session-the-congress-the-persian-gulf-crisis-and-the-federal-budget

11. Social Security Administration, "OASDI and SSI Program Rates & Limits, 2020," https://www.ssa.gov/policy/docs/quickfacts/prog_highlights/RatesLimits2020.html

12. Office of Management and Budget, "Historical Tables," https://www.white house.gov/omb/historical-tables/

13. U.S. Department of Treasury, Bureau of the Fiscal Service, "The Debt to the Penny and Who Holds It," https://treasurydirect.gov/NP/debt/current

14. Peter G. Peterson Foundation, "Spending," https://www.pgpf.org/ finding-solutions/understanding-the-budget/spending

15. Center for Education Reform, "Laws and Legislation," https://edreform. com/issues/choice-charter-schools/laws-legislation

16. U.S. Census Bureau, "Current Population," https://www.census.gov/pop clock/print.php?component=counter

17. Avalon Project: Documents in Law, History and Diplomacy, "Military-Industrial Complex Speech, Dwight D. Eisenhower, 1961," https://avalon.law.yale.edu/20th_century/eisenhower001.asp

18. "Use It and Lose It: The Outsize Effect of U.S. Consumption on the Environ-

ment," *Scientific American,* September 14, 2012, https://www.scientificamerican.com/article/american-consumption-habits/

19. Fife, *Winning the War on Poverty,* 84–114.

EPILOGUE

1. "Seneca Falls Convention," History.com, November 10, 2017, https://www.history.com/topics/womens-rights/seneca-falls-convention; and National Park Service, "The First Women's Rights Convention," Lucretia Mott, Harriet Cady Eaton, Margaret Pryor, Elizabeth Cady Stanton, et al., https://www.nps.gov/wori/historyculture/the-first-womens-rights-convention.htm

2. National Park Service, "First Women's Rights Convention."

3. For an excellent biography of Elizabeth Cady Stanton, see Elisabeth Griffith, *In Her Own Right: The Life of Elizabeth Cady Stanton* (New York: Oxford University Press, 1984).

4. "Seneca Falls Convention."

5. National Park Service, "Declaration of Sentiments," https://www.nps.gov/wori/learn/historyculture/declaration-of-sentiments.htm (updated February 26, 2015).

6. Hudson, *American Democracy in Peril;* and Laird, *Politics of Knowledge.*

Bibliography

Following this list of general sources are sections on Primary Documents Consulted, U.S. Government Sources, and Legal Cases.

African American Registry. "February 8, 1898: 'Grandfather Clause' Enacted." https://aaregistry.org/story/grandfather-clause-enacted
"American Newspapers, 1800–1860: City Newspapers." University of Illinois. https://www.library.illinois.edu/hpnl/tutorials/antebellum-newspapers-city/
"Americans Are Poorly Informed about Basic Constitutional Provisions." University of Pennsylvania, Annenberg Public Policy Center, September 12, 2017. https://www.annenbergpublicpolicycenter.org/americans-are-poorly-informed-about-basic-constitutional-provisions/
Barrett, Ted. "In Reversal from 2016, McConnell Says He Would Fill a Potential Supreme Court Vacancy in 2020." CNN.com, May 29, 2019. https://www.cnn.com/2019/05/28/politics/mitch-mcconnell-supreme-court-2020/index.html
Bellah, Robert N., Richard Madsen, William M. Sullivan, Ann Swidler, and Steven M. Tipton. *Habits of the Heart: Individualism and Commitment in American Life.* Berkeley: University of California Press, 1985.
Bilder, Mary Sarah. *Madison's Hand: Revising the Constitutional Convention.* Cambridge, MA: Harvard University Press, 2015.
Blake, Aaron. "A New Study Suggests Fake News Might Have Won Donald Trump the 2016 Election." *Washington Post,* April 3, 2018. https://www.washingtonpost.com/news/the-fix/wp/2018/04/03/a-new-study-suggests-fake-news-might-have-won-donald-trump-the-2016-election/
Bomboy, Scott. "Justice Antonin Scalia Rails again about Flag-Burning 'Weirdoes.'" National Constitution Center, August 28, 2019. https://constitutioncenter.org/blog/justice-antonin-scalia-rails-again-about-flag-burning-weirdoes/
Brenan, Megan. "Nurses Keep Healthy Lead as Most Honest, Ethical Profession."

Gallup, December 26, 2017. https://news.gallup.com/poll/224639/nurses-keep-healthy-lead-honest-ethical-profession.aspx

Brennan Center for Justice, New York University Law School. "Promote Fair Courts." 2019. https://www.brennancenter.org/issues/fair-courts

Brennan Center for Justice, New York University Law School. "New Voting Restrictions in America." October 1, 2019. https://www.brennancenter.org/new-voting-restrictions-america

Brewer, Garry D., and Peter deLeon. *The Foundations of Policy Analysis*. Homewood, IL: Dorsey Press, 1983.

Buckley, F. H. "The Efficient Secret: How America Nearly Adopted a Parliamentary System, and Why It Should Have Done So." *British Journal of American Legal Studies* 1 (2012): 349–410.

C. R. "A Keynes for All Seasons: Keynes Was Much More Empirical in His Thinking Than Even Keynesian Economists Are Willing to Admit." *The Economist*, November 26, 2013. https://www.economist.com/free-exchange/2013/11/26/a-keynes-for-all-seasons

Calder, Thomas. "Asheville Archives: President Theodore Roosevelt Arrives in the Mountains." *Mountain Xpress*, September 18, 2018. https://mountainx.com/news/asheville-archives-president-theodore-roosevelt-arrives-in-the-mountains/

Caltech/MIT Voting Technology Project. "Reports." https://www.vote.caltech.edu/reports

Center for Civic Education. "Constitutional Democracy." http://www.civiced.org/lesson-plans/constitutional-democracy

Center for Education Reform. "Laws and Legislation." https://edreform.com/issues/choice-charter-schools/laws-legislation/

"Charles E. Merriam: Political Science, 1874–1953." University of Chicago Library. https://www.lib.uchicago.edu/projects/centcat/fac/facch15_01.html

"Chinese Exclusion Act." History.com, August 24, 2018. https://www.history.com/topics/immigration/chinese-exclusion-act-1882

"*Citizens United v. FEC*." History.com, March 26, 2018. https://www.history.com/topics/united-states-constitution/citizens-united

"Civics Knowledge Predicts Willingness to Protect Supreme Court." University of Pennsylvania, Annenberg Public Policy Center, September 13, 2018. https://annenbergpublicpolicycenter.org/civics-knowledge-survey-willingness-protect-supreme-court

"Congress Enacts the Indian Citizenship Act." This Day in History: June 2, 1924. History.com, February 9, 2010. https://www.history.com/this-day-in-history/the-indian-citizenship-act

Cornell University Law School, Legal Information Institute. "Second Amendment." https://www.law.cornell.edu/wex/second_amendment

Crabtree, Steve. "Gallup Brain: Strom Thurmond and the 1948 Election." Gallup, December 17, 2002. https://news.gallup.com/poll/7444/gallup-brain-strom-thurmond-1948-election.aspx

Dahl, Robert A. *How Democratic Is the American Constitution?* 2nd ed. New Haven: Yale University Press, 2003.

"The Delegates Who Didn't Sign the U.S. Constitution." ConstitutionFacts.com. https://www.constitutionfacts.com/us-constitution-amendments/those-who-didnt-sign-the-constitution

"The Duties of American Citizenship." Yale University, Gilder Lehrman Center for the Study of Slavery, Resistance, and Abolition. https://glc.yale.edu/duties-american-citizenship

Farrand, Max. *The Records of the Federal Convention of 1787*, 3 vols. New Haven: Yale University Press, 1911.

"FDR Orders Japanese Americans into Internment Camps." This Day in History: February 19, 1942. History.com, November 16, 2009. https://www.history.com/this-day-in-history/roosevelt-signs-executive-order-9066

Fife, Brian L. *Desegregation in American Schools: Comparative Intervention Strategies.* New York: Praeger, 1992.

Fife, Brian L. *Reforming the Electoral Process in America: Toward More Democracy in the 21st Century.* Santa Barbara, CA: Praeger, 2010.

Fife, Brian L. "The Supreme Court and School Desegregation since 1896." *Equity and Excellence in Education* 29, no. 2 (1992): 46–55.

Fife, Brian L. *Winning the War on Poverty: Applying the Lessons of History to the Present.* Santa Barbara, CA: Praeger, 2018.

Gallup Poll. "Confidence in Institutions." Gallup, n.d. https://news.gallup.com/poll/1597/confidence-institutions.aspx

Gallup Poll. "Congress and the Public." Gallup, n.d. https://news.gallup.com/poll/1600/congress-public.aspx

Gallup Poll. "Presidential Approval Ratings—Gallup Historical Statistics and Trends." Gallup, n.d. https://news.gallup.com/poll/116677/presidential-approval-ratings-gallup-historical-statistics-trends.aspx

Gallup Poll. "Satisfaction with the United States." Gallup, n.d. https://news.gallup.com/poll/1669/general-mood-country.aspx

Gallup Poll. "Supreme Court." Gallup, n.d. https://news.gallup.com/poll/4732/supreme-court.aspx

Gawthrop, Louis C. *Public Service and Democracy: Ethical Imperatives for the 21st Century.* New York: Chatham House, 1998.

"Government 101: How a Bill Becomes a Law." *Vote Smart.* https://votesmart.org/education/how-a-bill-becomes-law#.XO2d-IhKiM8

Grant, Jane A. *The New American Social Compact: Rights and Responsibilities in the Twenty-First Century.* Lanham, MD: Rowman & Littlefield, 2008.

"Great Depression History." History.com, October 29, 2009. https://www.history.com/topics/great-depression/great-depression-history

Griffith, Elisabeth. *In Her Own Right: The Life of Elizabeth Cady Stanton.* New York: Oxford University Press, 1984.

Grodzins, Morton. *The American System: A New View of Government in the United States.* Chicago: Rand McNally, 1966.

"Gross Domestic Product, 2018." World Bank. https://databank.worldbank.org/data/download/GDP.pdf

"Guide to the Charles E. Merriam Papers, 1893–1957." University of Chicago Library. https://www.lib.uchicago.edu/e/scrc/findingaids/view.php?eadid=ICU.SPCL.MERRIAMCE

Ho, Daniel E., and Kevin M. Quinn. "Did a Switch in Time Save Nine?" *Journal of Legal History* 2, no. 1 (2010): 69–113.

Hochschild, Jennifer L., and Katherine Levine Einstein. "Do Facts Matter? Information and Misinformation in American Politics." *Political Science Quarterly* 130, no. 4 (2016): 585–624.

Hochschild, Jennifer L., and Katherine Levine Einstein. *Do Facts Matter? Information and Misinformation in American Politics.* Norman: University of Oklahoma Press, 2015.

Holmes, Oliver Wendell. "The Path of the Law." *Harvard Law Review* 10, no. 8 (1897): 457–78.

Howe, Daniel Walker. "What Hath God Wrought." *American Heritage* 59, no. 4 (2010). https://www.americanheritage.com/what-hath-god-wrought

Hudson, William E. *American Democracy in Peril: Eight Challenges to America's Future*, 8th ed. Thousand Oaks, CA: CQ Press, 2017.

Itkowitz, Colby. "Sen. Klobuchar: Democrats Shouldn't Have Gone 'Nuclear' on Judicial Nominees." *Washington Post*, September 2, 2018. https://washingtonpost.com/politics/2018/09/02/sen-klobuchar-democrats-shouldnt-have-gone-nuclear-judicial-nominees/?utm_term=.c3f911bbef2e

Jones, Jeffrey M. "U.S. Preference for Stricter Gun Laws Highest since 1993." Gallup, March 14, 2018. https://news.gallup.com/poll/229562/preference-stricter-gun-laws-highest-1993.aspx

King, Martin Luther, Jr. "I Have a Dream." Speech, August 28, 1963, Washington, DC. Available at Gilder Lehrman Institute of American History, https://www.gilderlehrman.org/sites/default/files/inline-pdfs/king.dreamspeech.excerpts.pdf

Klein, Christopher. "The State Where Women Voted Long before the 19th Amendment." History.com, August 26, 2015. https://www.history.com/news/the-state-where-women-voted-long-before-the-19th-amendment

Kochin, Michael S., and Michael Taylor. *An Independent Empire: Diplomacy and War in the Making of the United States.* Ann Arbor: University of Michigan Press, 2020.

Krauss, Clifford. "The House Bank; Committee Names All Who Overdrew at the House Bank." *New York Times*, April 17, 1992. https://www.nytimes.com/1992/04/17/us/the-house-bank-committee-names-all-who-overdrew-at-the-house-bank.html

"Ku Klux Klan." History.com, October 29, 2009. https://www.history.com/topics/reconstruction/ku-klux-klan

Laird, Richard K. *The Politics of Knowledge: When Loyalty Minimizes Learning.* Lanham, MD: Lexington Books, 2019.

"Laws Governing Recall." Ballotpedia, n.d. https://ballotpedia.org/Laws_governing_recall

"Literacy Tests and the Right to Vote." Connecticut History.org. https://connecticuthistory.org/literacy-tests-and-the-right-to-vote

Manuel, Frank E., and Fritzie P. Manuel. *James Bowdoin and the Patriot Philosophers.* Philadelphia: American Philosophical Society, 2004.

Marshall, Thurgood. "Reflections on the Bicentennial of the United States Constitution." *Harvard Law Review* 101, no. 1 (1987): 1–5.

Merriam, Charles E. *The Making of Citizens: A Comparative Study of Methods of Civic Training.* Chicago: University of Chicago Press, 1931.

"Merrick Garland." Ballotpedia, 2019. https://ballotpedia.org/Merrick_Garland

Mitofsky, Warren J. "Was 1996 a Worse Year for Polls Than 1948?" *Public Opinion Quarterly* 62, no. 2 (1998): 230–49.

National Conference of State Legislatures. "Initiative, Referendum, and Recall." September 20, 2012. http://ncsl.org/research/elections-and-campaigns/initiative-referendum-and-recall-overview.aspx

National Conference of State Legislatures. "NCSL Fiscal Brief: State Balanced Budget Provisions." October 2010. http://www.ncsl.org/research/fiscal-pol icy/state-balanced-budget-requirements-provisions-and.aspx

National Conference of State Legislatures. "Same Day Voter Registration." June 28, 2019. http://www.ncsl.org/research/elections-and-campaigns/same-day-registration.aspx#_Toc522006760

National Conference of State Legislatures. "Voter Registration Deadlines." November 1, 2019. https://www.ncsl.org/research/elections-and-cam paigns/voter-registration-deadlines.aspx

National Constitution Center. "Centuries of Citizenship: A Constitutional Time-line." N.d. https://constitutioncenter.org/timeline/html/cw08_12159.html

National Constitution Center. "On This Day: Congress Officially Creates the U.S. Army." September 29, 2019. https://constitutioncenter.org/blog/on-this-day-congress-officially-creates-the-u-s-army

National Council for the Social Studies. "Creating Effective Citizens: A Position Statement of National Council for the Social Studies." N.d. http://www.socialstudies.org/sites/default/files/publications/se/6505/650511.html

Neustadt, Richard E. *Presidential Power and the Modern Presidents: The Politics of Leadership from Roosevelt to Reagan.* New York: Free Press, 1980.

"New Deal." History.com, October 29, 2009. https://www.history.com/topics/great-depression/new-deal

New England Historical Society, "The First Town Meeting Still Going in Six States," http://www.newenglandhistoricalsociety.com/oldest-town-meeting-6-states

Newport, Frank. "75 Years Ago, the First Gallup Poll." Gallup, October 20, 2010. https://news.gallup.com/opinion/polling-matters/169682/years-ago-first-gallup-poll.aspx

Nix, Elizabeth. "'Dewey Defeats Truman': The Election Upset behind the Photo." History.com, November 1, 2018. https://www.history.com/news/dewey-defeats-truman-election-headline-gaffe

Nix, Elizabeth. "7 Things You Might Not Know about the U.S. Supreme Court." History.com, October 8, 2013. https://www.history.com/news/7-things-you-might-not-know-about-the-u-s-supreme-court

O'Connor, Sandra Day, and Lee H. Hamilton. "A Democracy without Civics?" *Christian Science Monitor,* September 18, 2008. https://www.csmonitor.com/Commentary/Opinion/2008/0918/p09s01-coop.html

"Patriot Act." History.com, December 19, 2017. https://www.history.com/topics/21st-century/patriot-act

"Past Attempts at Reform." Fairvote.org. https://www.fairvote.org/past_attempts _at_reform

Peter G. Peterson Foundation. "Spending." N.d. https://www.pgpf.org/finding-solutions/understanding-the-budget/spending

Pew Charitable Trusts. "Why Are Millions of Citizens Not Registered to Vote?" June 21, 2017. https://www.pewtrusts.org/en/research-and-analysis/issue-briefs/2017/06/why-are-millions-of-citizens-not-registered-to-vote

"Poll Taxes." Smithsonian Institution, National Museum of American History. http://americanhistory.si.edu/democracy-exhibition/vote-voice/keeping-vote/state-rules-federal-rules/poll-taxes

"Presidential Historians Survey: 2017." C-SPAN. https://www.c-span.org/presidentsurvey2017/

President's Committee on Administrative Management. January 1937. *Report of the President's Committee on Administrative Management.* Washington, DC: Government Printing Office, 1937.

Pruitt, Sarah. "Fast Facts on the 'First 100 Days.'" History.com, April 27, 2017. https://www.history.com/news/fast-facts-on-the-first-100-days

Putnam, Robert D. "Bowling Alone: America's Declining Social Capital." *Journal of Democracy* 6, no. 1 (1995): 65–78.

Putnam, Robert D. *Bowling Alone: The Collapse and Revival of American Community.* New York: Simon & Schuster, 2000.

"Report of the President's Committee on Administrative Management (The Brownlow Committee Report, 1937)." Teaching American History.org. https://teachingamericanhistory.org/library/document/report-of-the-presidents-committee-on-administrative-management-the-brownlow-committee-report/

Ricci, David M. *Good Citizenship in America.* New York: Cambridge University Press, 2004.

"Roosevelt Announces 'Court-Packing' Plan." This Day in History: February 5, 1937. History.com, February 9, 2010. https://www.history.com/this-day-in-history/roosevelt-announces-court-packing-plan

Roosevelt, Theodore. "The Duties of American Citizenship." Speech delivered at Buffalo, New York, January 26, 1883. Gilder Lehrman Center for the Study of Slavery, Resistance, and Abolition, Yale University. https://glc.yale.edu/duties-american-citizenship

Roosevelt, Theodore. *Theodore Roosevelt: An Autobiography.* New York: Macmillan, 1913.

Rosenberg, Gerald. "Much Ado about Nothing? The Emptiness of Rights' Claims in the Twenty-First Century United States." *Studies in Law, Politics, and Society* 48 (Special Issue) (2009): 1–41.

Schattschneider, E. E. *Party Government.* New Brunswick, NJ: Transaction, 2009.

Schlozman, Kay Lehman. "Vox Populi: Public Opinion and the Democratic Dilemma." Brookings, June 1, 2003. https://www.brookings.edu/articles/vox-populi-public-opinion-and-the-democratic-dilemma/

"Seneca Falls Convention." History.com, November 10, 2017. https://www.history.com/topics/womens-rights/seneca-falls-convention

Silverstein, Helena. *Unleashing Rights: Law, Meaning, and the Animal Rights Movement.* Ann Arbor: University of Michigan Press, 1996.

Skocpol, Theda. *Protecting Soldiers and Mothers: The Political Origins of Social Policy in the United States.* Cambridge, MA: Harvard University Press, 1992.

Smith, Adam. *The Wealth of Nations*, 2 vols. New York: E. P. Dutton, 1910. First published 1776.

"Smith v. Allwright: White Primaries." *Texas Politics Project*. http://texaspolitics. utexas.edu/archive/html/vce/features/0503_01/smith.html

"States with Initiative or Referendum." Ballotpedia, 2019. https://ballotpedia. org/States_with_initiative_or_referendum

Stauffer, Anne, Justin Theal, and Brakeyshia Samms. "Federal Funds Hover at a Third of State Revenue." Pew Charitable Trusts, October 8, 2019. https:// www.pewtrusts.org/en/research-and-analysis/articles/2019/10/08/ federal-funds-hover-at-a-third-of-state-revenue

"Supreme Court Survey: 2018." C-SPAN/PSB, August 2018. https://www.c-span. org/scotussurvey2018/

Thomas, Ken. "Trump Tags US Media as Nation's 'Biggest Enemy' after Summit." Associated Press, June 13, 2018. https://apnews.com/f9614436c6364903a f7f513ab72f8ddf/Trump-tags-US-media-as-nation's-'biggest-enemy'-after-summit

Thomas Jefferson-Monticello, "Extract from Thomas Jefferson to Edward Carrington." http://tjrs.monticello.org/letter/1289

Timm, Jane C. "McConnell Went 'Nuclear' to Confirm Gorsuch, but Democrats Changed Senate Filibuster First." NBC News, June 28, 2018. https://www. nbcnews.com/politics/donald-trump/mcconnell-went-nuclear-confirm-gor such-democrats-changed-senate-filibuster-rules-n887271

Tocqueville, Alexis de. *Democracy in America*. 1835. Reprint, Chicago: University of Chicago Press, 2000.

"Trail of Tears." History.com, November 9, 2009. https://www.history.com/ topics/native-american-history/trail-of-tears

"Trends in World Military Expenditure, 2018." Stockholm International Peace Research Institute, April 2019. https://www.sipri.org/sites/default/ files/2019-04/fs_1904_milex_2018.pdf

U.S. Elections Project. "Voter Turnout." http://www.electproject.org/home/ voter-turnout

"Use It and Lose It: The Outsize Effect of U.S. Consumption on the Environment." *Scientific American*, September 14, 2012. https://www.scientificameri can.com/article/american-consumption-habits/

"Voting Rights Act of 1965." History.com, November 9, 2009. https://www.his tory.com/topics/black-history/voting-rights-act

Walzer, Michael. "Civility and Civic Virtue in Contemporary America." *Social Research* 41, no. 4 (1974): 593–611.

Warren, Samuel D., and Louis D. Brandeis. "The Right to Privacy." *Harvard Law Review* 4, no. 5 (1890): 193–220.

Weible, Christopher M., Tanya Heikkila, Peter deLeon, and Paul A. Sabatier. "Understanding and Influencing the Policy Press." *Policy Sciences* 45, no. 1 (2012): 1–21.

"Why Do We Still Let the Electoral College Pick Our President?" *Stanford News*, August 20, 2012. https://news.stanford.edu/2012/08/20/ rakove-electoral-college-082012/

INTERNET SOURCES: PRIMARY DOCUMENTS CONSULTED

American Presidency Project

https://www.presidency.ucsb.edu/
"Executive Order 8248: Reorganizing the Executive Office of the President—September 8, 1939."
"George Bush: Address before a Joint Session of the Congress on the Persian Gulf Crisis and the Federal Budget Deficit, September 11, 1990."
"John F. Kennedy: Inaugural Address—January 20, 1961."

Avalon Project: Documents in Law, History, and Diplomacy

https://avalon.law.yale.edu/
The Federalist Papers: No. 10, November 23, 1787.
The Federalist Papers: No. 51, February 8, 1788.
The Federalist Papers: No. 52, February 8, 1788.
The Federalist Papers: No. 68, March 14, 1788.
The Federalist Papers: No. 69, March 14, 1788.
The Federalist Papers: No. 70, March 18, 1788.
The Federalist Papers: No. 78, May 28, 1788.
"The Judiciary Act: September 24, 1789."
"Military-Industrial Complex Speech, Dwight D. Eisenhower, 1961."
"Washington's Farewell Address: 1796."

U.S. GOVERNMENT SOURCES

FEDERAL JUDICIAL CENTER
"Circuit Riding (September 24, 1789)." https://www.fjc.gov/history/timeline/circuit-riding
"FDR's "Court-Packing" Plan (February 5, 1937)." https://www.fjc.gov/history/timeline/fdrs-court-packing-plan
"Landmark Legislation: The Judges' Bill." https://www.fjc.gov/history/legislation/landmark-legislation-judges-bill-0
"Landmark Legislation: Judiciary Act of 1801." https://www.fjc.gov/history/legislation/landmark-legislation-judiciary-act-1801
LIBRARY OF CONGRESS
"The American Revolution, 1763–1783." N.d. https://www.loc.gov/teachers/classroommaterials/presentationsandactivities/presentations/timeline/amrev/
"James Madison and the Federal Constitutional Convention of 1787." N.d. https://www.loc.gov/collections/james-madison-papers/articles-and-essays/james-madison-and-the-federal-constitutional-convention-of-1787
Morse, Samuel Finley Breese. *First Telegraphic Message—May 24, 1844.* Image. https://www.loc.gov/item/mmorse000107
Public Law 76-19. "Reorganization Act of 1939." April 3, 1939. https://www.loc.gov/law/help/statutes-at-large/76th-congress/session-1/c76s1ch36.pdf

Public Law 89-97. "Social Security Amendments of 1965." July 30, 1965. https://www.govinfo.gov/content/pkg/STATUTE-79/pdf/STATUTE-79-Pg286.pdf

MISCELLANEOUS DEPARTMENTS

Congressional Budget Office. *The Federal Work Force: Its Size, Cost, and Activities.* Washington, DC: Government Printing Office, March 1977.

Congressional Research Service. *History of Civil Service Merit Systems of the U.S. and Selected Foreign Countries.* Washington, DC: Government Printing Office, December 31, 1976.

Congressional Research Service. "Federal Workforce Statistics Sources: OPM and OMB." March 25, 2020. https://crsreports.congress.gov/product/pdf/R/R43590

Federal Election Commission. "Contribution Limits for 2019–2020." https://www.fec.gov/resources/cms-content/documents/contribution_limits_chart_2019-2020.pdf

Federal Election Commission. "Making Independent Expenditures." https://www.fec.gov/help-candidates-and-committees/making-independent-expenditures/

Office of Management and Budget. "Historical Tables." https://www.whitehouse.gov/omb/historical-tables/

Social Security Administration. 2020. OASDI and SSI Program Rates & Limits, 2020. https://www.ssa.gov/policy/docs/quickfacts/prog_highlights/RatesLimits2020.html

U.S. Department of Health and Human Services. "2020 Poverty Guidelines." https://aspe.hhs.gov/2020-poverty-guidelines

U.S. Department of Homeland Security, U.S. Citizenship and Immigration Services. "Citizenship Rights and Responsibilities." https://www.uscis.gov/citizenship/learners/citizenship-rights-and-responsibilities

U.S. Department of Justice. "Introduction to the Federal Court System." https://www.justice.gov/usao/justice-101/federal-courts

U.S. Department of Labor, Bureau of Labor Statistics. "Highlights of Women's Earnings in 2017." https://www.bls.gov/opub/reports/womens-earnings/2017/home.htm

U.S. Department of Treasury, Bureau of the Fiscal Service. "The Debt to the Penny and Who Holds It." https://treasurydirect.gov/NP/debt/current

U.S. CENSUS BUREAU

"Current Population." https://www.census.gov/popclock/print.php?component=counter

"History: 1790 Overview." https://www.census.gov/history/www/through_the_decades/overview/1790.html

Statistical Abstract of the United States: 2012. Section 7: Elections. https://www.census.gov/prod/2011pubs/12statab/election.pdf

U.S. COURTS

"Authorized Judgeships." https://www.uscourts.gov/judges-judgeships/authorized-judgeships

"The Evarts Act: Creating the Modern Appellate Courts." https://www.uscourts.gov/educational-resources/educational-activities/evarts-act-creating-modern-appellate-courts

U.S. HOUSE OF REPRESENTATIVES

"Committees." https://www.house.gov/committees

"Democratic Whips (1899 to Present)." https://history.house.gov/People/Office/Democratic-Whips/

"History of the House." https://www.house.gov/the-house-explained/history-of-the-house

"The House Explained." https://www.house.gov/the-house-explained

"List of Speakers of the House." https://history.house.gov/People/Office/Speakers-List/

"Majority Leaders of the House (1899 to Present)." https://history.house.gov/People/Office/Majority-Leaders/

"Minority Leaders of the House (1899 to Present)." https://history.house.gov/People/Office/Minority-Leaders/

"Party Divisions in the House of Representatives." http://history.house.gov/institution/Party-Divisions/Party-Divisions/

"The Permanent Apportionment Act of 1929." https://history.house.gov/Historical-Highlights/1901-1950/The-Permanent-Apportionment-Act-of-1929/

"Republican Whips (1897 to Present)." https://history.house.gov/People/Office/Republican-Whips/

U.S. NATIONAL ARCHIVES AND RECORDS ADMINISTRATION

"Electoral College." https://www.archives.gov/federal-register/electoral-college/roles.html

"Garrison's Constitution: The Covenant with Death and How It Was Made." https://www.archives.gov/publications/prologue/2000/winter/garrisons-constitution-1.html

"Pennsylvania Assembly: Reply to the Governor, 11 November 1755." *Founders Online,* https://founders.archives.gov/documents/Franklin/01-06-02-0107

U.S. NATIONAL PARK SERVICE

"Declaration of Sentiments." https://www.nps.gov/wori/learn/historyculture/declaration-of-sentiments.htm (updated February 26, 2015).

"The First Women's Rights Convention." Lucretia Mott, Harriet Cady Eaton, Margaret Pryor, Elizabeth Cady Stanton, et al. https://www.nps.gov/wori/learn/historyculture/the-first-womens-rights-convention.htm

"Stonewall National Monument." https://www.nps.gov/places/stonewall-national-monument.htm

U.S. SENATE

"Committees." https://www.senate.gov/committees/index.htm

"Filibuster and Cloture." https://www.senate.gov/artandhistory/history/common/briefing/Filibuster_Cloture.htm

"Majority and Minority Leaders." https://www.senate.gov/artandhistory/history/common/briefing/Majority_Minority_Leaders.htm

"Party Divisions." https://www.senate.gov/history/partydiv.htm

"President Pro Tempore." https://www.senate.gov/reference/Index/President_Pro_Tempore.htm

"The President of the Senate's Role in the Legislative Process." https://www.senate.gov/general/Features/Part_1_VP.htm

"Supreme Court Nominations: Present–1789." https://www.senate.gov/pagelayout/reference/nominations/Nominations.htm

U.S. SUPREME COURT

"Building History." https://www.supremecourt.gov/about/buildinghistory.aspx

"Justices: 1789–Present." https://www.supremecourt.gov/about/members_text.aspx

THE WHITE HOUSE

"Presidents." https://www.whitehouse.gov/1600/Presidents

LEGAL CASES

Barron v. Baltimore, 32 U.S. 243 (1833).

Bowers v. Hardwick, 478 U.S. 186 (1986).

Bradwell v. Illinois, 83 U.S. 130 (1873).

Brown v. Board of Education of Topeka, KS, 347 U.S. 483 (1954).

Buckley v. Valeo, 424 U.S. 1 (1976).

Citizens United v. FEC, 558 U.S. 310 (2010).

Dred Scott v. Sandford, 60 U.S. 393 (1857).

Dunn v. Blumstein, 405 U.S. 330 (1972).

Escobedo v. Illinois, 378 U.S. 478 (1964).

Gideon v. Wainwright, 372 U.S. 335 (1963).

Gitlow v. New York, 268 U.S. 652 (1925).

Gratz v. Bollinger, 539 U.S. 244 (2003).

Grutter v. Bollinger, 539 U.S. 306 (2003).

Guinn v. United States, 238 U.S. 347 (1915).

Harper v. Virginia Board of Elections, 383 U.S. 663 (1966).

Lawrence v. Texas, 539 U.S. 558 (2003).

Marbury v. Madison, 5 U.S. 137 (1803).

McCulloch v. Maryland, 17 U.S. 316 (1819).

Milliken v. Bradley, 418 U.S. 717 (1974).

Miranda v. Arizona, 384 U.S. 436 (1966).

Obergefell v. Hodges, 576 U.S. ____ (2015).

Palm Beach County Canvassing Board v. Harris, 772 So. 2d 1220 (Fla. 2000).

Plessy v. Ferguson, 163 U.S. 537 (1896).

Regents of University of California v. Bakke, 438 U.S. 265 (1978).

Roe v. Wade, 410 U.S. 113 (1973).

Schenck v. United States, 249 U.S. 47 (1919).

Smith v. Allwright, 321 U.S. 649 (1944).

Texas v. Johnson, 491 U.S. 397 (1989).

U.S. Term Limits, Inc. v. Thornton, 514 U.S. 779 (1995).

U.S. v. Nixon, 418 U.S. 683 (1974).

West Coast Hotel Company v. Parrish, 300 U.S. 379 (1937).

Index

accountability, 25, 47, 52, 70, 83–84, 123, 162
activism, 6–7, 37, 76, 166–67
Adams, John, 115, 117, 132–33
Adams, John Quincy, 55, 95
affirmative action, 39–40
Affordable Care Act, 145
African Americans
   affirmative action and, 39–40
   citizenship, 18
   suffrage, 31, 49–50
   violence against, 6, 50
   See also racial discrimination; segregation laws
Agricultural Adjustment Administration, 150
Aid to Families with Dependent Children (AFDC), 151
Alabama, 66
alienation, 63
amendments. *See* constitutional amendments
American Civil Liberties Union, 46
amicus curiae briefs ("friend of the court"), 140
Annapolis Convention, 12
appellate courts, 135
appellate jurisdiction, 130
Arizona, 66
Arkansas, 66
arms, right to bear, 34, 43–44, 46. *See also* Second Amendment
arms race, 155

Articles of Confederation and Perpetual Union, 11, 17, 23, 94, 128
Asian Americans, 38–39
assembly, freedom of, 34, 75
astroturf lobbying, 81
attack journalism, 80
authoritarian regimes, 25, 70

baby boom generation, 156
Bakke, Regents of the University of California v. (1978), 40
balanced budget, 157
Banfield, Edward, 85
banking crisis, 86
Bank of the United States, 18
Barron v. Baltimore (1833), 32–33
Benton, Thomas Hart, 93
bicameral legislature, 15, 89
Bill of Rights, 13, 30–34, 46, 53. *See also* civil liberties
bills, legislative process for, 102–4, 109
Bipartisan Campaign Reform Act, 59
block grants, 21
Bork, Robert, 143
Boston Tea Party, 10–11
Bowdoin, James, 12
Bowers v. Hardwick (1986), 37
Bradley, Joseph, 36
Bradwell v. Illinois (1873), 36
Brandeis, Louis, 39
Brennan, William, 45, 142
Breyer, Stephen, 140
Brownlow, Louis, 118

Brown v. Board of Board of Education of Topeka, KS (1954), 32, 131
Buchanan, James, 120
Buckley v. Valeo (1976), 59
budget deficits, 156–57
bureaucracy, 115–22, 127
Bush, George H. W., 155
Bush, George W., 56, 152, 161

cabinet, 115–17, 121
California, 64
candidates. *See* political campaigns
Carrington, Edward, 69
categorical grants, 21
caucuses, 53
centralization of government, 17
centrists, 89
charter schools, 158–59
Chávez, César, 38
checks and balances, 2, 4, 14, 69, 83, 105, 123, 162
Child Nutrition Act (1966), 152
China, 159–60
Chinese Americans, 38–39
Chinese Exclusion Act (1882), 38
circuit courts of appeal, 135, 142, 143–44
"citizen homework"
    civil liberties and civil rights, 45–46
    Congress and political parties, 109
    Constitution, 27
    federalism, 27
    mass media, interest groups, and public opinion, 85–86
    presidency and executive branch, 126–27
    social, economic, and foreign policy, 165
    Supreme Court and federal judiciary, 146–47
    voting and elections, 67–68
citizenship, defined, 1
citizenship, responsibilities of, xiii–xiv, 1–9, 162–63, 166–68
    civic obligations, 65–66
    civil liberties and civil rights, 41–44
    Congress and political parties, 105–7
    Constitution and federalism, 22–26
    disinterest in politics and, 2–3
    mass media, interest groups, and public opinion, 82–84
    presidency and executive branch, 122–25
    public policy and, 123
    social, economic, and foreign policy, 162–63

Supreme Court and federal judiciary, 140–44
voting and elections, 64–66
Citizenship and Immigration Services, 65
Citizens United v. Federal Election Commission (2010), 59
civil cases, 134
civil disobedience, nonviolent, 35
Civilian Conservation Corps, 150–51
Civilian Works Administration, 150
civil liberties, 28–46
    citizen homework, 45–46
    citizen responsibilities and, 41–44
    civic obligations and, 65
    current issues, 39–41
    defined, 28
    expansion of, 44
    historical evolution of, 30–34
    judicial activists and, 136
    knowledge matters, 44–45
    security and, 29–30
civil rights, 28–46
    citizen homework, 45–46
    citizen responsibilities and, 41–44
    current issues, 39–41
    defined, 28
    historical evolution of, 34–39
    knowledge matters, 44–45
    legislation on, 34–37, 94
Civil Rights Act (1957), 94
Civil Rights Act (1964), 35, 37
civil rights advocates, 6, 76
civil servant, 118
civil service (merit) system, 118, 121–22, 124
Civil War, 18–19, 120
Civil War Amendments, 30
Civil War veterans, 150
Clay, Henry, 93
clear and present danger test, 29
Cleveland, Grover, 55–56, 124
climate change, 158–59
Clinton, Bill, 56, 73, 79, 119, 142
Clinton, Hillary, 56
closed primaries, 53
cloture, 94
Cold War, 155–56
communism, 154–55
compromise. *See* political compromises
Compromise of 1877, 31
computer-assisted telephone interviewing (CATI), 78
concurring opinion (Supreme Court), 131

confederal system of government, 11
Confederate Congress, 11–12
conference committees, 104
conflict, political, 24–26, 43–44, 149. *See also* political compromises
Congress, 87–109
　approval ratings, 106, 108
　citizen homework, 109
　citizen responsibilities and, 105–7
　conference committees, 104
　constitutional amendments and, 16
　creation of, 14, 18–19, 49, 89–90, 105
　current issues, 102–4
　enumerated powers, 90
　federal courts and, 128, 134
　functions of, 102
　historical evolution of, 89–94
　implied powers, 90
　incumbents, 57–58
　knowledge matters, 107–8
　necessary and proper clause, 18
　oversight of executive branch, 121–22
　powers of, 14–15, 90
　public approval ratings, 48–49
　regulation of economy, 20
　sessions of, 94
　standing committees, 90, 103
　subcommittees, 90, 103
　taxes and, 90, 164 (*see also* taxes)
　term limits, 105–7
　See also House of Representatives; Senate
Connecticut Compromise. *See* Great (or Connecticut) Compromise
conservatives, 82, 96, 153–54, 158, 159
Constitution, 9–27
　Article I (establishing Congress), 14, 18–19, 49, 89–90, 105
　Article II (establishing presidency), 14, 54, 113, 125
　Article III (establishing Supreme Court), 14, 128–29, 132–33
　Article V (on amendments), 52, 107 (*see also* constitutional amendments)
　Article VI (federal law supersedes state law), 17, 22
　checks and balances, 2, 4, 14, 69, 83, 105, 123, 162
　citizen homework, 27
　citizen responsibilities and, 22–26, 41
　historical evolution of, 10–17
　humanness of creators, 23–24
　importance of, 9–10, 26

interpretation of, 28–29, 94, 129, 135–37
　knowledge matters, 26
　as "living" document, 136
　reverence of, 22–23
　separation of powers, 83
　supremacy clause, 134
constitutional amendments
　civil liberties and, 136
　Congress and, 16
　judicial restrainists and, 136
　list of, 16–17
　process for, 15–16, 52–53, 63
　Supreme Court jurisdiction and, 134
　See also Bill of Rights; *specific amendments*
Constitutional Convention. *See* Philadelphia Convention
consumer rights, 76
containment, 154–55
continuing resolution, 156–57
Coolidge, Calvin, 112
cooperative federalism, 21–22
corruption, 118
counsel, right to, 33–34
courts. *See* federal judiciary; Supreme Court
Criminal Anarchy Law (New York), 32–33
criminal cases, 134
cruel and unusual punishment, protection against, 34
C-SPAN, 126, 127, 140, 146
current events, 83–84
Curtis, Charles, 93

Dahl, Robert, 114
Day, Benjamin, 71
Declaration of Independence, 11, 25
Declaration of Sentiments, 166–67
de facto segregation, 32. *See also* segregation laws
defendants, 128
deficit spending, 153
de jure segregation, 32. *See also* segregation laws
Delaware, 11, 12, 90
democracy
　accountability and (*see* accountability)
　characteristics of, 1–2
　citizen participation and (*see* citizenship, responsibilities of)
　conflict and, 24–26, 43
　containment of communism and, 154–55
　defined, 9

democracy (*continued*)
  direct, 63, 71
  dysfunctional, 4
  expansion of, 25, 136, 166–67
  Jacksonian, 51
  Jeffersonian, 51
  national security and, 161
  pluralist, 73, 81
  public support for, 1–2
Democratic Party
  affirmative action and, 39
  citizen homework, 109
  economic policy, 153
  formation of, 95
  gender gap and, 56–57
  judicial nominations and, 144
  liberals, 82
  open seats and, 57
  overview of, 88
  Senate floor leader and, 93
  "Solid South," 51
  strength of national government and, 102
  white primary in Texas, 50–51
  See also elections
Democratic-Republican Party, 94–95, 115
Department of Defense, 121
deregulation, 153
devolution (of federal law), 22
Dewey, Thomas, 78–79
dictatorships. *See* authoritarian regimes
diplomacy, 160, 164
direct democracy, 63, 71
discretionary spending, 157–58, 165
discrimination
  gender-based, 36–37, 166–67
  against immigrants, 38
  against lesbian and gay Americans, 37
  racial, 6, 31–32, 35–40, 50–51, 66
  See also segregation laws
dissenting opinion (Supreme Court), 131
district courts, 134, 135
District of Columbia, 52, 55
doctrine of preemption (Bush Doctrine), 160–61
Dole, Bob, 79
domino theory, 155
Douglas, William, 145
Dred Scott v. Sandford (1857), 18–19
dual federalism, 19–20
due process clause, 30, 32–33, 37, 39
Dunn v. Blumstein (1972), 62

economic policy
  citizen homework, 165
  citizen responsibilities and, 162–63
  current issues, 156–62
  defined, 148
  historical evolution of, 152–54
  knowledge matters, 163–65
  See also federal budget; New Deal
education, 158–59
Eighteenth Amendment, 16
Eighth Amendment, 16, 30
Einstein, Katherine, 7
Eisenhower, Dwight D., 161–62
elected officials
  campaigns (*see* political campaigns)
  identification of, 67–68
  political parties and, 96–101
  term limits, 71
  See also Congress; House of Representatives; presidency; Senate
Election Day, 47, 49
  same-day voter registration, 62–63, 64
elections, 47–68
  citizen homework, 67–68
  citizen responsibilities and, 64–66
  closed primaries, 53
  current issues, 59–64
  fraud in, 5, 31, 66
  general, 47
  historical evolution of, 53–59
  horse race journalism, 80
  knowledge matters, 66–67
  as measure of public opinion, 77
  open primaries, 53
  popular vote, 55–56
  primary, 47
  qualifications for candidates, 54
  rules and restrictions in, 5–6
  winner-take-all system, 53, 63, 89
  See also political campaigns; presidential elections; voter registration laws; voter suppression; voter turnout; voting
Electoral College, 14–15, 31, 51, 54–56, 87, 114–15, 123
electoral process
  democratization of, 6
  restrictions on, 5–6
  See also political campaigns; presidential elections; voter registration laws; voter suppression; voter turnout; voting
Elementary and Secondary Education Act (1965), 152

Eleventh Amendment, 16
empathy, 43
entitlements, 151, 156–58, 163
enumerated powers
    of Congress, 90
    of president, 113
equal protection clause, 6, 28, 32, 34, 36–37, 39
equal time provision, 80–81
Escobedo, Danny, 33
Escobedo v. Illinois (1964), 33
Evarts Act (Judiciary Act of 1891), 135
executive agreements, 120
executive branch, 110–27
    cabinet, 115–17, 121
    citizen homework, 126–27
    citizen responsibilities and, 122–25
    creation of, 14
    current issues, 119–22
    historical evolution of, 115–19
    knowledge matters, 125–26
    See also presidency
Executive Office of the President (EOP),
    118–19, 121. *See also* presidency
executive orders, 120
executive privilege, 121
expression, freedom of, 45

Facebook, 83
facts, 7. *See also* knowledge
"fake news," 70, 85
Farrand, Max, 13
federal budget, 121, 156–57, 163
    balanced, 157
    deficits, 156–57
Federal Communications Commission
    (FCC), 80
Federal Election Commission (FEC),
    58
Federal Emergency Relief Administration,
    150
federal government
    bureaucracy, 115–22, 127
    due process clause, 30, 32
    public opinion on role of, 77
    size of, 117
    See also national government
federalism, 9–27
    citizen homework, 27
    citizen responsibilities and, 22–26
    current issues, 20–22
    defined, 9–10

dual, 19–20
    elections and, 49
    historical evolution of, 17–20
    layer cake, 19
    marble cake, 21
    nation-centered, 18–19
    state-centered, 18–19
    See also national government; state
        governments
Federalist Papers, 13–14, 27, 81, 83, 87, 105,
    110–11, 123, 128–29, 132
Federalist Party, 94–95, 115, 132
federal judiciary, 128–47
    citizen homework, 146–47
    citizen responsibilities and, 140–44
    current issues, 135–40
    district courts, 134
    historical evolution of, 134–35
    knowledge matters, 145–46
    partisanship in, 142
    three-tiered system, 135
Federal Judiciary Center, 147
federal poverty level, 152, 165
Federal Reserve Board, 152
Fifteenth Amendment, 16, 30–31, 50
Fifth Amendment, 16
    due process clause, 20, 30, 32
    privacy rights and, 136
filibuster, 93–94, 102, 144
fire alarm oversight, 121–22
First Amendment, 16, 30
    campaign finance and, 59
    civil liberties, 28, 34
    Establishment Clause (separation of
        church and state), 158
    privacy rights and, 39, 136
    See also freedom of assembly; freedom of
        religion; freedom of speech; freedom
        of the press
fiscal policy, 152
fiscal year, 156
flag burning, 44–45
flat tax, 159
Florida, 31, 66
Ford, Gerald, 145
foreign policy
    citizen homework, 165
    citizen responsibilities and, 162–63
    current issues, 156–62
    defined, 148
    historical evolution of, 154–56
    knowledge matters, 163–65

Fourteenth Amendment, 16
  definition of citizenship, 1
  due process clause, 30, 32–33, 37, 39
  equal protection clause, 6, 28, 32, 34,
    36–37, 39
  privacy rights and, 39, 136
Fourth Amendment, 16, 30, 34
  privacy rights and, 39, 136
franking privilege, 58
Franklin, Benjamin, 24–25, 29, 41
freedom of assembly, 34, 75
freedom of expression, 45
freedom of religion, 33–34
freedom of speech, 29, 32–34, 59
freedom of the press, 34, 69–70
freedoms. See civil liberties; civil rights
free rider, 81
French and Indian War. See Seven Years' War
fundraising
  election campaigns, 57–59, 108
  interest groups, 76

Gallup, George, 76
Gallup Poll surveys, 48, 70–71, 78, 106
Garfield, James, 118
Garland, Merrick, 142–43
gay rights movement, 37
gender discrimination, 36–37, 166–67
gender gap, 56–57
general elections, 47. See also elections
Georgia, 66
Gerry, Elbridge, 13
Gideon v. Wainwright (1963), 33
Ginsburg, Ruth Bader, 140
Gitlow v. New York (1925), 32–33
globalization, 160
global warming, 158
going public (presidential strategy), 121
Gore, Al, 56
Gorsuch, Neil, 144
grandfather clause, 50
Grant, Jane, 41
grants-in-aid, 21
grassroots lobbying, 81
Gratz v. Bollinger (2003), 40
Great Britain, 10–11, 92, 94–95
Great (or Connecticut) Compromise
    (bicameral legislature), 15, 89–90
Great Depression, 86, 120, 150–51, 153–54.
    See also New Deal
greater common good, 29, 43, 65, 81, 83,
    112

Great Society, 151–52
Green Party, 89
Grodzins, Morton, 19
Gross Domestic Product (GDP), 160
Grutter v. Bollinger (2003), 40
Guiteau, Charles, 118
Gulick, Luther, 118
gun control, 34, 43–44, 75

Hamilton, Alexander, 13–14, 94, 110–12,
    115, 123, 125, 128–29, 132, 140–41, 144
Hamilton, Lee, 22–23
Harding, Warren, 73, 112
hard money, 58
Harlan, John Marshall, 31–32
Harrison, Benjamin, 55–56
Hayes, Rutherford B., 31, 55
Head Start, 152
Health and Human Services (HHS)
    Department, 152
health care, 151
Hearst, William Randolph, 72–73
history, study of, 26
Hochschild, Jennifer, 7
Holmes, Oliver Wendell, Jr., 26, 29
Hoover, Herbert, 112, 151
horse race journalism, 80
House of Representatives
  citizen homework, 109
  creation of, 89–90
  current issues, 102–4
  election of members, 9, 51, 87–88
  incumbents, 57–58
  majority leader, 91
  majority whip, 92
  midterm elections, 60
  minority leader, 92
  minority whip, 92
  party divisions in, 96–101
  presidential elections and, 114–15
  qualifications for candidates, 54, 91
  Rules Committee, 93, 103
  speaker, 91
  Ways and Means Committee, 92
  winner-take-all system, 89
  See also Congress
Housing and Urban Development (HUD)
    Department, 152

ideological bias, 80
Illinois, 66
immigrants, 38–39, 50

implied powers (Congress), 90
incumbents, 57–58
independent expenditures, 58–59
independents, 89, 107
Indiana, 54, 66
Indian Citizenship Act, 38
Indian Removal Act (1830), 38
individualism, 8, 41–43, 65, 88
initiatives, 63
inside strategy (lobbying), 81
interest groups, 69–86
    amicus curiae briefs ("friend of the
        court"), 140
    citizen homework, 85–86
    citizen responsibilities and, 82–84
    current issues, 79–82
    defined, 69
    elections and, 64
    historical evolution of, 74–76
    knowledge matters, 84–85
    lobbying, 70–71, 79, 81, 85
    regulatory capture and, 122
internationalism, 160
internet, 73, 79, 83
internment camps, 38
Iowa, 53, 66
Iraq War, 161
iron triangle, 81
isolationism, 120, 154

Jackson, Andrew, 38, 55, 88, 95, 112,
    117
Jacksonian democracy, 51
Japanese Americans, 38–39
Jay, John, 13
Jefferson, Thomas, 69, 72, 94–95, 115,
    132–33
Jeffersonian democracy, 51
Jim Crow era, 6, 31–32, 34, 51
Jobs Corps, 152
Johnson, Andrew, 120
Johnson, Lyndon, 151–52
journalism. See mass media; press
judicial activism, 136
judicial branch, 14. See also federal judi-
    ciary; Supreme Court
judicial philosophy, 135–36, 143
judicial restraint, 136–37
judicial review, 132–34
Judiciary Act (1789), 133–34
Judiciary Act (1801), 132
Judiciary Act (1891), 135

Judiciary Act (1925), 130
jury trial, right to, 34

Kansas, 66
Kasich, John, 56
Kavanaugh, Brett, 144
Kennedy, John F., 7, 73, 86
Keynes, John Maynard, 153
Keynesian economics, 153
King, Martin Luther, Jr., 35–36
King Caucus, 53
knowledge
    citizen action and, 1
    of facts, 7
    importance of, 4–5
    levels of, 3, 22–23
    scientific, 84–85
    of Supreme Court, 140
"knowledge matters"
    civil liberties and civil rights, 44–45
    Congress and political parties, 107–8
    Constitution and study of history, 26
    mass media, interest groups, and public
        opinion, 84–85
    presidency and executive branch, 125–26
    social, economic, and foreign policy,
        163–65
    Supreme Court and federal judiciary,
        145–46
    voting and elections, 66–67
Knox, Henry, 115
Kochin, Michael, 10
Korean War, 155
Ku Klux Klan (KKK), 51

laissez-faire capitalism, 152
lame duck, 132, 142
Landon, Alfred, 76–77
Lasswell, Harold, 85
Latinos, 38, 40
Lawrence v. Texas (2003), 37
laws
    federal law superseding state law, 17, 22
    interpretation of, 28–29, 94, 129, 135–37
    judicial review of, 132
    mandatory spending, 157–58, 165
    presidential persuasion and, 113
    process for passage of, 102–4, 109
    public policy and, 148
    signing statement and, 120–21
layer cake federalism, 19
legal counsel, right to, 33–34

legal precedents, 141
legislative branch, 14
  envisioned supremacy of, 105, 122, 125
  functions of, 102
  See also Congress; House of Representatives; Senate
lesbian and gay Americans, 37. *See also* same-sex marriage
liberals, 82, 153–54, 158, 159
libertarianism, 65
Libertarian Party, 89
liberties. *See* civil liberties
Lincoln, Abraham, 19, 88, 95, 112, 120
literacy rates, 72
literacy tests (for voting), 50
Literary Digest, 76–77
living Constitution, 136
lobbying, 70–71, 79, 81, 85
local governments, 10
Louisiana, 31
Lynd, Robert, 85

Madison, James, 11–14, 24, 53, 74–75, 81, 83, 85, 87, 105–6, 123, 133, 149
Maine, 18–19, 63
majority leader (House), 91–92
majority leader (Senate), 93
majority opinion (Supreme Court), 131
majority whip (House), 92
mandatory spending, 157–58, 165
marble cake federalism, 21
Marbury v. Madison (1803), 132–34, 145
Marshall, John, 18, 133
Mason, George, 13, 115
Massachusetts, 11, 90
mass media, 69–86
  attack journalism, 80
  citizen homework, 85–86
  citizen responsibilities and, 82–84
  credibility of, 70, 85
  current issues, 79–82
  defined, 69
  equal time provision, 80–81
  "fake news," 70, 85
  hard news, 80
  historical evolution of, 71–73
  horse race journalism, 80
  knowledge matters, 84–85
  leaking and, 80
  soft news, 80
  See also internet; press
McConnell, Grant, 85

McConnell, Mitch, 142, 144
McCulloch v. Maryland (1819), 18
Medicaid, 151
Medicare, 151, 154, 156, 157
merit system, 118
Merriam, Charles E., 2–3, 4, 118
Mexican Americans, 38, 50
midterm elections, 60
military spending, 159–61, 165
Milliken v. Bradley (1974), 35
minimum wage, 20
minority leader (House), 92
minority leader (Senate), 93
minority whip (House), 92
Miranda, Ernesto, 33
Miranda v. Arizona (1966), 33
Mississippi, 66
Missouri, 18–19, 66
Missouri Compromise (1820), 18–19
moderates, 82, 89
monarchies, 25, 112
monetary policy, 152
Montana, 66
Morse, Samuel, 72
Muhlenberg, Frederick, 91
mutually assured destruction, 155
Myrdal, Gunnar, 85

name recognition, 57–58
national debt, 156, 157–58, 163–64, 165
national government
  centralization of, 17
  partisan views on, 88
  powers of, 9–10
  strength of, compared to states, 89–90, 94–95, 102, 153 (*see also* federalism)
  See also federal government
National Public Radio, 83
National Recovery Administration, 150
National Republican Party, 95
National Rifle Association, 75
national security, 121, 159, 161
nation-centered federalism, 18–19
Native Americans, 1, 37–38, 40
Natural Alliance Party, 89
Nebraska, 66
necessary and proper clause, 18
Neustadt, Richard, 113
The New American Social Compact (Grant), 41
New Deal, 20–21, 150–51, 153
New England town meetings, 63

New Hampshire, 66
New Jersey, 12
New Jersey Plan (unicameral legislature),
    15, 89–90
newspapers, 71–72, 79. See also mass media;
    press
New York, 12, 32–33
New York Times, 83
Nineteenth Amendment, 6, 16, 51
Ninth Amendment, 16, 39, 136
Nixon, Richard, 73, 86, 121, 153
nominating conventions, 53–54
nonviolent civil disobedience, 35
North Carolina, 66
North Dakota, 60, 64, 66
nuclear option (regarding judicial nomi-
    nees), 144
nuclear weapons, 155–56

Obama, Barack, 120, 142, 144
Obergefell v. Hodges (2015), 39, 140
O'Connor, Sandra Day, 22–23, 40
October term (Supreme Court), 131
Office of Economic Opportunity, 152
Office of Management and Budget
    (OMB), 103, 121
Ohio, 66
Oklahoma, 38
open primaries, 53
open seats (Congress), 57
oral arguments (Supreme Court), 131
original intent (Constitution), 136–37
original jurisdiction (Supreme Court), 130,
    133–34
outside strategy (lobbying), 81
oversight, 121–22
Oyez Project, 146

partisanship, 144. See also political parties
patronage system, 117–18
Paul, Ron, 56
Payne, Sereno, 92
Pendleton Civil Service Act (1883), 118
Pennsylvania, 11, 12, 90
penny press, 71
Persian Gulf War, 155–56
persuasion, presidential power of, 113
Philadelphia Convention, 12–13, 15, 24–25,
    53, 89–90, 105, 114–15, 149–50
    Committee of the Whole, 110
Pierce, Franklin, 120
plaintiffs, 128

plea bargaining, 140
Plessy v. Ferguson (1896), 31–32, 34
pluralist democracy, 73, 81
pocket veto, 104
police patrol oversight, 121–22
policy-making institutions, 128–29, 136. See
    also Congress; presidency
political action committees (PACs), 59,
    81–82
political campaigns, 53–59
    commercials, 67
    equal time provision (FCC regulation),
        80–81
    fundraising and spending, 57–59, 108
    incumbent candidates, 57–58
    name recognition and, 57–58
    public policy ideas and, 148
    third-party, 89
    See also elections; presidential elections;
        voting
political compromises, 14–15, 114, 149–50
political loyalty, 117–18
political parties, 87–109
    citizen homework, 109
    citizen responsibilities and, 105–7
    conflicts between, 149
    current issues, 102–4
    defined, 88
    historical evolution of, 94–102
    ideological polarization, 82
    judicial nominations and, 144
    knowledge matters, 107–8
    minor (third), 89
    newspapers and, 71–72
    presidential elections and, 115
    selection of nominees, 53
    See also Democratic Party; Republican
        Party
political reform, 6–7, 59, 76, 166–67
political socialization, 82
polling, 48, 70–71, 76–79, 106. See also
    public opinion
poll taxes, 50. See also public opinion
popular vote, 55–56
Postal Service (USPS), 121
poverty, 150–52, 159, 164, 165
Powell, Colin, 56
Powell, Lewis, 143
power, exercise of, 125–26
precedents, legal, 141
preemption, doctrine of (Bush Doctrine),
    160–61

presidency, 110–27
  citizen homework, 126–27
  citizen responsibilities and, 122–25
  creation of, 14, 54, 113
  current issues, 119–22
  enumerated powers, 113
  executive agreements, 120
  executive orders, 120
  executive privilege, 121
  going public, 121
  historical evolution of, 110–15
  judicial review of, 132
  judiciary appointments and, 135
  knowledge matters, 125–26
  legislative process and, 103–4
  list of presidents, 1789–2020, 116
  persuasion and, 113, 123–24
  power of, 121–24, 125–26
  qualifications for, 54, 113
  signing statements, 120–21
  stewardship theory and, 112–13
  term limits, 71, 111
  Whig theory and, 112
  See also executive branch; Executive
    Office of the President (EOP)
presidential approval ratings, 119–20
presidential debates (televised), 73, 86
presidential elections
  disputed, 31
  framers' vision of, 110–11
  gender gap and, 56–57
  historical evolution of, 53–59
  process for, 113–15
  Russian influence in 2016 campaign,
    66, 83
  televised debates, 73, 86
  in U.S. history, 67
  voter turnout, 60
  See also elections; Electoral College;
    voting
press
  criticism of, 70
  freedom of, 34, 69–70
  ideological bias and, 80
  See also internet; mass media
primary elections, 47. See also elections
privacy rights, 34, 39, 46, 82, 136, 145
privatization, 158–59
Progressive Era, 2–3
Progressive Party, 79
progressive tax, 159
Prohibition, 16–17, 53

public opinion, 69–86
  citizen homework, 85–86
  citizen responsibilities and, 82–84
  on Congress, 106, 108
  current issues, 79–82
  defined, 69
  on federal bureaucracy, 122
  historical evolution of, 76–79
  knowledge matters, 84–85
  on lobbyists, 70–71
  presidential approval ratings, 119–20
  public policy outcomes and, 148
  satisfaction with political system, 5–6,
    48–49
  on Supreme Court, 146
public policy, 148–65
  citizen involvement and, 162–63
  current challenges, 6
  defined, 148
  global impact of, 163
  scientific knowledge and, 84–85
  stages of policy process, 148–49
public safety, 44
public security, 32–33
public service, 7–8, 65
Public Works Administration, 150

racial discrimination, 6, 31–32, 35–40, 50–
  51, 66–67. See also segregation laws
racism, 31, 51, 146
radio, 73, 83
Randolph, Edmund, 13, 115
random sample (in polls), 77–78
RDD (random digit dialing) sampling, 78
Reagan, Ronald, 96, 119, 143, 152–53
Reaganomics, 153
recall elections, 63
Reconstruction, 31, 34
red tape, 122
referendum rights, 63–64
reform movements, 166–67
regressive tax, 159
regulations, 117. See also laws
regulatory capture, 122
Reid, Harry, 144
religion, freedom of, 33–34
Reorganization Act (1939), 118
republican form of government
  citizen engagement and, 168
  defined, 9
  presidential power and, 123
  See also citizenship, responsibilities of

Republican Party
affirmative action and, 39
African American equality and, 51
citizen homework, 109
conservatives, 82
economic policy, 153
formation of, 95
gender gap and, 56–57
judicial nominations and, 142–44
open seats and, 57
overview of, 88
Senate floor leader and, 93
strength of national government and, 102
See also elections
Resettlement Administration (RA), 84–85
Revolutionary War, 10–11
revolving door syndrome, 81
Rhode Island, 66, 90
Ricci, David, 3–4
Richardson, James, 92
rights. *See* civil liberties; civil rights
Roberts, Owen, 20
robo-calls, 78
Roe v. Wade (1973), 39
Roosevelt, Franklin D.
Democrats and, 95
economic policy, 152–53
Executive Office of the President and, 118
mass media and, 73, 86
New Deal and, 20–21, 84, 150–51
persuasiveness, 113
proactive presidency, 111–12
public opinion on, 76–77
ranking of, 120
Supreme Court justices and, 145
World War II internment camps and, 38
Roosevelt, Theodore, xiii–xiv, 120, 125–26
stewardship theory and, 112–13
rule making, 117
rule of four (Supreme Court), 131, 143
Rules Committee (House), 93, 103
Russia, 66

same-day voter registration, 62
same-sex marriage, 39, 82, 88, 145
Sanders, Bernie, 56
Scalia, Antonin, 45, 142
Schattschneider, E. E., 108
Schenck v. United States (1919), 29
school vouchers, 158

scientific knowledge, 84–85
searches and seizures, unreasonable, 34
Second Amendment, 16, 28–30, 34. *See also* arms, right to bear
Second Continental Congress (1777), 11
segregation laws, 31–32, 34–35, 51, 145. *See also* racial discrimination
selective incorporation, 33
self-incrimination, protection against, 33–34
Senate
citizen homework, 109
cloture, 94
confirmation of Supreme Court justices, 140–44
creation of, 89–90
current issues, 102–4
debate procedures, 93–94
direct election of members, 88
election of members, 9, 51
filibusters, 93–94, 102, 144
incumbents, 57–58
majority leader, 93
midterm elections, 60
minority leader, 93
president of (vice president of U.S.), 92
president pro tempore, 93
qualifications for candidates, 54, 91
See also Congress
senatorial courtesy, 144
Seneca Falls Convention (1848), 6, 49, 67, 166
separation of powers, 14, 128–29, 162
September 11, 2001 terrorist attacks, 160
Seventeenth Amendment, 16, 51, 88
Seventh Amendment, 16
Seven Years' War, 10
Shays' Rebellion, 12
signing statements, 120–21
Sixteenth Amendment, 16
Sixth Amendment, 16, 30, 33–34
slavery
abolition of, 6, 30, 34, 120
antislavery groups, 76
political parties and, 95
state-centered federalism and, 18–19
three-fifths compromise, 15
Smith, Adam, 152–53
Smith v. Allwright (1944), 51
Socialist Party, 89
social media, 83

social policy
  citizen homework, 165
  citizen responsibilities and, 162–63
  current issues, 156–62
  defined, 148
  gender gap and, 56–57
  historical evolution of, 150–52
  knowledge matters, 163–65
  See also New Deal
social reform, 6–7, 76
Social Security, 151, 154, 156, 157
sodomy laws, 37
soft money, 58
"Solid South," 51
South Carolina, 31, 66
South Dakota, 66
Soviet Union, 154–56
speaker (House), 91
speech, freedom of, 29, 32–34, 59
spending. *See* economic policy
spoils system, 117–18
Spotted Eagle, Faith, 56
standing (in federal court), 128
standing committees (Congress), 90, 103
Stanton, Elizabeth Cady, 166–67
state-centered federalism, 18–19
state courts, 140
state governments
  due process clause, 30, 32
  federal revenue and, 20–22
  powers of, 9–10
  strength of, 89–90 (*see also* states' rights)
  See also federalism
state judges, 128
state legislatures
  electoral process and, 49–51, 53
  gun control and, 29
  ratification of constitutional amendments, 15–16, 53
  regulation of businesses, 20
  sodomy laws and, 37
  U.S. senators selected by, 51, 87
  voter registration and, 64
states' rights, 18–19, 22, 77
  Democrats and, 88
  political parties and, 94–95
  same-sex marriage and, 39
Steinbeck, John, 85
Stevens, John Paul, 107
stewardship theory, 112–13
Stonewall rebellion (1969), 37
subcommittees (Congress), 90, 103

suffrage
  African American men, 31, 49–50
  defined, 49
  women, 2–3, 6, 36, 49, 51–52, 166–67
  See also voting
The Sun, 71
super PACs, 59
superpowers, 155, 159, 163
supply-side economics, 153
supremacy clause (Constitution), 134
Supreme Court, 128–47
  citizen homework, 146–47
  citizen responsibilities and, 140–44
  concurring opinion, 131
  creation of, 14, 128–29, 132
  current issues, 135–40
  dissenting opinion, 131
  historical evolution of, 130–34
  judicial review, 132–34
  jurisdiction, 130, 133–34
  knowledge matters, 145–46
  lifetime tenure, 124, 130, 141–42, 145–46
  list of chief justices and associate justices, 137–39
  majority opinion, 131
  nomination and confirmation of justices, 130, 140–44
  number of judges on, 20–21, 134
  October term, 131
  oral arguments, 131
  rule of four, 131, 143
  writ of certiorari, 131
Supreme Court, rulings
  on civil liberties and civil rights, 29–37, 39–40, 44–45, 145–46
  on congressional term limits, 107
  on election campaigns, 59
  on executive privilege, 121
  on voting rights, 50

Taft, William Howard, 112, 130
Taney, Roger, 18–19
Tawney, James, 92
taxes
  as civic responsibility, 65
  on colonists, 10–11
  economic policy and, 148, 152–53
  flat, 159
  "no taxation without representation," 10, 52
  poll (fee for voting), 50

progressive, 159
public policy and, 164
regressive, 159
Shay's Rebellion and, 12
social policy and, 151, 156, 158–59
state, 21
three-fifths compromise and, 15
Taylor, Michael, 10
telegraph, 72
telephone surveys, 77–78
television, 73, 79
Tennessee, 66
Tenth Amendment, 16, 18–19
term limits
  in Congress, 105–7
  presidency, 71, 111
terrorism, international, 156, 160
Texas, 50–51, 66
Texas v. Johnson (1989), 44
Third Amendment, 16
third-party candidates, 89
Thirteenth Amendment, 6, 16, 30
three-fifths compromise, 15
Thurmond, Strom, 93–94
Tilden, Samuel, 31, 55
Tocqueville, Alexis de, 8, 42, 75
Toobin, Jeffrey, 46
Trail of Tears, 38
trial courts, 134
Truman, Harry, 79, 119–20
Trump, Donald, 56, 60, 70, 124, 142, 152, 160
Twelfth Amendment, 16, 55
Twentieth Amendment, 17
Twenty-fifth Amendment, 17
Twenty-first Amendment, 17
Twenty-fourth Amendment, 17, 50
Twenty-second Amendment, 17, 71, 111
Twenty-seventh Amendment, 17
Twenty-sixth Amendment, 17, 52
Twenty-third Amendment, 17, 52, 55

Underwood, Oscar, 92, 93
unicameral legislature, 11–12, 15, 90
University of California, Davis, 40
University of Michigan, 40
University of Pennsylvania Annenberg
  Public Policy Center Survey, 22, 46
USA Freedom Act, 30
USA Patriot Act, 30
U.S. Postal Service (USPS), 121

U.S. Term Limits, Inc. v. Thornton (1995), 107
U.S. v. Nixon (1974), 121

Vermont, 21
veto, 104
vice president, 92
Vietnam War, 52, 152, 155
violence
  against African Americans, 6, 50
  against Chinese Americans, 38
  mass shootings, 34, 43
Virginia, 11, 12, 66, 90
Virginia Plan (bicameral legislature), 15, 89–90
volunteering, 64–65
voter registration laws, 60, 62–64, 68
voter suppression, 5–6, 66–67
voter turnout, xiv, 47–48, 59–64, 67, 79, 123–24
voting, 47–68
  citizen homework, 67–68
  citizen responsibilities and, 64–66
  current issues, 59–64
  historical evolution of, 49–53
  knowledge matters, 66–67
  racial discrimination in, 35–38, 50–51, 66
  as responsibility and right, 47
  restrictions on, 114
  See also suffrage
voting age population, 60
Voting Rights Act (1965), 35, 50, 67

Wallace, Henry, 79
Walzer, Michael, 4
War on Poverty, 151–52. *See also* poverty
Warren, Earl, 33
Warren, Samuel, 39
Washington, George, 12, 89, 94, 110–11, 115, 117, 120, 145, 154
Washington Post, 83
Watergate era, 106, 121
Ways and Means Committee (House), 92
welfare state, 152, 154. *See also* social policy
West Coast Hotel Company v. Parrish (1937), 20
West Virginia, 66
Whig Party, 95
Whig theory, 112
whips (House), 92
white primary, 50–51
white supremacy, 51

Wilson, Woodrow, 94
winner-take-all system, 53, 63, 89
Wisconsin, 66
women
   abortion rights, 39, 82, 88, 145
   discrimination against, 36–37, 166–67
   See also gender gap

women's rights, 76, 166
World War II, 38, 120, 154
writ of certiorari (Supreme Court), 131
Wyoming, 52

yellow journalism, 72

Printed and bound by CPI Group (UK) Ltd, Croydon, CR0 4YY

13/04/2025

14656536-0002